The Power of Profit

Ali Anari · James W. Kolari

The Power of Profit

Business and Economic Analyses, Forecasting, and Stock Valuation

 Springer

Ali Anari
Texas A&M University
Mays Business School
College Station TX 77843
USA
manari@mays.tamu.edu

James W. Kolari
Texas A&M University
Mays Business School
College Station TX 77843
USA
jkolari@mays.tamu.edu

ISBN 978-1-4419-0648-9   e-ISBN 978-1-4419-0649-6
DOI 10.1007/978-1-4419-0649-6
Springer New York Dordrecht Heidelberg London

Library of Congress Control Number: 2009938545

Printed on acid-free paper

Springer is part of Springer Science+Business Media (www.springer.com)

To Faye, Karie, Armita, and Wes

Preface

In recent years the USA and global economy have been shocked by financial crises that severely damaged credit markets and financial institutions. The upshot has been unprecedented in post-Great Depression era declines in output, capital stock, and profits among business firms around the world. Critics point to a variety of potential culprits to explain the current economic and financial crises, such as poor corporate governance mechanisms, excessive management compensation incentives, short-run wealth maximization, irresponsible financial practices, lack of regulatory oversight of systemic risk, and macroeconomic and monetary policy breakdowns. Naturally, a debate is emerging about how to instill more prudent management practices in an effort to avoid repeating the catastrophes of the last few years. These difficult times therefore provide an opportunity to consider new ideas and see whether they are useful in better managing business practices in the future.

This book seeks to contribute to this debate by carefully examining the role of profit in business firms in particular and the economy in general. It combines the efforts of a macroeconomist (Ali Anari) and finance professor (James W. Kolari), who share a common interest in business and economic analysis, forecasting, and stock valuation. The authors' previous work experiences in business firms, as well as consulting and academic research activities, motivated the development of a profit system model that takes into account interactions between fundamental business variables, including output, capital stock, profit rate, profit margin, and total profit. The profit system model is a tool that business firms can use to analyze and forecast these fundamental variables. To our knowledge, no such model exists that integrates these important business variables, even though they are inextricably dependent on one another. We believe that the profit system model has many practical applications to business firms and industries, in addition to the aggregate business sector and national economy. Also, stock investors can utilize the profit system model for estimating and forecasting the valuation of the stock market as a whole in addition to individual firms' stocks. It is our hope that readers will implement this new model in their daily business and investment practices and find other innovative applications also.

We would like to thank our editor, Nicholas Philipson, for his enthusiastic support during this project. We met briefly with him in Houston a few years ago, explained the basic ideas to him, and immediately gained a friend who understood what we were trying to do. Also, we thank Charlotte Cusumano, who provided editorial assistance.

Contents

Chapter 1
The Role of Profit in Advanced Market Economies

During our careers as business economists before entering university research programs, we observed that profitability criteria are key variables not only in investment decisions but also in production decisions *after* investments are made and goods and services come on stream. Profitability not only determines the level of investments but also the level of output. In our academic careers, we have found that, while there is an extensive theoretical and empirical literature on the relationships between profitability criteria and capital formation activities,[1] as manifested by project evaluation courses in universities, scant attention has been paid to the relationships between profits and production activities *after* capital formation projects are implemented. Consequently, a major gap in the literature exists to the extent that the predictive and analytic power of profit has not been fully exploited on both the microlevel of the firm and the macrolevel of the economy. Given the importance of profit in advanced market economies, where the bulk of national output is produced by the business or for-profit sector, this book investigates how profit measures can be utilized to better understand business activities. To exploit the power of profit, we propose a profit system model of the firm founded on three premises:

1. *Profit rate determines capital formation investment.* At the project evaluation stage, investment projects are selected based on the firm's required hurdle rates of return on capital (hereafter profit rates) to attain the firm's objective. Alternative firm objectives include profit maximization, sales maximization, and so on,

---

[1] For further discussion on the role of profit as a driving force in capital formation activities in business firms, see Smith (1776), Ricardo (1815), Marx (1867), Schumpeter (1934), Keynes (1936), Solow (1957), Sraffa (1960), Friedman (1962), Baumol (1974), and Samuelson (1974). Keynes' (1936) assertion that investment and employment opportunities depend on the marginal efficiency of capital sparked substantial research on the relationship between required profit rates and capital formation, for example, see neo-Keynesian and neoclassical studies by Jorgenson (1963, 1967, 1971), Hall and Jorgenson (1967), Lucas and Prescott (1971), Abel, Mankiw, Summers, and Zeckhauser (1989), and Feldstein (1996). Relatedly, the cost of capital is a key determinant of investment in models of capital formation based on Tobin's q ratio of the value of a company given by financial markets to its total assets, for example, see Alchian (1955), Brainard and Tobin (1968), Tobin (1969), Abel (1979), Summers (1981), Hayashi (1982), Shapiro (1986), and Asimakopulos (1971, 1991).

A. Anari, J.W. Kolari, *The Power of Profit*, DOI 10.1007/978-1-4419-0649-6_1,
© Springer Science+Business Media, LLC 2010

subject to various constraints by the firm's stakeholders, including shareholders, workers, suppliers, customers, and others.

2. *Profit rate determines the level of output.* After capital investments are made, firms combine fixed stocks of capital with different quantities of labor in order to attain their required profit rates. Firms continually compare realized profit rates with ex ante hurdle profit rates used to select investment projects. Realized profit rates lower than target or hurdle rates lead to reduced production activities or abandonment of unprofitable activities. They also consider expected profit rates on alternative investment projects if on-going economic activities are abandoned and resources tied up are released and employed in alternative economic activities. Of course, higher ex post realized profit rates compared to ex ante hurdle profit rates lead to higher levels of output by existing and entering firms.

3. *Profit rate, profit margin, total profit, sales, and capital stocks of a firm are determined simultaneously.* Profit rate, profit margin, and total profit depend on the levels of sales and capital, which in turn depend on profit rate and profit margin. Each of these fundamental variables is determined by the other three variables.

Employing two approaches – mathematical economics and accounting definitions – we derive in Chapter 2 a fundamental relationship among five key economic and business variables: output, capital stock, profit rate, profit margin, and total profit. We show that a firm's output is equal to the product of profit rate and the market value of capital stock divided by profit margin, while the value of capital stock is equal to the product of profit margin and output divided by profit rate. Models of profit rate, profit margin, and total profit are derived from the same fundamental relationship also. A number of other relationships among the five fundamental variables are derived in which the impact of inflation on these variables is studied. The set of profit system models of output, capital stock, profit rate, profit margin, and total profit together constitute an integrated model of a business firm in which the values of each of these variables depend on the values of the other variables. We show how this profit system model of the firm can be extended to include the labor market for the firm. The empirical representation of this integrated profit system model is a dynamic system of equations which can be applied to firms, industries, or the whole business sector depending on the level of aggregation.

Chapter 3 uses the profit system to build a macroeconomic model of the business sector. The business sector in the model is the sum of all for-profit business firms' activities in the nation. We augment this business sector model with a nonprofit sector model that includes the government sector, nonprofit organizations, and the owner-occupied housing sector. The combination of the business sector and nonprofit sector models represents the whole national economy. This model is subsequently applied to the US economy for macroeconomic forecasting, monetary and fiscal policy analysis, and business cycle analysis. In brief, based on annual data for the period 1959–2008, we find that the model can closely mimic historical in-sample series of US nominal and real output for the business sector, nonprofit sector, and national economy, as well as the capital stock, profit rates, profit margins, and total profit for the business sector. It can also be used to explore the channel of inflation transmission through capital stock and associated expected profits in the business sector. We subsequently employ the model for forecasting purposes under different monetary policy regimes represented by Federal funds rate targets and alternative fiscal stimulus assumptions. The severe economic contraction and financial crises in 2008 are included in these analyses. Our empirical results show that profit is a pivotal variable driving US output and investment that should be included in macroeconomic analyses of the national economy. Based on these findings, we conclude that our parsimonious profit system model of the economy using a small set of variables performs well in terms of in-sample analyses and out-of-sample forecasts.

Chapter 4 applies the profit system model to the aggregate corporate sector. Our corporate sector model is developed along lines similar to the business sector model in Chapter 3, which is broader in scope due to the inclusion of corporate and noncorporate business. Some inputs from the national macroeconomic model are utilized, including national output, the Federal funds rate, and the growth rate of nonfinancial debt outstanding. Aside from forecasting fundamental business variables, a major motivation for building a corporate sector model is to use it in aggregate stock valuation of the corporate sector.

Chapter 5 presents the results of applying the profit system model to 12 US industries. In-sample estimates and out-of-sample forecasts of fundamental business variables are provided to demonstrate the application of our model to a wide variety of business firms.

Chapter 6 shows how to apply our profit system model of the corporate sector to the valuation of the aggregate stock market. Our profit system stock valuation model is based on the well-known discounted cash flow (DCF) approach to valuation. Using data for the period 1959–2008, the profit system model provides in-sample estimates and out-of-sample forecasts of DCF inputs, including total corporate profits, the growth rate of profits, and the profit rate. These data for the corporate sector are developed in Chapter 4. To our knowledge no other stock market valuation model is supported by a formal business model of the business sector to estimate and forecast profit variables that are essential ingredients in DCF valuation. We develop both long-run and short-run stock valuation models and compare the results to the actual values of aggregate US stock market indices. The results suggest that our profit system stock valuation model can be used to analyze stock market movements and provide insights into whether aggregate stock market indices are over- or undervalued relative to fundamental values predicted by profits. Also, short-run and long-run forecasts of stock market values can be produced.

Chapter 7 applies the profit system model to two large US corporations that are included in the Dow Jones Industrial Average Index. For these two firms we extract long-run trends in the fundamental business variables of sales, profits, and capital stocks. The relationships between the stock values of these corporations and the long-run paths of their discounted profits over time are then investigated using DCF methods developed in Chapter 6. We also discuss potential firm-level applications of our profit system to strategic business planning, budgetary control, and capital budgeting decisions.

Chapter 8 provides a summary and implications. The macro–micro approach chosen for the empirical application of our profit system model – that is, initially applying the model to the aggregate US economy and then to the corporate sector, industries, and individual firms – is advantageous. The model is applied to the aggregate US economy to obtain forecasts of the Federal funds rate and growth rate of nonfinancial debt outstanding. These financial variables help capture the influence of the financial sector on the real economy. Also, we find that their forecasts are important inputs to the corporate sector, industry, and individual firm models. While the macroeconomic application of the model is interesting from the standpoint of providing a simple, parsimonious model of the national economy, readers who are not interested in macroeconomic issues can skip to subsequent chapters that focus on corporate sector, industry, and firm analyses.

The empirical results in Chapters 3, 4, 5, 6, and 7 strongly support our theoretical profit system models on both the macrolevel and the microlevel. These results should not be surprising. The importance of profits arises from the fact that they summarize all information on the supply and demand sides of goods and services. Profits contain expense information related to the quantities and prices of inputs on the supply side and revenue information related to the quantities and prices of outputs on the demand side as well as other information on input and output markets. Generally speaking, the more capitalistically developed and free an economy, the larger the share of national output produced by the business sector. Over the past two centuries, the economic transformation of developing economies to industrialized market economies has raised the significance of the business sector in national economies. More recently, global economic problems in 2008 and 2009 have caused profits for many business firms to fall precipitously to relatively low levels in historic terms. How will firms adjust to falling profits? What effects will the economic and financial crises have on future business capital investment, output, profit rates, profit margins, total profits, and employment? Our profit system model can be used to gain insights into these and other related questions.

Exploiting the power of profit for business and economic analysis, forecasting, and stock valuation is the goal of this book. In this way we seek to contribute to our understanding of profit and its impacts on business activities.

Chapter 2
Profit System Models of the Firm, Industry, and Business Sector

This chapter proposes an integrated profit system model of the firm consisting of dynamic relationships among fundamental business variables. The first part of the chapter derives theoretical profit system models of production, capital stock, profit rate, profit margin, total profit, and employment for firms in the business sector, in addition to related models of employee compensation and other business variables. The second part of the chapter provides empirical profit system models that capture the relationships between these variables as a system of dynamic equations. These empirical models can be applied to individual firms, industries, and the whole business sector.

For managers of firms, these new empirical models provide a battery of methods to better understand the interrelationships between sales, fixed tangible assets, and profits. Importantly, the models can be used to not only analyze recent business decisions but forecast critical operating variables too. What production is needed by a firm to meet forecasted sales? How much investment in new capital is needed to meet forecasted capital stocks? What profit guidance is expected for the next period? On the industry and business sector levels these empirical models can be used by a wide variety of interested parties for business and economic analyses, forecasting, policy analyses, impact studies, and stock valuation. We demonstrate a number of these practical uses in forthcoming chapters.

2.1 Theoretical Foundation of Profit System Models of the Firm

We begin with the simple identity that firm output is equal to the product of the profit rate and market value of capital stock divided by the profit margin. This production identity can be rearranged to easily derive models of capital stock, profit rate, profit margin, and employment in the business sector. Together, these models constitute an integrated profit system model of firms.

There are two approaches to derive our profit system model of production: a mathematical economic approach and an accounting approach. Readers who are not interested in the mathematical economic approach can skip to the accounting approach.

A. Anari, J.W. Kolari, *The Power of Profit*, DOI 10.1007/978-1-4419-0649-6_2,

2.1.1 Mathematical Economic Approach to Obtaining a Profit System Model of Production

Output for a firm is commonly represented by the Cobb–Douglas production function:[1]

$$Y_t = A_t K_t^S H_t^{1-S}, \tag{2.1}$$

where Y is the output, A is the total factor productivity, K is the amount of capital, H is the amount of labor hired, and S is a parameter less than 1. Output can be defined as either sales or value added (e.g., dollar revenues from goods and services sold minus dollar costs of goods and services purchased). Assuming that each unit of output is priced at \$1 and that the wage rate is equal to the marginal product of labor, the *accounting profit function* (Z) conventionally computed by business firms is

$$Z_t = A_t K_t^S H_t^{1-S} - (1-S)A_t K_t^S H_t^{-S} H_t = S A_t K_t^S H_t^{1-S} = S Y_t, \tag{2.2}$$

where the dollar value of the marginal product of labor $(1-S)A_t K_t^S H_t^{-S}$ equals the wage rate. Note that S is capital's share of output or profit margin (i.e., profit divided by output).

Dividing equation (2.2) by K_t yields the profit rate R_t as

$$R_t = \frac{S Y_t}{K_t}. \tag{2.3}$$

Hence, a profit system model of production can be written as

$$Y_t = \frac{R_t K_t}{S_t}. \tag{2.4}$$

Thus, output in the Cobb–Douglas production function is equal to the product of the profit rate and capital stock divided by the profit margin for a business firm. In the Cobb–Douglas production function, the profit margin or capital's share of output S is a constant. However, as shown in equation (2.4), we assume (for practical reasons explained shortly) that the profit margin is a variable that varies over time S_t.[2] This key assumption changes equation (2.3) to a model of profit rates with time-varying S_t as follows:

$$R_t = \frac{S_t Y_t}{K_t}. \tag{2.5}$$

---

[1] See Solow (1957) and Felipe and Holz (2001).
[2] In a recent paper McGratten and Prescott (2000) allow profit margins to vary in the Cobb–Douglas function.

2.1.2 Accounting Approach to Obtaining a Profit System Model of Production

The average profit rate R_t in period t commonly calculated by firms can be alternatively defined as the dollar value of nominal profit or earnings Z_t in period t generated from a stock of capital divided by the total market value of the capital stock K_t, or

$$R_t = \frac{Z_t}{K_t}. \tag{2.6}$$

Profit margin in period t is defined as nominal profit Z_t divided by the dollar value of nominal output in either sales or value-added terms:

$$S_t = \frac{Z_t}{Y_t}. \tag{2.7}$$

Solving for Z_t in equations (2.6) and (2.7), we alternatively obtain

$$Z_t = R_t K_t = S_t Y_t. \tag{2.8}$$

No matter how profit is defined (before or after charging interest costs, taxes, depreciation, etc.), the identities (2.6) and (2.7) result in equation (2.4) as long as the same figure for profit is used for computation of R_t and S_t. Derivation of the output model (2.4) from accounting identities (2.6) and (2.7) shows that it is not necessary to make any assumptions to derive the output model (2.4). In particular, it is not necessary to assume profit maximization.

Equation (2.4) can be viewed as a profit system model of managers' production behavior in the business sector. Consider a firm that has capital stock K. The firm's capital stock is the bundle of investment goods selected by the firm in the past based on expected hurdle profit rates. The firm's management is expected to attain the profit rate R used for selecting investment projects, which means that R is the target profit rate. Multiplying the expected target profit rate by the amount of capital stock gives the expected target total profit, or $Z_t = R_t K_t$. In order to attain the expected target profit, the firm must achieve a target level of sales or output derived by multiplying the expected target profit ($Z_t = R_t K_t$) and expected sales to profit ratio ($1/S_t = Y_t/Z_t$) to get $Y_t = R_t K_t / S_t$, namely, equation (2.4). While ex post realized profit rates and profit margins can be negative on a firm basis or even on an industry basis, expected target profit rates and profit margins are positive, due to the fact that firms do not embark on production activities unless they anticipate positive profits in the future.

Equation (2.4) shows that higher output depends on a higher profit rate and a smaller profit margin (or larger labor share of output). Also, equation (2.4) reveals that a falling profit rate does not necessarily lead to falling output. The adverse impact on output of falling profit rates in the numerator of equation (2.4) can be offset by a smaller profit margin in the denominator of equation (2.4), which means a growing share of labor. These observations are important for two reasons. First, falling profit rates have been considered as a prelude to the collapse of the capitalist system due to Marx's assertion that falling profit rates would eventually lead to the collapse of the capitalist system.[3] This assertion does not take into account declining profit margin effects that can boost output. Second, many economists have assumed that the impacts on output of changes in profit margins and profit rates are the same. The profit system model of production shows that *both* profit rates and profit margins are key determinants of output with distinctly different impacts on output.

2.1.3 Profit System Model of Capital Stock

Solving for K in terms of the other variables in equation (2.4) gives the value of the stock of capital as the discounted value of profit, or

$$K_t = \frac{S_t Y_t}{R_t}, \tag{2.9}$$

where the numerator shows profit as the product of output and the profit margin, and the denominator is the discount rate equal to the average profit rate. Similar to the accelerator theory of investment,[4] which posits that changes in capital stock (i.e., investment) depend on changes in output, equation (2.8) likewise shows that capital stock is a function of output. Investment in neoclassical theories depends on the required profit rate.[5] The capital stock in equation (2.8) depends on both the profit rate and the profit margin. While our model shares similarities to these well-known investment theories, it proposes that both output and profitability drive capital investment via the functional relation defined in equation (2.9).

2.1.4 Profit System Model of Profit Margins

By solving equation (2.4) for the profit margin, we obtain

$$S_t = \frac{R_t K_t}{Y_t}. \tag{2.10}$$

This equation implies that S_t can be viewed as a variable related to R_t, K_t, and Y_t in any period t. Measurement of the actual time series of S_t for the USA confirms that capital's share of output (as well as labor's share) is a variable. Willis and Wrobleski

---

[3] For example, see Marx (1894), Gillman (1957), Duménil and Lévy (1993), Shaikh and Tonak (1994), Wolff (2003), and Mohun (2003, 2006).

[4] See Clark (1917) and Chenery (1952).

[5] See Jorgenson and Yun (2001).

(2007) report that, in the US nonfinancial corporate business sector, capital (labor) shares fluctuate within a range of 16 percent (84 percent) to 22 percent (78 percent). The authors offer some potential explanations for this variability, including delayed adjustments in wages and salaries over time, business cycle uncertainty, and changing risk-sharing arrangements between workers and firms throughout the business cycle. In this regard, former Federal Reserve Bank Chairman Alan Greenspan once observed that profit margins vary over time with the business cycle: "... in the U.S., profit margins ... have begun to stabilize, which is an early sign we are in the later stages of a cycle."[6] Finally, relevant to Section 2.2 on the empirical application of the above equations, the assumption that the profit margin is not a constant per equation (2.10) allows more accurate forecasts of not only S_t but Y_t, R_t, and K_t, as defined in equations (2.4), (2.5), and (2.9), respectively.

2.1.5 Profit System Model of Employment

Dividing both sides of equation (2.4) by H_t, the number of hours of employment or the number of employees hired in period t, results in the following equations:

$$\frac{Y_t}{H_t} = \frac{R_t K_t}{S_t H_t} \qquad (2.11)$$

and

$$B_t = \frac{R_t K_t}{S_t H_t}, \qquad (2.12)$$

where labor productivity in period t is

$$B_t = \frac{Y_t}{H_t}. \qquad (2.13)$$

Solving for H_t gives employment determined by profit rates, capital stock, profit margins, and labor productivity:

$$H_t = \frac{R_t K_t}{S_t B_t}. \qquad (2.14)$$

Equation (2.14) reveals a positive relationship between employment and both profit rates and capital stock in the numerator but a negative relationship between employment and both labor productivity and capital's share of output (profit margin) in the denominator.

Comparison of equations (2.4) and (2.14) shows that, while business output Y_t is determined by R_t, S_t, and K_t, employment is determined by these variables plus labor productivity.

---

[6] See the *Wall Street Journal*, February 28, 2007, p. C1.

2.1.6 Other Key Business Variables: Sales Tax, Depreciation, Total Employment Compensation, and Wage Rate

A number of useful relationships can be defined with the above variables. Total sales tax T_t is the product of sales tax rate τ_t and total output of the business sector Y_t:

$$T_t = \tau_t Y_t. \tag{2.15}$$

Total depreciation expense G_t is the product of depreciation rate g_t and total nominal capital stock K_t:

$$G_t = g_t K_t. \tag{2.16}$$

Total employees' compensation C_t is

$$C_t = Y_t - Z_t - G_t - T_t, \tag{2.17}$$

where output Y is measured in value-added terms. If Y is measured in sales, the cost of goods and services purchased is deducted from Y. Lastly, the wage rate per hour of employment in nominal terms is

$$W_t = \frac{C_t}{H_t}. \tag{2.18}$$

2.1.7 Profit System Channel of Inflation Transmission

Anari and Kolari (2002) have argued that home owners, when renting their houses, add expected inflation over the rental period to real rents. This inflation adjustment is similar to Fisher's (1930) famous observation that lenders add expected inflation to real interest rates when lending funds to borrowers. Since home prices are the discounted values of expected rents, higher rents containing an inflation premium lead to higher home prices. In general, the same model of transmission of inflation from profit to capital stock can be applied to other types of capital stock. Thus, equation (2.9) can be written as

$$K_t = \frac{S_t \bar{Y}_t \widehat{P}_t}{R_t}, \tag{2.19}$$

where output in real terms is

$$\bar{Y}_t = \frac{Y_t}{\widehat{P}_t} \tag{2.20}$$

and $\widehat{P}_t$ is the output price index (deflator) in period t that takes into account the general price level (i.e., inflation). In equation (2.19) owners of capital stock multiply expected profit in real terms $(S_t \bar{Y}_t)$ by an index of expected inflation $(\widehat{P}_t)$.

Consequently, the nominal value of K_t in equation (2.19) contains information about expected inflation. The impact of inflation on capital stock is transmitted to nominal output in equation (2.4) when firms use nominal values of capital stock to determine their target profits and output levels.

2.1.8 Profit System Models of Deflated Output, Deflated Capital Stock, and Deflated Labor Productivity

Output and capital stock in the Cobb–Douglas production function (2.1) are in real terms. By contrast, firms and market participants normally use actual (nominal) output and capital stock in equations (2.6) and (2.7) for computing profit rates and profit margins. As shown in forthcoming chapters, the distinction between real and nominal terms becomes important when the profit system model is applied to industries (or group of firms) and the whole business sector (or all firms). For these reasons we next provide profit system models in deflated terms.

Solving for real output ($\bar{Y}_t$) in equation (2.19) gives

$$\bar{Y}_t = \frac{R_t K_t}{S_t \widehat{P}_t} \tag{2.21}$$

or

$$\bar{Y}_t = \frac{R_t \bar{K}_t}{S_t}, \tag{2.22}$$

where deflated capital stock is

$$\bar{K}_t = \frac{K_t}{\widehat{P}_t} \tag{2.23}$$

and $\widehat{P}_t$ is the output price deflator. Equations (2.21) and (2.22) show that we can compute output in real terms from capital stocks deflated by the output price deflator. Note that capital stock deflated by an output price deflator in equation (2.23) is not capital stock in real terms.

Equation (2.22) results in the following three equations for deflated capital stocks, profit rates, and profit margins, respectively, when deflated output and capital stock are used:

$$\bar{K}_t = \frac{S_t \bar{Y}_t}{R_t} \tag{2.24}$$

$$R_t = \frac{S_t \bar{Y}_t}{\bar{K}_t} \tag{2.25}$$

$$S_t = \frac{R_t \bar{K}_t}{\bar{Y}_t}. \tag{2.26}$$

For transforming output in nominal terms to real terms, we need a price model for the good or service under consideration – that is, a price function which shows the relationship between price levels and a number of variables. In the second part of this chapter, we present a model of prices based on Wicksell's (1898) theory of the relationships between prices and interest rates and then employ this price model in applications of our profit system model to the aggregate business sector in the Chapter 3 and the corporate sector in Chapter 4. When this model is applied on the microlevel to an individual firm, it can be augmented by adding the firm's specific variables determining the prices of outputs, such as unit labor cost, unit material cost, unit energy cost, and so on.

Using equation (2.22) and relationships (2.11), (2.12), (2.13), and (2.14) results in the following employment equation when employment is determined by deflated capital stock, profit rate, profit margin, and labor productivity in real terms:

$$H_t = \frac{R_t \bar{K}_t}{S_t \bar{B}_t}. \tag{2.14a}$$

2.1.9 Total Profit Equations

Equation (2.8) shows that total profit in current dollars is given by

$$Z_t = S_t Y_t \tag{2.8a}$$

or

$$Z_t = R_t K_t. \tag{2.8b}$$

Dividing both sides of equation (2.8a) and (2.8b) by a price index for output gives deflated total profit:

$$\bar{Z}_t = S_t \bar{Y}_t \tag{2.8c}$$

or

$$\bar{Z}_t = R_t \bar{K}_t. \tag{2.8d}$$

2.1.10 Profit System Economic Equilibrium

Since capital formation projects are expected to generate output and profit over the useful economic lives of projects, the variables R_t, S_t, and Y_t in equation (2.9) are expected values wherein expectations are formed at the initial stage of project evaluation. Consequently, equation (2.9) can be written as

$$K_t = \frac{E_t(S)E_t(Y)}{E_t(R)}, \tag{2.27}$$

where $E_t(S), E_t(Y)$, and $E_t(R)$ are expected values or steady states of S_t, Y_t, and R_t as of time t over the useful economic lives of projects, respectively.

Substituting K_t from equation (2.27) into equation (2.4) gives

$$Y_t = \frac{R_t E_t(S) E_t(Y)}{S_t E_t(R)}, \tag{2.28}$$

where R_t and S_t are the realized values of the profit rate and profit margin, respectively. Equation (2.28) shows that output in the steady state wherein $E_t(Y) = Y_t$ (i.e., expected output is equal to realized output) occurs when the expected profit rate and profit margin are equal to their realized values or $E_t(R) = R_t$ and $E_t(S) = S_t$. In a competitive economy, if realized profit rates are higher than expected profit rates, higher output by existing firms and entering firms that seek profit opportunities will lead to reduced profit rates, while lower than expected profit rates will lead to reduced output and abandonment of business activities.

The speed of attaining equilibrium, at which realized profit rate and profit margins are equal to their expected values when business investment projects were selected, depends on the gestation period of capital formation projects. Over the past three centuries, industrialization of formerly agrarian economies has resulted in the selection and implementation of business investment projects with long gestation periods. For instance, it takes 7 years to build a nuclear power station, which means that it may take more than 7 years to find out whether the realized profit rate on a nuclear power plant is greater than the expected profit rate when the investment project was selected.

In the capitalist system profit rates not only determine the level of capital formation activity but also the level of production activity *after* capital formation projects come on stream. As Schumpeter (1942) has argued, selection of investment projects is a gamble with results only known in the future. Sometime after projects are implemented, entrepreneurs realize that some projects should not have been selected. The realization that the realized profit rates are lower than expected hurdle rates leads to abandonment of unprofitable or less profitable activities and the release of resources locked up in these activities, a process he famously dubbed "creative destruction."

In the for-profit sector, the price system can equilibrate supply and demand to the extent that price movements reflect profit rate movements. Changes in prices may have no effect on the supply of and demand for goods and services if price changes do not lead to changes in profit rates – for instance, when higher costs of energy inputs are offset by lower labor costs due to higher labor productivity.

2.1.11 Profit System Theory of Economic Growth

There is a vast literature on the subject of economic growth that is beyond the scope of this book.[7] Here we seek to focus on applying our profit system model to the problem of understanding economic growth. To do this we rewrite equation (2.5) as

---

[7]For example, see Schumpeter (1934), Solow (1956), Swan (1956), Barro (1997), Foley (1999), Charles (2002), Lucas (2004), Aghion and Durlauf (2005), and many others.

follows:

$$R_t = S_t A_t K_t^{S-1} H_t^{1-S} = S_t A_t \left(\frac{H_t}{K_t} \right)^{1-S}. \tag{2.5a}$$

Together, the set of equations for output Y_t, capital stock K_t, profit rate R_t as represented by equation (2.5a), profit margin S_t, employment H_t, and wage rate W_t can be viewed as a profit system theory of economic growth. Equation (2.5a) shows that higher total factor productivity A_t results in higher profit rates for a given level of capital and labor. Higher profit rates lead to higher output in equation (2.4). Higher output in equation (2.17) implies higher employee compensation and higher wages in equation (2.18). Higher labor productivity B_t in equation (2.14) is associated with less labor employed for a given level of output, which increases the availability of labor inputs for new economic activities. Thus, the set of equations for Y_t, K_t, R_t, S_t, H_t, and W_t represents a growth process that has taken place over the past two centuries in industrialized economies. As an example, productivity growth in the agrarian sector resulted in more agricultural goods produced with less labor, thereby releasing more labor to be employed in the manufacturing and services sectors accompanied by growing real wage rates. Economic growth in our profit system model is driven by profit and attained by the selection of more profitable projects and abandonment of less profitable activities making entrepreneurship an important factor in economic growth. This Schumpeterian creative destruction has been described by former Federal Reserve Chairman Alan Greenspan as "... the process by which the cash flow from obsolescent, low-return capital is invested in high-return, cutting-edge technology."[8]

2.1.12 Profit System Theory of Business Cycles

According to equations (2.4) and (2.9), fluctuations in both profit rates and profit margins generate fluctuations in output per equation (2.4) and capital stock per equation (2.9). Note that changes in profit rates and profit margins have opposing effects on output and capital stock, as the profit rate is in the numerator of output equation but the denominator of capital stock equation, while profit margin is in the denominator of output but the numerator of capital stock. Thus, a change in profit could generate a business cycle through the interaction between output and capital stock in response to a change in profit. According to Samuelson (1939a), interactions between multiplier effects and accelerator effects may generate business cycles. Increases in investment are expected to result in higher output (the multiplier effect), whereas increases in output are expected to result in higher investments (the accelerator effect). Relating these concepts to our profit system model of business activity, the interactions between output per equation (2.4) and capital stock per

---

[8] Swan (1956).

equation (2.9) are due to changes in profit rates and profit margins, whose changes
are due to simultaneous changes in output and capital stock also. To demonstrate the
effects of these interactions, Chapter 3 applies our profit system model to business
cycle analysis in the US economy.

2.1.13 Financial Sector Variables: Interest Rate and Credit

So far we derived all the components of a profit system model of the firm as if
the economy consisted of a goods and services market plus a labor market. But
advanced market economies have another important component – namely, the financial sector. Before proceeding to the next section's empirical representations of our
model, it is worthwhile to look at the relationship between its key variables and the
financial sector. When an economy has a financial system in which consumption
and capital stocks can be financed by borrowing loanable funds, then the cost and
availability of credit become important variables affecting profit rate, profit margin,
capital stock, and output. Higher (lower) interest rate charges on borrowed funds
decrease (increase) total profits in the numerator of equations (2.6) and (2.7) and,
in turn, lead to lower (higher) profit rate and profit margin. Changes in the cost of
capital or interest rate affect output and capital stocks through their impacts on profit
rate and profit margin on the supply side. On the demand side higher (lower) interest
rates on consumer loans result in lower (higher) demand for goods and services.

   The important roles played by the cost and availability of credit in the financial
system necessitate their inclusion in the empirical profit system model of the firm
discussed in Section 2.2.

2.2 Empirical Profit System Models in the Form
of Dynamic Equations

Profit system models of output, capital stock, profit rate, and profit margin can be
used by an individual firm for planning, forecasting, and research on business output, capital stock, total profit, profit rate, and profit margin. The dependency of these
fundamental variables on one another in the profit system models derived above
means that in the real world the magnitudes of these variables are determined simultaneously. For this reason systems of dynamic equations containing five equations
for the five variables (i.e., output, capital stock, total profit, profit rate, and profit
margin) are the most appropriate and potentially useful empirical representation of
profit system models.

2.2.1 General Approach

As an initial step to developing empirical versions of our theoretical profit system
models, we take the logarithms of both sides of capital stock equation (2.9), output equation (2.4), profit rate equation (2.5), profit margin equation (2.10), and total

profit equation (2.8), resulting in the following simple contemporaneous relationships (i.e., relationships in the same period) between the logarithms of Y_t, K_t, R_t, S_t,
and Z_t:

$$k_t = y_t - r_t + s_t \qquad (2.29)$$

$$y_t = r_t - s_t + k_t \qquad (2.30)$$

$$r_t = y_t + s_t - k_t \qquad (2.31)$$

$$s_t = -y_t + r_t + k_t \qquad (2.32)$$

$$z_t = r_t + k_t = y_t + s_t, \qquad (2.33)$$

where the coefficients of the principle variables in the model (y_t, r_t, s_t, k_t) are either
± 1 as posited by theory, and there is no residual error. Note that we have two
alternative specifications for total profit in (2.33).

Next, it is reasonable to assume that, given the profit system models represented
by equations (2.9), (2.4), (2.5), (2.10), and (2.8) and their log-linear versions (2.29),
(2.30), (2.31), (2.32), and (2.33), firms and market participants use lagged values of
the profit rate, profit margin, capital stock, and output to form conditional expectations or forecasts of their current and future values. The simplest approach to
modeling expectations when forecasting each variable in period t is to use the values
of other variables in the previous period $t - 1$ as follows:

$$k_t = \alpha_0 + \alpha_1 y_{t-1} + \alpha_2 r_{t-1} + \alpha_3 s_{t-1} \qquad (2.34)$$

$$y_t = \beta_0 + \beta_2 r_{t-1} + \beta_3 s_{t-1} + \beta_4 k_{t-1} \qquad (2.35)$$

$$r_t = \theta_0 + \theta_1 y_{t-1} + \theta_3 s_{t-1} + \theta_4 k_{t-1} \qquad (2.36)$$

$$s_t = \eta_0 + \eta_1 y_{t-1} + \eta_2 r_{t-1} + \eta_4 k_{t-1} \qquad (2.37)$$

$$z_t = v_0 + v_1 r_{t-1} + v_2 k_{t-1} = v_0 + v_1 y_{t-1} + v_2 s_{t-1}, \qquad (2.38)$$

where the left-hand-side variables are expected values or forecasts of capital stock,
output, profit rate, profit margin, and total profits, respectively, for period t using the
values of the other variables in the previous period $t - 1$. A constant term is added
to each equation for econometric estimation of the equations. Note that, when lags
of the variables are used for forming expectations, the coefficients on the lagged
variables are no longer equal to plus or minus unity and residual error exists. To
minimize residual errors in these equations, other variables can be included in the
set of variables used for forecasting the fundamental business variables.

Equations (2.34), (2.35), (2.36), (2.37), and (2.38) can provide estimates of
expectations or forecasts of capital stock, output, profit rate, profit margin, and

total profit. Different econometric methods can be applied to their estimation. When using a system approach for estimating all the equations, we can reduce the number of equations (and hence coefficients) to be estimated by using the forecasts of the variables generated in the model based on a priori information that contemporaneous relationships between the logarithms of the principle variables in the model (y_t, k_t, r_t, s_t, z_t) are either ± 1, as shown in equations (2.29), (2.30), (2.31), (2.32), and (2.33). For instance, equations (2.37) and (2.38) can be derived from estimates of equations (2.34), (2.35), and (2.36). Instead of estimating equation (2.37), we can compute equation (2.37) by using the forecast of k_t from equation (2.34), forecast of y_t from equation (2.35), and forecast of r_t from equation (2.36). In turn, this forecast of profit margin s_t can then be used for forecasting total profit z_t per equation (2.33) as the sum of the forecast of profit margin s_t and forecast of output from equation (2.35). Alternatively, the forecast of total profit z_t per equation (2.33) can be computed as the sum of the forecast of capital stock k_t from equation (2.34) and forecast of profit rate r_t from equation (2.36). These specifications result in the following system of equations:

$$k_t = \alpha_0 + \alpha_1 y_{t-1} + \alpha_2 r_{t-1} + \alpha_3 s_{t-1} \tag{2.39.1}$$

$$y_t = \beta_0 + \beta_2 r_{t-1} + \beta_3 s_{t-1} + \beta_4 k_{t-1} \tag{2.39.2}$$

$$r_t = \theta_0 + \theta_1 y_{t-1} + \theta_3 s_{t-1} + \theta_4 k_{t-1} \tag{2.39.3}$$

$$s_t = k_t + r_t - y_t \tag{2.39.4}$$

$$z_t = r_t + k_t = y_t + s_t, \tag{2.39.5}$$

The empirical representation of these profit system models of the firm in system equations (2.39) can be extended to include more lags of the fundamental variables as well as other variables which may improve the forecasts of the fundamental variables.

2.2.1.1 Profit System Models of the Goods and Services Market

Profit system models of the goods and services market can be specified in either nominal (current dollar) or deflated (constant dollar) terms. Table 2.1 provides a simple model specification with output and capital stock variables in nominal terms. System equations (2.39) are augmented with financial sector variables. As already noted, our fundamental business variables can be affected by financial sector variables, such as the interest rate and total nonfinancial debt outstanding. In empirical application of the model to the US economy, we conducted variable addition tests and found that these variables are influential with respect to capital stock, output, and profit rate. Consequently, we included these variables in the profit system model. Lag orders for these financial sector variables are determined empirically.

Table 2.1 Basic profit system model of the goods and services market with output and capital stock in current dollars

The following system of equations provides a profit system model of the goods and services market in current dollars. Financial sector variables (i.e., the Federal funds rate and growth rate of nonfinancial debt outstanding in nominal terms) are included in the model with lag (L) structures determined empirically.

Capital stock model

$$k_t = \alpha_0 + \alpha_1 y_{t-1} + \alpha_2 r_{t-1} + \alpha_3 s_{t-1} + \alpha_5 \dot{D}_{t-L} + \alpha_6 F_{t-L} \qquad (2.1.1)$$

Output model

$$y_t = \beta_0 + \beta_2 r_{t-1} + \beta_3 s_{t-1} + \beta_4 k_{t-1} + \beta_5 \dot{D}_{t-L} + \beta_6 F_{t-L} \qquad (2.1.2)$$

Profit rate model

$$r_t = \theta_0 + \theta_1 y_{t-1} + \theta_3 s_{t-1} + \theta_4 k_{t-1} + \theta_5 \dot{D}_{t-L} + \theta_6 F_{t-L} \qquad (2.1.3)$$

Profit margin model

$$s_t = r_t + k_t - y_t \qquad (2.1.4)$$

Total profit model

$$Z_t = R_t \times K_t = Y_t \times S_t \qquad (2.1.5)$$

Variables are defined as follows:

$Y(y)$ = sales or output in current dollars (log)
$K(k)$ = capital stock in current dollars (log)
$R(r)$ = profit rate (log)
$S(s)$ = profit margin (log)
Z = total profit
F = Federal funds rate in percent (financial sector variable)
$\dot{D}$ = growth rate of nonfinancial debt outstanding in percent (financial sector variable),
where K_t = antilog k_t, Y_t = antilog y_t, R_t = antilog r_t, and S_t = antilog s_t

This basic profit system model can be used when we are interested only in the goods and services market and seek to analyze and forecast the fundamental variables in nominal terms. Empirical applications of this model to individual firms are presented in Chapter 7. There the model is estimated for two large US corporations (namely, IBM and Johnson & Johnson), and the resultant historical simulations of these firms' profits are used for valuing their stock prices.

Table 2.2 simplifies the model in Table 2.1 by using the forecast of log capital stock from equation (2.2.1) in equation (2.2.2)'s forecast of log output. Also, the forecast of log capital stock from equation (2.2.1) and log output from equation (2.2.2) are used in equation (2.2.3)'s forecast of log profit margin. The advantage of this alternative model is that the number of coefficients to be estimated is reduced by two; consequently, the model may be useful when the number of observations in the sample period is small. The disadvantage of the model is that error in forecasting capital stock from equation (2.2.1) may lead to errors in forecasting output

Table 2.2 Alternative basic profit system model of the goods and services market with output and capital stock in current dollars

The following system of equations provides a profit system model of the goods and services market in current dollars. Financial sector variables (i.e., the Federal funds rate and growth rate of nonfinancial debt outstanding in nominal terms) are included in the model with lag structure (L) determined empirically.

Capital stock model

$$k_t = \alpha_0 + \alpha_1 Y_{t-1} + \alpha_2 r_{t-1} + \alpha_3 s_{t-1} + \alpha_5 \dot{D}_{t-L} + \alpha_6 F_{t-L} \tag{2.2.1}$$

Output model

$$y_t = \beta_0 + \beta_2 r_{t-1} + \beta_3 s_{t-1} + k_t + \beta_5 \dot{D}_{t-L} + \beta_6 F_{t-L} \tag{2.2.2}$$

Profit rate model

$$r_t = \theta_0 + y_t + \theta_3 s_{t-1} - k_t + \theta_5 \dot{D}_{t-L} + \theta_6 F_{t-L} \tag{2.2.3}$$

Profit margin model

$$s_t = r_t + k_t - y_t \tag{2.2.4}$$

Total profit model

$$Z_t = R_t \times K_t = Y_t \times S_t \tag{2.2.5}$$

Variables are defined as follows:

$Y(y)$ = sales or output in current dollars (log)
$K(k)$ = capital stock in current dollars (log)
$R(r)$ = profit rate (log)
$S(s)$ = profit margin (log)
Z = total profit
F = Federal funds rate in percent (financial sector variable)
$\dot{D}$ = growth rate of nonfinancial debt outstanding in percent (financial sector variable),
where K_t = antilog k_t, Y_t = antilog y_t, R_t = antilog r_t, and S_t = antilog s_t

in equation (2.2.2) and likewise in forecasting profit margin in equation (2.2.3). In Chapter 5 we apply this alternative model to 12 US industries.

Firms and market participants normally use local-currency-denominated, or nominal, values of output and capital stocks for making business decisions. For this reason we use nominal values of these variables in the basic profit system models in Tables 2.1 and 2.2. However, it is essential to distinguish between local-currency-denominated (nominal) and deflated or constant dollar (real) values when the model is applied to the aggregate national economy, aggregate business sector, and aggregate corporate sector.

Table 2.3 presents the basic profit system model of the goods and services market with output and capital stock deflated using an output price index. Derivation of this model is similar to the model presented in Table 2.1. Taking logarithms of both sides of capital stock equation (2.24), output equation (2.22), profit rate equation (2.25), profit margin equation (2.26), and total profit equations (2.8c) and (2.8d) results in the following contemporaneous relationships (i.e., relationships in the same period)

Table 2.3 Basic profit system model of the goods and services market with output and capital stock in constant dollars

---

The following system of equations provides a profit system model of the goods and services market in which output, capital stock, and total profit are deflated (i.e., values are deflated for changes in the general price level due to inflation). Financial sector variables (i.e., the Federal funds rate and growth rate of nonfinancial debt outstanding in deflated terms) are included in the model with lag structure (L) determined empirically.

Deflated capital stock model

$$\bar{k}_t = \alpha_0 + \alpha_1 \bar{y}_{t-1} + \alpha_2 r_{t-1} + \alpha_3 s_{t-1} + \alpha_5 \dot{\bar{D}}_{t-L} + \alpha_6 F_{t-L} \qquad (2.3.1)$$

Deflated (real) output model

$$\bar{y}_t = \beta_0 + \beta_2 r_{t-1} + \beta_3 s_{t-1} + \beta_4 \bar{k}_{t-1} + \beta_5 \dot{\bar{D}}_{t-L} + \beta_6 F_{t-L} \qquad (2.3.2)$$

Profit rate model

$$r_t = \theta_0 + \theta_1 \bar{y}_{t-1} + \theta_3 s_{t-1} + \theta_4 \bar{k}_{t-1} + \theta_5 \dot{\bar{D}}_{t-L} + \theta_6 F_{t-L} \qquad (2.3.3)$$

Profit margin model

$$s_t = \bar{k}_t + r_t - \bar{y}_t \qquad (2.3.4)$$

Deflated total profit model

$$\bar{z}_t = v_0 + v_1 r_{t-1} + v_2 \bar{k}_{t-1} \text{ or } \bar{z}_t = v_0 + v_1 \bar{y}_{t-1} + v_2 s_{t-1}, \qquad (2.3.5)$$

Variables are defined as follows:

$\bar{k} = $ log deflated capital stock $\bar{K}$
$\bar{y} = $ log deflated (real) output $\bar{Y}$
$r = $ log profit rate R (equal to total profit divided by capital)
$s = $ log profit margin S (equal to total profit divided by output)
$\bar{z} = $ log deflated (real) total profit $\bar{Z}$
$F = $ Federal funds rate in percent (financial sector variable)
$\dot{\bar{D}} = $ growth rate of deflated nonfinancial debt outstanding in percent (financial sector variable),
where $\bar{K} = $ antilog $\bar{k}$, $\bar{Y} = $ antilog $\bar{y}$, $R = $ antilog r, $S = $ antilog s, and $\bar{Z} = $ antilog $\bar{z}$

---

between the logarithms of deflated $\bar{K}_t$, deflated (real) $\bar{Y}_t$, R_t, S_t, and deflated total profit $\bar{Z}_t$:

$$\bar{k}_t = \bar{y}_t - r_t + s_t \qquad (2.40)$$

$$\bar{y}_t = r_t - s_t + \bar{k}_t \qquad (2.41)$$

$$r_t = \bar{y}_t + s_t - \bar{k}_t \qquad (2.42)$$

$$s_t = -\bar{y}_t + r_t + \bar{k}_t \qquad (2.43)$$

$$\bar{z}_t = r_t + \bar{k}_t = s_t + \bar{y}_t, \qquad (2.44)$$

where the coefficients of the contemporaneous relationships between the logarithms of the principle variables in the model ($\bar{y}_t$, $\bar{k}_t$, r_t, s_t, and $\bar{z}_t$) are either ± 1 as posited by theory.

As before, the simplest models of expectations or forecasts for each variable in period t use the values of other variables in the previous period $t - 1$ as follows:

$$\bar{k}_t = \alpha_0 + \alpha_1 \bar{y}_{t-1} + \alpha_2 r_{t-1} + \alpha_3 s_{t-1} \tag{2.45}$$

$$\bar{y}_t = \beta_0 + \beta_2 r_{t-1} + \beta_3 s_{t-1} + \beta_4 \bar{k}_{t-1} \tag{2.46}$$

$$r_t = \theta_0 + \theta_1 \bar{y}_{t-1} + \theta_3 s_{t-1} + \theta_4 \bar{k}_{t-1} \tag{2.47}$$

$$s_t = \omega_0 + \omega_1 \bar{y}_{t-1} + \omega_2 r_{t-1} + \omega_4 \bar{k}_{t-1} \tag{2.48}$$

$$\bar{z}_t = v_0 + v_1 r_{t-1} + v_2 \bar{k}_{t-1} = v_0 + v_1 \bar{y}_{t-1} + v_2 s_{t-1}, \tag{2.49}$$

where the left-hand-side variables are expected values or forecasts of deflated capital stock, deflated output, profit rate, profit margin, and deflated total profit in period t. A constant term is added to each equation for purposes of econometric estimation. Again, when lags of the variables are used for forming expectations, the coefficients associated with the lagged variables are no longer equal to plus or minus unity and forecasting errors exist. To minimize forecast errors other variables can be incorporated in the set of variables used for forecasting the fundamental business variables.

Equations (2.45), (2.46), (2.47), (2.48), and (2.49) can be used for forming expectations or forecasting deflated capital stock, deflated output, profit rate, profit margin, and deflated total profit. Different econometric methods can be employed to estimate these equations. As before, when using a system approach for estimating all the equations, we can reduce the number of equations (and coefficients) to be estimated by using the forecasts of some of the variables generated in the model to forecast other variables. For instance, to forecast profit margin s_t per equation (2.43), we can use the forecast of $\bar{k}_t$ from equation (2.45), forecast of $\bar{y}_t$ from equation (2.46), and forecast of r_t from equation (2.47). In this way we obtain the following profit system model:

$$\bar{k}_t = \alpha_0 + \alpha_1 \bar{y}_{t-1} + \alpha_2 r_{t-1} + \alpha_3 s_{t-1} \tag{2.50.1}$$

$$\bar{y}_t = \beta_0 + \beta_2 r_{t-1} + \beta_3 s_{t-1} + \beta_4 \bar{k}_{t-1} \tag{2.50.2}$$

$$r_t = \theta_0 + \theta_1 \bar{y}_{t-1} + \theta_3 s_{t-1} + \theta_4 \bar{k}_{t-1} \tag{2.50.3}$$

$$s_t = \bar{k}_t + r_t - \bar{y}_t \tag{2.50.4}$$

$$\bar{z}_t = v_0 + v_1 r_{t-1} + v_2 \bar{k}_{t-1} \text{ or } \bar{z}_t = v_0 + v_1 \bar{y}_{t-1} + v_2 s_{t-1}. \tag{2.50.5}$$

The empirical profit system model comprised of dynamic equations (2.50) can be extended to include more lags of the fundamental variables and other variables to improve forecasts of the fundamental variables. Table 2.3 provides an example of such a system of equations. In this model output, capital stock, and total profit variables are deflated by an output price deflator. Also, the system of equations is augmented with financial sector variables (i.e., the Federal funds rate and the growth rate of deflated nonfinancial debt outstanding).

2.2.1.2 Extended Profit System Model with Goods and Services Plus Labor Markets

The previous basic profit system models can be combined and extended to include a labor market as shown in Table 2.4. In this model deflated capital stock and real output are first computed. Equations (2.4.1), (2.4.2), (2.4.3), (2.4.4), and (2.4.5) are

Table 2.4 Extended profit system model with goods and services plus labor markets

Goods market equations

Deflated capital stock model

$$\bar{k}_t = \alpha_0 + \alpha_1 \bar{y}_{t-1} + \alpha_2 r_{t-1} + \alpha_3 s_{t-1} + \alpha_5 \dot{\bar{D}}_{t-L} + \alpha_6 F_{t-L} \qquad (2.4.1)$$

Deflated (real) output model

$$\bar{y}_t = \beta_0 + \beta_2 r_{t-1} + \beta_3 s_{t-1} + \beta_4 \bar{k}_{t-1} + \beta_5 \dot{\bar{D}}_{t-L} + \beta_6 F_{t-L} \qquad (2.4.2)$$

Profit rate model

$$r_t = \theta_0 + \theta_1 \bar{y}_{t-1} + \theta_3 s_{t-1} + \theta_4 \bar{k}_{t-1} + \theta_5 \dot{\bar{D}}_{t-L} + \theta_6 F_{t-L} \qquad (2.4.3)$$

Profit margin model

$$s_t = \bar{k}_t + r_t - \bar{y}_t \qquad (2.4.4)$$

Deflated total profit model

$$\bar{z}_t = v_0 + v_1 r_{t-1} + v_2 \bar{k}_{t-1} \text{ or } \bar{z}_t = v_0 + v_1 s_{t-1} + v_2 \bar{y}_{t-1} \qquad (2.4.5)$$

Additional goods and services market equations

Price model

$$\hat{p}_t = \varphi_0 + \varphi_1 \hat{p}_{t-1} + \varphi_2 \hat{p}_{t-2} + \varphi_3 \hat{F}_{t-L} \qquad (2.4.6)$$

Nominal capital stock model

$$k_t = \bar{y}_t + s_t + \hat{p}_t - r_t \qquad (2.4.7)$$

Nominal output model

$$y_t = k_t + r_t - s_t \qquad (2.4.8)$$

Nominal total profits model

$$z_t = \bar{z}_t + \hat{p}_t \qquad (2.4.9)$$

Sales tax model

$$T_t = \tau_t Y_t \qquad (2.4.10)$$

Depreciation expense model

$$G_t = g_t K_t \qquad (2.4.11)$$

Table 2.4 (continued)

Labor market equations

Total employment compensation model

$$C_t = Y_t - Z_t - G_t - T_t \tag{2.4.12}$$

Total employment model

$$h_t = \omega_0 + \omega_1 r_{t-1} + \omega_2 s_{t-1} + \omega_4 \bar{k}_{t-1} + \omega_5 \bar{b}_{t-1} \tag{2.4.13}$$

Labor productivity model

$$\bar{b}_t = \bar{y}_t - h_t \tag{2.4.14}$$

Wage rate model

$$w_t = c_t - h_t \tag{2.4.15}$$

Variables are defined as follows:

$\bar{k}$ = log deflated capital stock $\bar{K}$

$\bar{y}$ = log deflated (real) output $\bar{Y}$

r = log profit rate (equal to total profit divided by capital stock) R

s = log profit margin (equal to total profit divided by output) S

$\bar{z}$ = log deflated (real) total profit $\bar{Z}$

z = log nominal total profit Z

F = Federal funds rate in percent (financial sector variable)

$\bar{F}$ = deflated (real) Federal funds rate in percent (financial sector variable)

$\dot{D}$ = growth rate of deflated nonfinancial debt outstanding in percent (financial sector variable)

$\hat{P}$ = log general price level deflator $\hat{P}$

k = log nominal capital stock K

y = log nominal output Y

T = total sales tax

G = capital depreciation expenses

C = total employees' compensation

h = log of the number of hours of employment or the number of employees hired

τ = sales tax rate

g = capital depreciation rate

$\bar{b}_t$ = log labor productivity

w = log wage rate

c = log total employees' compensation C,

where K = antilog k, $\bar{K}$ = antilog $\bar{k}$, Y = antilog y, $\bar{Y}$ = antilog $\bar{y}$, R = antilog r, S = antilog s, Z = antilog z, $\bar{Z}$ = antilog $\bar{z}$, $\hat{P}$ = antilog $\hat{P}$, H = antilog h, $\bar{B}$ = antilog $\bar{b}$, W = antilog w, and C = antilog c.

the same as those in the basic profit system model in Table 2.3. Equation (2.4.6) is a general form of a price level (inflation) function for the output of the firm, industry, or business sector with lagged prices used for forecasting prices in period t. Inflation in this price model is determined by the real interest rate represented by the deflated Federal funds rate (Wicksell 1898). In applications of the model to individual firms, other variables such as labor cost, energy cost, and labor productivity can be added to the equation. Equation (2.4.7) is the expectation or forecasted model in log form of nominal capital stock k_t based on equation (2.19). In words, equation (2.4.7) sums log output in real terms and log profit margin (i.e., equal to log total profit in real terms, or $\bar{y}_t + s_t$), plus the expected log of output price $\widehat{p}_t$ (i.e., equal to the expected value of log total profit in nominal terms z_t), and then divides or discounts using log profit rate r_t to yield log capital stock in nominal terms.

Equation (2.4.8) computes the log of nominal output y_t from log nominal capital stock k_t, profit rate r_t, and profit margin s_t. Equation (2.4.9) gives the log of total profit in nominal terms z_t as the sum of log deflated total profit $(\bar{z}_t)$ plus log output price $\widehat{p}_t$.

Notice that labor equations are added to the aforementioned goods and services market equations. The variables estimated in logarithms are transformed into levels and used in equations (2.4.10), (2.4.11), and (2.4.12) for estimating the expected values of total sales tax (T), total depreciation expenses (G), and total employee compensation (C) in the business sector. Equation (2.4.13) is the empirical representation of the log of employment (h_t) based on log-linearized employment equation (2.14a) using values of deflated capital stock, profit rate, profit margin, and labor productivity. Equation (2.4.14) gives the log of labor productivity $(\bar{b})$ as the difference of log real output and log employment, or $\bar{y}_t - h_t$. And, equation (2.4.15) defines the log of wage rate (w_t) (i.e., wage per hour or per person W_t) as the difference between log total employee compensation and log employment, or $c_t - h_t$.

We apply this extended profit system model to the aggregate US business sector in Chapter 3's macroeconomic analyses of the national economy. In Chapter 4 the goods and services market part of this model is applied to the US corporate sector, which focuses on larger firms in the business sector. For these purposes the Appendix provides a general form of the extended profit system model that takes into account different forecast horizons and variable lag lengths.

Another approach for developing the extended business model is to start with the profit system model of the goods and services market in current dollars in Table 2.1, initially estimate forecasts of output and capital stocks in nominal terms, and then deflate these values using an output price deflator as in equation (2.4.6) in Table 2.4 to derive deflated values of output, capital stock, and profit rates. Subsequently, other variables can be estimated as shown in Table 2.4.

The empirical application of the above profit system models to firms and industries requires the estimation of the profit system macroeconomic model of the USA due to the fact that financial sector forecasts of the real Federal funds rate and growth rate of nonfinancial debt must be generated on a macrobasis. If these forecasts can be obtained from other sources, then the macromodel is not needed for firm and industry analyses.

In application of our models to individual firms, it is possible that the firm has losses rather than profits in some periods. Since firms embarking on production and capital formation activities anticipate positive expected profit, we treat losses as missing values. The economic intuition for this data adjustment is that losses are missed profit targets. In Chapter 7 we apply the model to a firm when there are losses in the time series of profits.

2.3 Summary

This chapter developed a profit system model of the firm consisting of output, capital stock, profit rate, profit margin, and total profit equations. No assumptions about profit maximization are required to derive the model. Although the modeling process began with the Cobb–Douglas production function, our model can be alternatively derived via an accounting approach. The model is applicable to firms, industries, and the business sector as a whole.

We presented empirical profit system models of the firm consisting of five fundamental business variables. Each of these five variables can be estimated from lags of the other variables. Also, we can include other relevant variables to minimize the forecast error terms in equations. For example, our experience with the model in application to the US business sector in Chapter 3 suggests that the Federal funds rate and growth rate of nonfinancial debt outstanding have explanatory power and improve the predictive power of the model. In general, lagged values of the variables contain almost all information needed for the model's estimation and application.

Additional contributions of our profit system model of the firm are as follows:

- *A new model of inflation transmission* is proposed using capital stock and output models. One of the least understood areas of economics is the channels of inflation transmission in the economy. The initial source of inflation transmission in our model is the attempt by owners of capital stock to adjust the rental values of their capital to the expected inflation. Inflation expectations contained in capital stock are then transmitted to output when nominal capital stocks are used for output planning. By contrast, the initial source of inflation in many economic models is workers' expected inflation, which in the augmented Phillips curve and other inflation models leads to a wage-price spiral. Hence, our model extends previous approaches in terms of both the source and the transmission mechanism of inflation.
- *A profit system concept of equilibrium* is provided. Economic equilibrium was defined to exist when ex post realized profit rates equal ex ante hurdle profit rates used to select capital formation projects. Firms and market participants form expectations about our five fundamental variables (i.e., real and nominal output, deflated and nominal capital stock, profit rates, profit margins, and total profit) at the time of project evaluation. After projects become operational, the firm's objective is to realize the expected values of these variables. That is, the firm seeks to minimize the difference between variables' realized and expected values. In forming expectations with respect to these fundamental business variables, firms and market participants may also form expectations about other factors that might influence these variables and include these factors in equations for the fundamental business variables to minimize forecast error terms. At the time of this writing, a global recession caused realized profit rates in many industries to be lower than the expected profit rates at the initial stage of project evaluation. Consequently, gross domestic product and stock price indexes in most countries

have declined in response to realized profit rates that are lower than hurdle profit rates.

- A *profit system model of economic growth* is derived. According to this new model, higher total factor productivity leads to higher profit rate, which causes higher output and reduces labor inputs for a given level of output, thereby releasing more labor input to be employed in new projects. Hence, economic growth in our model is driven by profit, which is consistent with Schumpeter's creative destruction.
- A *profit system business cycle theory* is proposed. Utilizing our profit system models of the firm, the business cycle comes about through the interaction between the output and the capital stock equations that is triggered by a change in total profit affecting profit rates (in the output equation's numerator and the capital equation's denominator) and profit margins (in the output equation's denominator and the capital equation's numerator).
- In profit system models of the firm, the discount rate R_t is a time-varying variable rather than a parameter, and the profit margin S_t is time varying also. The technology variable A_t is contained in the profit rate as shown by equation (2.5a).

In general, the "power of profit" emanates from the central role it plays in firms, industries, and the business sector as a whole. We have sought in this chapter to exploit this focal measure of business activity in an effort to better understand how firms manage their output, capital, labor, and profit. The resultant profit system model of the firm is comprised of multiple, interconnected equations that can be utilized for analysis, planning, and forecasting of fundamental business variables. In forthcoming chapters we investigate these potential applications using US economic, industry, and firm data.

Appendix: General Form of the Extended Profit System Model with Goods and Services Plus Labor Markets

This appendix provides a general specification of the extended profit system model in Table 2.4. In the following model j is the forecast horizon, i is the lag order, and, for example, $E_t \bar{k}_{t+j}$ is the expected value of $\bar{k}$ in period $t + j$ estimated in period t. The subscripts 1, 2, 3, and 4 are assigned to coefficients for variables $\bar{y}$, r, s, and $\bar{k}$, respectively. Lags (L) of the Federal funds rate (F) and growth rate of deflated nonfinancial debt outstanding $(\dot{D})$ are determined empirically.

Table 2.5 General form of extended profit system model with goods and services plus labormarkets

Goods market equations
Deflated capital stock model

$$E_t \bar{k}_{t+j} = \alpha_0 + \Sigma_{i=1}^I \alpha_{1i} \bar{y}_{t+j-i} + \Sigma_{i=1}^I \alpha_{2i} r_{t+j-i} + \Sigma_{i=1}^I \alpha_{3i} s_{t+j-i} + \alpha_5 \dot{D}_{t-L} + \alpha_6 F_{t-L} \qquad (2.5.1)$$

Table 2.5 (continued)

Deflated (real) output model

$$E_t \bar{y}_{t+j} = \beta_0 + \Sigma_{i=1}^{I}\beta_{2i}r_{t+j-i} + \Sigma_{i=1}^{I}\beta_{3i}s_{t+j-i} + \Sigma_{i=1}^{I}\beta_{4i}\bar{k}_{t+j-i} + \beta_5 \dot{\bar{D}}_{t-L} + \beta_6 F_{t-L} \quad (2.5.2)$$

Profit rate model

$$E_t r_{t+j} = \theta_0 + \Sigma_{i=1}^{I}\theta_{1i}\bar{y}_{t+j-i} + \Sigma_{i=1}^{I}\theta_{3i}s_{t+j-i} + \Sigma_{i=1}^{I}\theta_{4i}\bar{k}_{t+j-i} + \theta_5 \dot{\bar{D}}_{t-L} + \theta_6 F_{t-L} \quad (2.5.3)$$

Profit margin model

$$E_t s_{t+j} = E_t r_{t+j} + E_t \bar{k}_{t+j} - E_t \bar{y}_{t+j} \quad (2.5.4)$$

Deflated (real) total profits model

$$E_t \bar{z}_{t+j} = E_t s_{t+j} + E_t \bar{y}_{t+j} \quad (2.5.5a)$$

or

$$E_t \bar{z}_{t+j} = v_0 + \Sigma_{i=1}^{I}v_{1i}s_{t+j-i} + \Sigma_{i=1}^{I}v_{2i}\bar{y}_{t+j-i} \quad (2.5.5b)$$

or

$$E_t \bar{z}_{t+j} = v_0 + \Sigma_{i=1}^{I}v_{1i}r_{t+j-i} + \Sigma_{i=1}^{I}v_{2i}\bar{k}_{t+j-i} \quad (2.5.5c)$$

Other goods and services market equations
Wicksellian price model

$$E_t \hat{p}_{t+j} = \varphi_0 + \Sigma_{i=1}^{I}\varphi_{1i}\hat{p}_{t+j-i} + \varphi_2 \bar{F}_{t-L} \quad (2.5.6)$$

Nominal capital stock model

$$E_t k_{t+j} = E_t \bar{y}_{t+j} + E_t s_{t+j} + E_t \hat{p}_{t+j} - E_t r_{t+j} \quad (2.5.7)$$

Nominal output model

$$E_t y_{t+j} = E_t k_{t+j} + E_t r_{t+j} - E_t s_{t+j} \quad (2.5.8)$$

Nominal total profits model

$$E_t z_{t+j} = E_t s_{t+j} + E_t y_{t+j} \quad (2.5.9)$$

Sales tax model

$$E_t T_{t+j} = \tau_{t+j}E_t y_{t+j} \quad (2.5.10)$$

Depreciation model

$$E_t G_{t+j} = g_t E_t K_{t+j} \quad (2.5.11)$$

Labor market equations
Employment compensation model

$$E_t C_{t+j} = E_t Y_{t+j} - E_t Z_{t+j} - E_t T_{t+j} - E_t G_{t+j} \quad (2.5.12)$$

Employment model

$$E_t h_{t+j} = \omega_0 + \omega_1 r_t + \omega_2 s_t + \omega_3 \bar{k}_t + \omega_4 \bar{b}_{t-1} \quad (2.5.13a)$$

or

$$E_t h_{t+j} = \omega_0 + \Sigma_{i=1}^{L}\omega_{1i}r_{t+j-i} + \Sigma_{i=1}^{L}\omega_{2i}s_{t+j-i} + \Sigma_{i=1}^{L}\omega_{3i}\bar{k}_{t+j-i} + \Sigma_{i=1}^{L}\omega_{4i}\bar{b}_{t+j-i} \quad (2.5.13b)$$

Labor productivity model

$$E_t \bar{b}_{t+j} = E_t \bar{y}_{t+j} - E_t h_{t+j} \quad (2.5.14)$$

Table 2.5 (continued)

Wage rate model

$$E_t w_{t+j} = E_t c_{t+j} - E_t h_{t+j} \tag{2.5.15}$$

Variables are defined as follows:

$\bar{k}=$ log deflated capital stock $\bar{K}$

$\bar{y} =$ log deflated (real) output $\bar{Y}$

$r =$ log profit rate (equal to total profit divided by capital stock) R

$s =$ log profit margin (equal to total profit divided by output) S

$\bar{z}=$ log deflated (real) total profit $\bar{Z}$

$z =$ log nominal total profit Z

$\widehat{p}=$ log price level deflator $\widehat{P}$

$k =$ log nominal capital stock K

$y =$ log nominal output Y

$T =$ total sales tax

$G =$ capital depreciation expenses

$C =$ total employees' compensation

$h =$ log of the number of hours of employment or the number of employees hired

$\tau =$ sales tax rate

$g =$ capital depreciation rate

$b =$ log labor productivity

$w =$ log wage rate

$c =$ log total employees' compensation C

$\dot{D} =$ growth rate of nonfinancial deflated debt outstanding in percent (financial sector variable)

$F =$ nominal Federal funds rate in percent (financial sector variable)

$\bar{F} =$ real Federal funds rate in percent (financial sector variable)

where $E_t \bar{K}_{t+j} =$ antilog $E_t \bar{k}_{t+j}$, $E_t K_{t+j} =$ antilog $E_t k_{t+j}$, $E_t \bar{Y}_{t+j} =$ antilog $E_t \bar{y}_{t+j}$, $E_t Y_{t+j} =$ antilog $E_t y_{t+j}$, $E_t R_{t+j} =$ antilog $E_t r_{t+j}$, $E_t S_{t+j} =$ antilog $E_t s_{t+j}$, $E_t Z_{t+j} =$ antilog $E_t z_{t+j}$, $E_t \bar{Z}_{t+j} =$ antilog $E_t \bar{z}_{t+j}$, $E_t \widehat{P}_{t+j} =$ antilog $E_t \widehat{p}_{t+j}$, $E_t H_{t+j} =$ antilog $E_t h_{t+j}$, $E_t \bar{B}_{t+j} =$ antilog $E_t \bar{b}_{t+j}$, and $E_t W_{t+j} =$ antilog $E_t w_{t+j}$.

Chapter 3
A Macroeconomic Profit System Model of Advanced Market Economies

This chapter provides a two-sector macroeconomic model consisting of a business sector and a nonprofit sector. This profit system model is developed from the micro-profit system model of the firm in Chapter 2. Using annual US macroeconomic data in the period 1959–2008, the empirical representation of the model is estimated, its reliability is tested, and different applications are investigated, including economic forecasting, monetary policy, fiscal policy, and business cycle analysis. In brief, the results demonstrate the crucial role of profits in the economy. Profit drives not only business sector and national output but is a prime determinant of capital stock and employment. Given the major influence of profits on the economy, it is not surprising that it also plays a role in the transmission of inflation. Moreover, we show that changes in profit can lead to business cycle fluctuations in economic activity.

3.1 Macroeconomic Profit System Model

Modern free-market economies are comprised of a for-profit or business sector and a nonprofit sector. According to the Bureau of Economic Analysis (BEA) of the US Department of Commerce and the Federal Reserve (Fed), the business sector in the USA consists of corporate and noncorporate sectors and government enterprises. The noncorporate sector is comprised of single proprietorships, partnerships, and rental housing sector. The nonprofit sector consists of general governments (federal, state, and local levels), as well as households and nonprofit institutions serving households. The value added of the household sector mainly consists of the imputed value of rent income of owner-occupied housing sector.

Excluding the farm sector, the US business sector accounted for 75.7 percent of the gross domestic product (GDP) of the US economy in 2008, which is not significantly different from its share in national output in 1959 (see Table 3.1). The share of the farm sector measured in terms of value added declined from 3.4 percent in 1959 to less than 1 percent in 2008. After 1959 the share of nonprofit sector increased from 19.4 to 23.5 percent of the nation's gross value added (GVA) due to the expansion of the share of households and institutions. The government's share of value added remained the same over the same period.

A. Anari, J.W. Kolari, *The Power of Profit*, DOI 10.1007/978-1-4419-0649-6_3,
© Springer Science+Business Media, LLC 2010

Table 3.1 Gross value added by sector of the US economy

	1959		2008	
	$Billion	Percent of total	$Billion	Percent of total
Gross domestic product	506.6	100.0	14,264.6	100.0
Business Sector	408.2	80.6	10,917.6	76.5
Nonfarm	390.9	77.2	10,791.2	75.7
Farm	17.3	3.4	126.3	0.9
Nonprofit Sector	98.4	19.4	3,347.0	23.5
Households and institutions	40.1	7.9	1,674.3	11.7
Households	29.8	5.9	929.2	6.5
Nonprofit institutions serving households	10.3	2.0	745.1	5.2
General government	58.3	11.5	1,672.7	11.7
Federal	31.9	6.3	515.9	3.6
State and local	26.5	5.2	1,156.8	8.1

Source: US Bureau of Economic Analysis, April 2009.

In the USA the income shares of compensation of employees and net operating surplus in the nation's gross domestic income have remained stable since 1959 (Table 3.2). Compensation of employees accounted for 56.3 percent of gross domestic income in 2007 compared with 55.5 percent in 1959. The net operating surplus

Table 3.2 Percentage share of gross domestic income

	1959	2007
Gross domestic income	100.0	100.0
Compensation of employees	55.5	56.3
Taxes on production and imports	8.1	7.3
Less: Subsidies	0.2	0.4
Net operating surplus	26.1	24.4
Private enterprises	25.9	24.4
Corporate profits, domestic industries[a]	10.5	9.3
Proprietors' income[a]	10.0	7.6
Net interest and miscellaneous payments (domestic industries)	1.9	6.5
Business current transfer payments (net)	0.3	0.7
Rental income of persons with capital consumption adjustment	3.2	0.3
Current surplus of government enterprises	0.2	−0.1
Consumption of fixed capital	10.5	12.4
Private	7.6	10.3
Government	2.9	2.1

[a]After inventory valuation and capital consumption adjustments.
Source: US Bureau of Economic Analysis, April 2009.

of businesses (or gross domestic income minus compensation of employees, sales taxes, and subsidies) in 2007 accounted for 24.4 percent of gross domestic income compared with 26.1 percent in 1959 (Table 3.2).

Given the existence of a business sector, a nonprofit sector, a monetary authority in advanced market economies, and a financial sector, the macroeconomic profit system model presented here is comprised of the following building blocks:

1. an aggregate profit system model of the business sector
2. a nonprofit sector model
3. macroeconomic aggregates
4. a monetary policy rule model, and
5. a model of total debt outstanding of the nonfinancial sector.

Table 3.3 shows all equations in this macroeconomic model. The final model is a small-scale, parsimonious model comprised of only 10 equations with their numbers bold face. Forthcoming sections explain the derivation of equations in the model.[1]

Table 3.3 Macroeconomic profit system model: equations and identities

Goods and services market:

$$\bar{k}_t = \alpha_0 + \alpha_1\bar{y}_{t-1} + \alpha_2\bar{y}_{t-2} + \alpha_3 r_{t-1} + \alpha_4 r_{t-2} + \alpha_5 s_{t-1} + \alpha_6 s_{t-2} + \alpha_7\dot{\bar{D}}_t \tag{3.3.1}$$

$$\bar{y}_t = \beta_0 + \beta_1 r_{t-1} + \beta_2 r_{t-2} + \beta_3 s_{t-1} + \beta_4 s_{t-2} + \beta_5\bar{k}_{t-1} + \beta_6\bar{k}_{t-2} + \beta_7 F_{t-1} + \beta_8\dot{\bar{D}}_t + \beta_9\bar{X}_t \tag{3.3.2}$$

$$r_t = \theta_0 + \theta_1\bar{y}_{t-1} + \theta_2 s_{t-1} + \theta_3\bar{k}_{t-1} + \theta_4 F_{t-1} \tag{3.3.3}$$

$$s_t = \bar{k}_t + r_t - \bar{y}_t \tag{3.3.4}$$

$$\bar{z}_t = v_0 + v_1 r_{t-1} + v_2\bar{k}_{t-1} \tag{3.3.5}$$

$$\hat{p}_t = \varphi_0 + \varphi_1\hat{p}_{t-1} + \varphi_2\hat{p}_{t-2} + \varphi_3\bar{F}_{t-2} + \varphi_4\dot{\hat{P}}_{t-1} \tag{3.3.6}$$

$$k_t = \bar{y}_t + s_t + \hat{p}_t - r_t \tag{3.3.7}$$

$$y_t = k_t + r_t - s_t \tag{3.3.8}$$

$$z_t = \bar{z}_t + \hat{p}_t \tag{3.3.9}$$

$$T_t = \tau_t Y_t \tag{3.3.10}$$

$$G_t = g_t K_t \tag{3.3.11}$$

Labor market:

$$C_t = Y_t - Z_t - G_t - T_t \tag{3.3.12}$$

$$h_t = \omega_0 + \omega_1 r_t + \omega_2 s_t + \omega_3\bar{k}_t + \omega_4\bar{b}_{t-1} \tag{3.3.13}$$

---

[1] As noted by Campbell and Krane (2005, p. 52), small models trade off identification of numerous factors that can influence economic output against simplicity of interpretation and specification robustness.

Table 3.3

$\bar{b}_t = \bar{y}_t - h_t$	(3.3.14)
$w_t = c_t - h_t$	(3.3.15)

Nonprofit sector goods and services market:

$$\bar{x}_t = \delta_0 + \delta_1 \bar{x}_{t-1} + \delta_2 \bar{x}_{t-2} + \delta_3 F_{t-1} + \delta_4 \dot{D}_t + \delta_5 \dot{Y}_{t-1}$$ (**3.3.16**)

$$\breve{P}_t = \gamma_0 + \gamma_1 \breve{P}_{t-1} + \gamma_2 \breve{P}_{t-2} + \gamma_3 \bar{F}_{t-2} + \gamma_4 \dot{P}_{t-1}$$ (**3.3.17**)

$$x_t = \breve{P}_t + \bar{x}_t$$ (3.3.18)

Macroeconomic aggregates:

$$G\bar{D}P_t = \bar{Y}_t + \bar{X}_t$$ (3.3.19)

$$GDP_t = Y_t + X_t$$ (3.3.20)

$$P_t = GDP_t / G\bar{D}P_t$$ (3.3.21)

Monetary rule:

$$F_t = \lambda_0 + \lambda_1 F_{t-1} + \lambda_2 F_{t-2} + \lambda_3 \dot{P}_{t-1} + \lambda_4 G\dot{D}P_{t-1}$$ (**3.3.22**)

$$\bar{F}_t = F_t - \dot{P}_t$$ (3.3.23)

Debt demand:

$$d_t = \eta_0 + \eta_1 d_{t-1} + \eta_2 d_{t-2} + \eta_3 gdp_{t-1} + \eta_4 F_{t-1}$$ (**3.3.24**)

Bold numbered equations are empirically estimated (see Tables 3.5 and 3.6), and other equations are derived from their forecasts. All equations are solved simultaneously and recursively in forecasting and simulation analyses (see Tables 3.7, 3.8, and 3.9 as well as Figs. 3.1 and 3.4). Variables are defined as follows:

$\bar{k} =$ log of deflated capital stock in the business sector ($\bar{K}$)
$\bar{y} =$ log of deflated output in the business sector ($\bar{Y}$)
$r =$ log of profit rate in the business sector (R)
$s =$ log of profit margin in the business sector (S)
$\dot{D} =$ growth rate of total nonfinancial debt outstanding in real terms ($\dot{D}$)
$F =$ Federal funds rate in nominal terms
$\dot{X} =$ growth rate of deflated output in the nonprofit sector ($\bar{X}$)
$\bar{z} =$ log of deflated total profit in the business sector ($\bar{Z}$)
$\widehat{P} =$ log of price index for business sector output ($\widehat{P}$)
$\breve{P} =$ inflation rate in the nonprofit sector equal to growth rate of price index ($\breve{P}$) for nonprofit sector output
$y =$ log of business sector output in current dollars (Y)
$k =$ log of capital stock in the business sector in current dollars (K)
$z =$ log of total profit in the business sector in current dollars (Z)
$T =$ sales tax in current dollars
$\tau =$ sales tax rate
$Y =$ business sector output in current dollars or antilog of y
$G =$ capital consumption (depreciation) in the business sector
$g =$ capital consumption rate (or depreciation rate) in the business sector
$K =$ capital stock in the business sector in current dollars or antilog of k

$\bar{Y}$ = deflated business sector output or antilog of $\bar{y}$
C = total employee compensation
Z = total profit in the business sector in current dollars or antilog of z
h = log of hours of employment index in the business sector (H)
$\bar{b}$ = log of labor productivity ($B = \bar{Y}/H$)
W = log of wage rate ($W = C/H$)
$\bar{x}$ = log of deflated nonprofit sector output ($\bar{X}$)
x = log of nonprofit sector output in current dollars (X)
$\dot{\bar{Y}}$ = growth rate of deflated business sector output
$\bar{X}$ = deflated nonprofit sector output or log of $\bar{x}$
$\breve{P}$ = log of price index for the nonprofit sector output ($\breve{P}$)
$\dot{P}$ = inflation rate in the business sector equal to growth rate of price index ($\widehat{P}$) for business
     sector output
$\breve{P}$ = price index for nonprofit sector output or antilog of $\breve{p}$
X = nonprofit sector output in current dollars or antilog of x
$G\bar{D}P$ = deflated gross domestic product in \$2000
GDP = gross domestic product in current dollars
P = price index for GDP (GDP price deflator)
$\dot{P}$ = GDP inflation rate
$G\dot{D}P$ = growth rate of GDP in real terms
$\bar{F}$ = real Federal funds rate
d = log of total debt outstanding in the nonfinancial sector in current dollars (D),
$\bar{D}$ = total nonfinancial debt outstanding in real terms
D = total debt outstanding in the nonfinancial sector in current dollars or antilog of d
gdp = log of GDP in current dollars.

3.1.1 Business Sector Profit System Model

A macroeconomic model of the business sector is an aggregate of all firms in the business sector. As such, the whole US business sector, including government-owned enterprises, is treated as a single firm in the business sector model. Aggregate output equals the value added of all firms and industries in the US business sector. Also, aggregate profits and capital stocks are the sum of profits and capital stocks of all firms in the US business sector as defined and measured by the BEA and Fed. These two organizations have recently compiled a number of national income and product tables which make possible the application of our profit system model to the US macroeconomy.

The business sector profit system model is comprised of all equations in the extended business model shown in Table 2.4 of Chapter 2. These equations are utilized here in Table 3.3 and referred to as equations (3.3.1)–(3.3.15) for representing goods and services plus labor markets in the macrobusiness model. The lag orders of variables in the estimated equations are determined empirically as discussed in forthcoming sections. The capital stock equation (3.3.1) for the business sector is estimated with two lags of the logarithms of fundamental variables and includes the contemporaneous growth rate of nonfinancial debt outstanding in real terms ($\dot{\bar{D}}$) but not the Federal funds rate as suggested by empirical results. The output and price equations are augmented to include the impact of the nonprofit sector on business sector output. The business sector's output equation (3.3.2) is estimated with two lags of the fundamental variables and is augmented by including the growth rate of real output of nonprofit sector ($\dot{X}$), as the nonprofit sector output (e.g., government expenditures) can impact the business sector's output in the short run. In the long run the business sector capital stock equation (3.3.1) includes investments for meeting the demand by the nonprofit sector for goods and services produced in the business sector. The business output equation includes the nominal Federal funds rate (F) and the growth rate of nonfinancial debt outstanding in real terms ($\dot{D}$). The business sector profit rate equation (3.3.3) is estimated with one lag of the logarithms of fundamental variables and includes the Federal funds rate (F) but not the growth rate of nonfinancial debt outstanding as suggested by empirical results. The business sector total profit equation (3.3.5) was estimated with one lag of logarithms of profit rate and deflated capital stock as suggested by empirical results. The business sector's price equation (3.3.6) is estimated with two lags of the logarithm of price index ($\widehat{P}$) and is augmented by including the nonprofit sector's inflation rate ($\overset{\smile}{P}$), as inflation in the business sector ($\hat{P}$) is expected to be influenced by nonprofit sector's inflation rate. We expect a negative relationship between the real Federal funds rate ($\bar{F}$) and the logarithm of business sector inflation ($\hat{p}$) consistent with Wicksell (1898) and a positive relationship between the logarithm of business sector inflation ($\hat{p}$) and the inflation rate ($\overset{\smile}{P}$) in nonprofit sector. The employment equation (3.3.13) is estimated with contemporaneous logarithms of profit rate, profit margin, deflated capital stock, and the first lag of log labor productivity as suggested by empirical results. This business sector model is next combined with a nonprofit sector model to obtain a macroeconomic profit system model.

3.1.2 Nonprofit Sector Model

Output in the nonprofit sector is the sum of output of the government sector (federal, state, and local levels), households and nonprofit institutions serving households, and the farm sector. The farm sector is included in the nonprofit sector due to the importance of subsidies and government agricultural policies as well as data consistency. According to Wagner's (1892) law, government activities tend to increase with economic expansion.[2] Given the exchange of goods and services between the business and the nonprofit sectors, the logarithm of real nonprofit sector output ($\bar{x}$) represented by equation (3.3.16) is determined by its own lags, growth rate of business sector's output in real terms ($\dot{Y}$), nominal Federal funds rate (F), and growth rate of nonfinancial debt outstanding in real terms ($\dot{D}$).

---

[2] See also Wagner and Weber (1977), Chang (2002), and others.

Similar to the business sector price model, the log of the price deflator for output in the nonprofit sector or $\breve{p}$ as specified in equation (3.3.17). Inflation $(\breve{p})$ in the nonprofit sector is expected to be influenced by the real Federal funds rate $(\bar{F})$ and the business sector inflation rate $(\hat{P})$. Like the price model for output in the business sector, we expect a negative relationship between the real Federal funds rate and the nonprofit sector inflation and a positive relationship between the nonprofit sector inflation and the inflation in the business sector.

Adding the log of the nonprofit sector price deflator $(\breve{p})$ to the log of real non-profit sector output $(\bar{x})$ gives the log of nominal nonprofit sector output (x) in equation (3.3.18).

3.1.3 Combined Business Sector Profit System Model and Nonprofit Sector Model

The expected aggregate national output of the economy is the sum of expected output in the business and nonprofit sectors. In equation (3.3.19) the aggregate $G\bar{D}P$ in real terms is computed as the sum of gross value added of the business sector $\bar{Y}$ and gross value added of the nonprofit sector $\bar{X}$, where $\bar{Y}$ and $\bar{X}$ are antilogs of $\bar{y}$ and $\bar{x}$ estimated from equations (3.3.2) and (3.3.16), respectively. Equation (3.3.20) gives the aggregate GDP in nominal terms as the sum of the gross value added of the business sector Y and nonprofit sector X both in nominal terms, where Y and X are antilogs of y and x estimated from equations (3.3.8) and (3.3.18), respectively. In equation (3.3.21) GDP in current dollars is divided by $G\bar{D}P$ in constant dollars to give the GDP price deflator (P). We italicize GDP to denote its usage as a variable in an empirical model.

Note that there are three price indices or deflators in the model: (1) a price deflator for the business sector output $(\hat{P})$, (2) a price deflator for the nonprofit sector output $(\breve{P})$, and (3) a GDP price deflator (P).

3.1.4 The Monetary Policy Model

Since 1980, the Fed has employed a Wicksellian approach for attaining price stability in the US economy, which targets interest rates in contrast to the Fisherian approach of targeting monetary aggregates to control inflation. Here we focus on changes in the Federal funds rate over time.[3] A review of the minutes of Federal Open Market Committee of the Federal Reserve Board of Governors shows that the Fed looks at and reacts to changes in the inflation rate and growth rate of real GDP

---

[3] See Taylor (1979, 1993), Khoury (1990), Mehra (1997), Hamilton and Jordà (2002), Woodford (2003), and others.

when contemplating changes in the Federal funds rate. Equation (3.3.22) is a simple version of a monetary rule which assumes that the nominal Federal funds rate (F) is determined by the inflation rate, defined here as the growth rate $(\dot{P})$ of the GDP price deflator (P), and the real GDP growth rate $(\dot{GDP})$. The real Federal funds rate in equation (3.3.23) is the difference between the nominal Federal funds rate (F) and the GDP inflation rate $(\dot{P})$ computed from the GDP price deflator P.

3.1.5 Debt Model

Demand for debt, like demand for any other goods or services, is expected to be positively determined by economic activity and negatively affected by the price of debt. In the present context total debt outstanding in nominal terms is expected to be positively related to nominal GDP and negatively related to the Federal funds rate according to the loanable funds theory of interest.[4] In equation (3.3.24) the log of nominal nonfinancial debt outstanding (d) is specified as a function of its two lags, log of GDP in nominal terms (gdp), and the Federal funds rate (F).

The nonfinancial debt outstanding variable is also a proxy for the demand side of the economy in the model as higher levels of demand for goods and services by households and firms lead to higher levels of demand for debts. Repaying debts results in lower demand for goods and services and lower levels of debt.

3.1.6 Macroeconomic Equilibrium

From an initial state of the economy, the dynamic relationships among the variables in the model result in a trajectory toward equilibrium. In the model financial sector variables affect economic activities, which have feedback effects on these variables. More specifically, the trajectory of macroeconomic equilibrium in the model is governed by the following interactions:

1. The nominal Federal funds rate and the growth rate of nonfinancial debt outstanding in real terms directly affect the logarithms of business sector deflated capital stock in equation (3.3.1), business sector real output in equation (3.3.2), business sector profit rate in equation (3.3.3), and real output of nonprofit sector in equation (3.3.16).
2. The real Federal funds rate directly influences inflation in the business sector in equation (3.3.6) and inflation in the nonprofit sector in equation (3.3.17).
3. The nominal Federal funds rate and growth rate of nonfinancial debt outstanding in real terms indirectly impact the logarithm of business sector profit margins in equation (3.3.4), as expected profit margins are computed from expected profit rates, expected deflated capital stock, and expected deflated output.

---

[4]See Ohlin (1937a, b, c), Robertson (1934, 1936, 1937), and Wicksell (1898, 1907a).

4. The nominal Federal funds rate and the growth rate of nonfinancial debt outstanding in real terms indirectly impact the logarithm of real business sector total profits in equation (3.3.5) via the lag of logarithms of profit rates and deflated capital stocks in the business sector.
5. The nominal Federal funds rate and growth rate of nonfinancial debt outstanding in real terms indirectly determine the logarithms of the nominal capital stock in the business sector in equation (3.3.7), nominal business output in equation (3.3.8), nominal total profit in equation (3.3.9), and nominal output of the nonprofit sector in equation (3.3.18), as logarithms of nominal values of outputs, capital stock, and total profits are computed by adding the expected logarithm of inflation to the expected deflated values of the respective variables.
6. The Federal funds rate in equation (3.3.22) is determined by the GDP inflation rate and the growth rate of GDP in real terms. The GDP inflation rate is determined by real GDP and nominal GDP in equation (3.3.21) computed from real and nominal outputs of the business sector and nonprofit sector in equations (3.3.19) and (3.3.20). These outputs are determined by the Federal funds rate and the growth rate of debt outstanding through channels (1) and (2). The growth rate of GDP in real terms is derived from the level of GDP in real terms in equation (3.3.19), where GDP in real terms is the sum of the outputs of the business sector and nonprofit sector in real terms which are affected by the Federal funds rate and the growth rate of nonfinancial debt outstanding through channels (1) and (2).
7. Total nonfinancial debt outstanding in nominal terms in equation (3.3.23) is affected by nominal GDP and the Federal funds rate.

In our macroeconomic profit system model these interactions among the variables lead to a steady-state equilibrium of the economy.

3.1.7 Channels of Inflation and Monetary Policy Transmission

The channels of transmission of inflation and monetary policy in our profit system model are as follows:

1. In equations (3.3.6) and (3.3.17) market participants use inflation information in the two periods preceding period t to form expectations on inflation in period t in the business and nonprofit sectors. Market participants take into account the potential negative impact of the real Federal funds rate on expected inflation (Wicksell 1898).
2. In equation (3.3.7) owners of capital stocks adjust expected profits in real terms $(\bar{y}_t + s_t)$ to expected inflation $(\widehat{p}_t)$ by adding the log of expected price $(\widehat{p}_t)$ to expected profit in real terms resulting in the log of expected profits in nominal terms $(\bar{y}_t + s_t + \widehat{p}_t)$. Discounting expected profits in nominal terms using the discount rate – that is, deducting the log of discount rate (r_t) from the log of nominal profits $(\bar{y}_t + s_t + \widehat{p}_t - r_t)$ – yields capital stock in nominal terms (k_t). In equation (3.3.8) expected inflation in nominal capital stock (k_t) is transmitted to

the nominal value of output (y_t). In equation (3.3.18) the output of nonprofit sector in real terms ($\bar{x}_t$) is adjusted for inflation ($\breve{p}_t$) to derive the output of nonprofit sector in nominal terms (x_t).

3. The nominal Federal funds rate is expected to have a negative impact on real business sector output in equation (3.3.2), business sector profit rates in equation (3.3.3), nonprofit sector real output in equation (3.3.16), and the amount of nonfinancial debt outstanding in equation (3.3.24).

4. According to monetary policy model (3.3.22), increases (decreases) in the GDP inflation rate ($\dot{P}$) and real growth rate ($\dot{GDP}$) lead to a higher (lower) nominal Federal funds rate (F).

5. Feedbacks from business sector real output equation (3.3.2) and nonprofit sector real output equation (3.3.16) to aggregate GDP in real terms in equation (3.3.19), as well as from business sector nominal output equation (3.3.8) and nonprofit sector nominal output equation (3.3.18) to aggregate GDP in nominal terms in equation (3.3.20) lead to changes in the GDP price deflator in equation (3.3.21) and GDP inflation rate in the monetary policy rule equation (3.3.22). Also, feedbacks from business sector real output equation (3.3.2) and nonprofit sector real output equation (3.3.16) to aggregate GDP in real terms in equation (3.3.19) lead to changes in the growth rate of GDP in real terms in the monetary policy model equation (3.3.22).

3.1.8 Wicksell's Cumulative Process in the Macroeconomic Profit System Model

Our profit system model of the macroeconomy contains Wicksell's cumulative process due to the key roles of the profit rate and the Federal funds rate. This cumulative process theory is based on comparing the cost of borrowing capital with the marginal productivity of capital. The marginal productivity of capital is the natural rate of interest, while the cost of borrowing is the money rate of interest. Profitability increases when the natural rate of return exceeds the money rate leading to higher demand and prices for capital goods. Wicksell did not precisely identify the channel of transmission of inflation from capital goods to consumption goods and the general level of inflation. In our model the business sector's output equation (3.3.2) and the profit rate equation (3.3.3) are the channels of transmission of his cumulative process. The Federal funds rate is a proxy for the money rate of interest, and the profit rate is a proxy for the marginal product of capital or natural rate of interest. Lower Federal funds rates in the business sector's profit rate equation (3.3.3) increase profit rates, which increase business sector output in equation (3.3.2). Also, lower Federal funds rates in the business sector's output equation (3.3.2) motivate higher business sector output. In turn, higher business sector output leads to higher business sector capital stock in equation (3.3.3).

3.1.9 The Government Sector and Profitability

Government macroeconomic policies (fiscal or monetary) play an important role in the economy by influencing the profitability of production and capital formation activities. Government purchases of goods and services from the business sector generate markets for these goods and services and affect the profitability of the supplying industries. As noted Chapter 2, economic project selection is a gamble, as the results will be known some time after the selection and implementation of investment projects. At any time there are some sectors of the economy that are marginally profitable and are near the brink of bankruptcy. In normal times as well as in mild recessions, Schumpeter's creative destruction tends to purge the economy from unprofitable economic activities so that resources locked up in these activities can be released and utilized in more efficient and more profitable economic activities. But when an economy falls into a deep recession, as in the Great Depression in the 1920s and 1930s as well as recent economic/financial crises in 2008 and 2009, then the liquidation of one sector of the economy can lead to the liquidation of other sectors of the economy and potential deepening of the recession. Under these conditions, government expenditures and fiscal policies can assist some sectors of the economy and thereby assist the business sector to recover from the recession.

The government monetary policy of targeting interest rates may be even more powerful than government expenditures in influencing the profitability of economic activities. Lowering interest rates makes more economic activities profitable leading to more production of goods and services and more investment expenditures.

In our macroeconomic profit system model presented in Table 3.3, the inclusion of the government sector's value added in the aggregate value added of the nonprofit sector in equation (3.3.16) makes possible analyses of the macroeconomic impacts of government expenditures. By plugging in various growth rates or magnitudes of the government sector's value added, we can simulate the estimated model to investigate how changes in government expenditures affect the expected trajectories of output, prices, profits, and employment. Higher (lower) levels of government expenditure are expected to lead to higher (lower) levels of nonprofit sector output in equation (3.3.16). Higher growth rates of nonprofit sector output lead to higher levels of the business sector output in equation (3.3.2) and through the impact of business output on business capital stock in equation (3.3.1) and business profit rate in equation (3.3.3) lead to higher levels of capital stock and profit rates. In forthcoming analyses we present simulation results of how government spending can affect macroeconomic aggregates.

3.2 Application of the Macroeconomic Profit System Model to the US Economy

We next apply the macroeconomic profit system model in the previous section to the US economy. US macroeconomic data series are described, the empirical model is estimated, model reliability is tested, and applications to forecasting, monetary policy, fiscal policy, and the business cycle are demonstrated.

3.2.1 Data

Annual data from the Fed and from the BEA of the US Department of Commerce are used for empirical application of the macroeconomic profit system model to the US economy.[5] The estimated model using annual data can be updated each quarter for the purpose of macroeconomic analysis.

The National Income and Product Accounts (NIPA) of the BEA provide annual data from 1929 and quarterly data from 1947 for the gross value added of all businesses, in addition to the gross value added and profits of corporate businesses disaggregated into financial and nonfinancial corporate sectors. The BEA also publishes annual data for fixed tangible assets of all types of businesses classified by the legal forms of businesses (i.e., corporate, single proprietorship, and partnerships). Using these data, the BEA has published several articles about the average accounting rate of return on tangible assets of nonfarm nonfinancial corporations in the USA.[6] The average accounting rate of return has been a key variable in several studies of capital stock formation.[7]

On the second week of each quarter, the Fed publishes annual data from 1945 and quarterly data from 1952 for profits and assets of corporate businesses and noncorporate businesses (series Z1), but the Fed does not publish tangible (buildings, equipment, and software) asset data for the financial corporate sector. The Fed obtains annual data on the tangible assets of US businesses from the BEA and converts the annual data to quarterly data. On its website the Fed maintains historical data sets for the profits and assets of corporate businesses (available in September 1996 and thereafter in each quarter), as well as for noncorporate businesses (available in the fourth quarter of 2001 and thereafter in each quarter). The data sets are released and updated on a quarterly basis and enable researchers to use preliminary as well as final revised data.

Using these data sources, we define the aggregate output or the GDP of the business sector in nominal terms Y and real terms $\bar{Y}$ as the gross value added of the nonfarm business sector in current and constant dollars, respectively. These data are gathered from Tables 1.3.5 and 1.3.6 of NIPA, respectively. The aggregate profit of the business sector Z is the sum of profits of domestic firms (nonfarm nonfinancial corporations, nonfarm noncorporate businesses, and financial corporations) from

---

[5]The Fed's website for data is http://www.federalreserve.gov/releases/Z1/. The BEA's website is http://www.bea.gov/.

[6]See Bureau of Economic Analysis (1999).

[7]For example, see Feldstein (1977), Abel et al. (1989), and Feldstein (1996). Poterba (1997) provides international comparisons of the rate of return to corporate capital and capital's share of output.

series Z1 of the Fed. Since profits of noncorporate businesses may include salaries and other compensation of owner–managers, the profit figures should be adjusted to exclude these side payments. Given that the mean profit rates for corporate and noncorporates businesses are expected to be equal over the long run, the unadjusted profit figures of noncorporate businesses are multiplied by an adjustment factor to equalize the two profit rates. The adjustment factor is the ratio of the mean corporate profit rate to the mean noncorporate profit rate, which is equal to 46.5 percent (i.e., 53.5 percent of unadjusted noncorporate profits are paid out as salaries and other compensation to owner–mangers). Dividing aggregate profit Z in nominal terms by the gross value added of US businesses Y in nominal terms gives the aggregate profit margin S of the US business sector.

The aggregate capital stock of business sector K consists of real estate, equipment, and software of corporate (nonfinancial and financial) and noncorporate firms plus government enterprises. In the second week of each quarter, the Fed releases annual and quarterly aggregate tangible capital stock data for the nonfarm nonfinancial corporate sector and the nonfarm noncorporate sector (series Z1). The only available data for the tangible capital of financial sector are the NAICS-based (North American Industrial Classification System) annual data released in August of each year by the BEA. The estimated capital stock of financial corporations should be adjusted to include land values, as the BEA does not include land values in their capital stock data. A comparison of corporate and noncorporate capital stock figures from the Fed (which includes land values) and from the BEA (which does not include land values) shows that capital stock data from the BEA should be multiplied by an adjustment factor of 1.18 to include land values. Thus, capital stock values for financial corporations are multiplied by this factor. We then summed nonfinancial and financial corporate plus noncorporate capital stocks to get the aggregate capital stock of the business sector. Dividing aggregate profit of the business sector Z by the aggregate capital stock K gives the time series of profit rates R.

The business sector employment time series (H) is business sector hours of all persons (HOABS) from the Fed available on a quarterly basis and converted to an annual basis. Labor productivity index is defined as the ratio of business sector output in real terms $(\bar{Y})$ divided by hours of all persons (H).

Total nonprofit sector output in nominal terms (X) is the difference between the total US GDP in nominal terms and business sector GDP in nominal terms (Y), both from Table 1.3.5 of the BEA. Total nonprofit sector output in real terms $(\bar{X})$ is the difference between the total US GDP in real terms and business sector GDP in real terms $(\bar{Y})$, both from Table 1.3.6 of the BEA.

The output price index $(\widehat{P})$ for business sector output is the ratio of nominal output (Y) to real output $(\bar{Y})$ in the business sector. The output price index $(\widecheck{P})$ for nonprofit sector output is the ratio of nominal output (X) to real output $(\bar{X})$ in the nonprofit sector.

The annual time series of the Federal funds rate (F) is the maximum of the average monthly rates in each year from the Fed. The annual time series of the total debt outstanding of the nonfinancial sector is the sum household debt (consumer credit plus home mortgage), business debt (corporate and noncorporate businesses), and state, local, and federal government debt from the Fed Z1 series.

Due to a change from standard industrial classification (SIC) to NAICS, there is some discontinuity in national account data.[8] The most consistent sets of data for application of the model to the US economy have been available since April 2006 when the BEA began to release time series of NAICS from 1952. Given the data availability at the time of writing this book, we compiled annual data series reported in the August of 2006, 2007, and 2008. These data sets can be updated each quarter when the Fed releases its Z1 data sets. We used post-1958 data due to a number of changes made in national macroeconomic data in 1959 by the BEA.[9]

The main problem in compiling quarterly data for this research is the unavailability of capital stocks of financial corporate sector on a quarterly basis. It is of course possible to generate quarterly data from annual data using various methods for converting low-frequency to high-frequency data. Using the cubic splice method, annual data for capital stocks in the financial corporate sector can be converted to quarterly data and added to the generated data to quarterly capital stocks of nonfinancial corporate and noncorporate sectors for estimating capital stocks in the business sector on a quarterly basis. However, in this book we focus on annual data in application of our model to the US economy due to the fact that profit and capital stock data supplied by the Fed and the BEA are originally estimated from annual data (and then transformed into quarterly data by various sampling and interpolation methods).

Table 3.4 provides a list of the variables and descriptive statistics for our macroeconomic model. There we see that profit margins in the US business sector ranged between 11.1 and 20.1 percent in the sample period from 1959 to 2008. Similarly, profit rates fell within the range of 4.1–10.3 percent. According to our models, wide fluctuations in profit margins and profit rates have the potential to substantially affect capital stock and output levels in the US business sector.

Table 3.4 Macroeconomic profit system model: list of variables and descriptive statistics based on 1959–2008 data series

		Descriptive statistics in levels of variables				
Level (log)	Description	Mean	Standard deviation	Median	Maximum	Minimum
$Y(y)$	GDP in the business sector in billions of current dollars	3,804.5	3,165.4	3,007.7	10,791.2	402.3

---

[8] During the transition period from 2004 to 2006, time series of nominal and real GDP in addition to fixed assets data released by the BEA were available from 1987.

[9] We should mention that any economic model must overcome data problems. In this regard, the formal model presented in this book could be more easily implemented if the BEA or Fed made available the capital stock of financial corporations on a quarterly basis.

Table 3.4 (continued)

Level (log)	Description		Descriptive statistics in levels of variables				
		Mean	Standard deviation	Median	Maximum	Minimum
$X(x)$	GDP in the nonprofit sector in billions of current dollars	1,187.3	982.7	925.5	3,473.4	124.1
GDP	Total GDP $= Y + X$ in billions of current dollars	4,991.8	4,147.7	3,933.2	14,264.6	526.4
$\bar{Y}(\bar{y})$	GDP in the business sector in billions of 2000 dollars	4,734.3	2,224.8	4,254.3	9,108.1	1,713.5
$\bar{X}(\bar{x})$	GDP in the nonprofit sector in billions of 2000 dollars	1,621.6	519.5	1,559.3	2,543.9	788.3
$G\bar{D}P$	Total $G\bar{D}P = \bar{Y} + \bar{X}$ in billions of 2000 dollars	6,355.9	2,738.9	5,813.6	11,652.0	2,501.8
$K(k)$	Capital stock in the business sector in billions of current dollars	8,305.5	6,812.8	7,462.7	25,160.1	853.7
$Z(z)$	Total profit in the business sector in billions of current dollars	563.7	519.2	368.9	1,926.9	72.1
$R(r)$	Profit rate in the business sector, percent	7.2	1.5	7.2	10.3	4.1
$S(s)$	Profit margin in the business sector, percent	15.5	2.4	15.5	20.1	11.1
$P(p)$	GDP price deflator $= GDP/G\bar{D}P$, index $= 100_{2000}$	63.9	33.4	66.4	122.4	20.8
$\hat{P}(\hat{p})$	Business sector price deflator $= Y/\bar{Y}$, index $= 100_{2000}$	65.3	32.1	69.7	118.5	23.2
$\check{P}(\check{p})$	Nonprofit sector price deflator $= X/\bar{X}$, index $= 100_{2000}$	60.8	37.3	57.6	136.5	15.3
F	Nominal Federal funds rate, percent	7.0	3.9	5.8	19.1	1.3
$\bar{F}$	Real Federal funds rate, percent	3.3	2.6	3.3	9.8	−2.3
$H(h)$	Hours of employment in the business sector, index $= 100_{2000}$	92.9	19.1	91.2	121.3	65.1

Table 3.4 (continued)

Level (log)	Description	Mean	Standard deviation	Median	Maximum	Minimum
			Descriptive statistics in levels of variables			
$\bar{B}(\bar{b})$	Labor productivity, index $= 100_{2000}$	75.6	22.2	71.3	124.4	40.8
$W(w)$	Wage rate in real terms, index $= 100_{2000}$	71.5	21.6	68.2	116.9	36.6
$D(d)$	Total nonfinancial sector debt outstanding in billions of current dollars	9,281.8	9,138.8	5,752.7	33,517.9	689.9

3.2.2 Estimation of the Macroeconomic Model

The most appropriate time for macroeconomic forecasting in the USA is September when the BEA completes its revisions of the past 3 years of national income and product data. We use the most updated data from the Fed and the BEA. All data were available as of April 2009, except the capital stock of financial corporate sector released on September 2008. The Fed's data on capital stock show that capital stocks of the nonfinancial corporate sector and nonfinancial noncorporate sector at the end of 2008 had decreased by 7.2 and 12.2 percent, respectively, from their values at the end of 2007. We measure the value of capital stock in the financial sector at the end of 2007 and adjust it by reducing its value by 10 percent to derive the value of capital stock in the financial corporate sector at the end of 2008. It should be noted that the capital stock of the financial corporate sector accounts for less than 7 percent of the total capital stock of the US business sector.

We employed ordinary least squares (OLS) regressions and Zellner's (1962) seemingly unrelated regressions (SUR) for estimating the macroeconomic model, as different econometric methods generate different coefficient estimates in the economic models.

Tables 3.5 and 3.6 present the estimated equations in our macroeconomic model using OLS and SUR methods, respectively. Initially, all equations in the model were specified and estimated with one lag of the focal variables in log terms ($\bar{y}$, $\bar{k}$, r, and s), and when the error terms in the equations were found to be serially correlated, the equations were re-estimated with two lags of the focal variables. Because the number of annual observations was not large, we tried to estimate all equations with minimum lags to avoid overparameterization of the model. We have no a priori information on the lag lengths for the Federal funds rate (F) and the growth rate of debt outstanding in real terms ($\dot{D}$) other than that there is a long lag between monetary policy actions and the response of macroeconomic aggregates as argued by Friedman (1961). Consequently, we determined the lag order empirically to get the most statistically significant estimated coefficients of the Federal funds rate and growth rate of nonfinancial debt outstanding, with the resultant lag orders for these two variables as shown in Tables 3.5 and 3.6.

Table 3.5 Estimated macroeconomic profit system model using OLS method: 1959–2008

$$\bar{k}_t = 0.228 + 1.567\,\bar{y}_{t-1} - 0.601\,\bar{y}_{t-2} - 1.635\,r_{t-1} + 0.805\,r_{t-2} +$$

(2.55)* (6.59)** (2.53)* (10.11)** (4.63)**

$$1.732\,s_{t-1} - 0.999\,s_{t-2} + 0.393\,\dot{\bar{D}}_t$$

(9.96)** (4.93)** (2.03)*

$R^2 = 0.99$ $\quad$ $DW = 2.13$

$$\bar{y}_t = 0.136 + 0.879\,r_{t-1} + 0.124\,r_{t-2} - 0.873\,s_{t-1} - 0.164\,s_{t-2} +$$

(1.88)+ (5.58)** (0.74) (4.60)** (0.82)

$$0.861\,\bar{k}_{t-1} + 0.121\,\bar{k}_{t-2} - 0.269\,F_{t-1} + 0.492\,\dot{\bar{D}}_t + 0.260\,\dot{\bar{X}}_t$$

(4.99)** (0.70) (1.90)+ (3.42)** (0.88)

$R^2 = 0.99$ $\quad$ $DW = 1.76$

$$r_t = -0.418 + 0.661\,\bar{y}_{t-1} + 0.571\,s_{t-1} - 0.717\,\bar{k}_{t-1} - 2.131\,F_{t-1}$$

(2.54)* (5.41)** (7.75)** (5.95)** (6.50)**

$R^2 = 0.92$ $\quad$ $DW = 2.05$

$$\bar{z}_t = 0.004 + 0.959\,r_{t-1} + 0.991\,\bar{k}_{t-1}$$

(0.01) (13.90)** (33.16)**

$R^2 = 0.95$ $\quad$ $DW = 1.56$

$$h_t = 0.048 + 0.901\,r_t - 0.921\,s_t + 0.929\,\bar{k}_t - 0.879\,\bar{b}_{t-1}$$

(0.56) (26.17)** (24.75)** (23.23)** (13.18)**

$R^2 = 0.99$ $\quad$ $DW = 1.77$

$$\hat{p}_t = -0.002 + 1.562\,\hat{p}_{t-1} - 0.564\,\hat{p}_{t-2} - 0.200\,\hat{\bar{F}}_{t-2} + 0.477\,\dot{\hat{P}}_{t-1}$$

(0.44) (16.70)** (6.05)** (3.11)** (4.41)**

$R^2 = 0.99$ $\quad$ $DW = 1.57$

Table 3.5 (continued)

$$\bar{x}_t = 0.127 + 1.120\,\bar{x}_{t-1} - 0.135\,\bar{x}_{t-2} - 0.003\,F_t + 0.039\,\dot{\bar{D}}_{t-1} + 0.123\,\dot{\bar{Y}}_{t-1}$$
$$\quad (3.17)^{**}\ (7.72)^{**}\quad (0.95)\qquad (0.07)\qquad (0.64)\qquad (2.11)^{*}$$
$$R^2 = 0.99 \qquad DW = 2.14$$

$$\breve{P}_t = 0.012 + 1.588\,\breve{P}_{t-1} - 0.591\,\breve{P}_{t-2} - 0.086\,\bar{F}_{t-2} + 0.194\,\hat{P}_{t-1}$$
$$\quad (2.47)^{*}\ (12.65)^{**}\quad (4.72)^{**}\quad (1.22)\qquad (1.99)^{*}$$
$$R^2 = 0.99 \qquad DW = 2.15$$

$$F_t = -0.014 + 0.838\,F_{t-1} - 0.191\,F_{t-2} + 0.499\,\dot{P}_{t-1} + 0.612\,G\dot{D}P_{t-1}$$
$$\quad (1.51)\ (5.90)^{**}\quad (1.50)\qquad (2.78)^{**}\quad (3.99)^{**}$$
$$R^2 = 0.78 \qquad DW = 1.97$$

$$d_t = -0.041 + 1.644\,d_{t-1} - 0.778\,d_{t-2} + 0.150\,gdp_{t-1} - 0.145\,F_{t-1}$$
$$\quad (1.80)^{+}\ (18.48)^{**}\quad (10.45)^{**}\quad (3.90)^{**}\quad (2.44)^{*}$$
$$R^2 = 0.99 \qquad DW = 1.70$$

Notes: Figures in parentheses are t-values associated with estimated coefficients, where the superscripts **, *, and + denote significance at the 1, 5, and 10 percent levels, respectively. DW denotes the Durbin–Watson test for serial correlation. The variables are defined as follows: $\bar{k}$ = log of deflated capital stocks in the business sector, $\bar{y}$ = log of real GDP in the business sector, r = log of profit rate in the business sector, s = log of profit margin in the business sector, $\dot{D}$=growth rate of debt outstanding in the nonfinancial sector in real terms, $\dot{X}$=growth rate of output of nonprofit sector in real terms, F = nominal Federal funds rate, $\breve{z}$= log of total profit of business sector in real terms, h = log of hours of employment, $\bar{b}$ = log of labor productivity, $\hat{p}$ = log of price deflator for output in the business sector, $\dot{P}$= inflation rate for output in the business sector, $\bar{F}$= real Federal funds rate, $\bar{x}$ = log of real GDP in the nonprofit sector, $\dot{Y}$=growth rate of business sector output in real terms, $\breve{p}$ = log of price deflator for output in the nonprofit sector, $\hat{P}$= inflation rate for output in the business sector, $\hat{p}$= inflation rate of GDP, $G\dot{D}P$= real GDP growth rate, d = log of debt outstanding in the nonfinancial sector in current dollars, and gdp = log of GDP in nominal terms.

Table 3.6 Estimated macroeconomic profit system model using SUR method: 1959–2008

$$\bar{k}_t = 0.235 + 1.560\,\bar{y}_{t-1} - 0.590\,\bar{y}_{t-2} - 1.632\,r_{t-1} + 0.798\,r_{t-2} +$$
$$(3.16)^{**}\ (7.86)^{**}\qquad (2.97)^{**}\qquad (12.60)^{**}\quad (5.82)^{**}$$
$$1.677\,s_{t-1} - 0.917\,s_{t-2} + 0.395\,\dot{\bar{D}}_t$$
$$(12.10)^{**}\quad (5.76)^{**}\qquad (2.54)^{*}$$

$R^2 = 0.99 \qquad DW = 2.05$

$DW = 2.05$

$$\bar{y}_t = 0.136 + 0.966\,r_{t-1} + 0.066\,r_{t-2} - 0.955\,s_{t-1} - 0.098\,s_{t-2} +$$
$$(2.65)^{**}\ (8.73)^{**}\qquad (0.57)\qquad (7.27)^{**}\qquad (0.72)$$
$$0.939\,\bar{K}_{t-1} - 0.045\,\bar{K}_{t-2} - 0.111\,F_{t-1} + 0.497\,\dot{\bar{D}}_{t-1} + 0.259\,\dot{\bar{X}}_t$$
$$(7.94)^{**}\qquad (0.38)\qquad (1.17)\qquad (5.22)^{**}\qquad (1.43)$$

$R^2 = 0.99 \qquad DW = 2.04$

$$r_t = -0.383 + 0.801\,\bar{y}_{t-1} + 0.672\,s_{t-1} - 0.834\,\bar{K}_{t-1} - 1.236\,F_{t-1}$$
$$(2.60)^{**}\ (8.86)^{**}\qquad (11.96)^{**}\quad (9.38)^{**}\quad (5.19)^{**}$$

$R^2 = 0.90 \qquad DW = 1.97$

$$\bar{z}_t = -0.038 + 0.959\,r_{t-1} + 0.995\,\bar{K}_{t-1}$$
$$(0.16)\ (15.76)^{**}\qquad (36.22)^{**}$$

$R^2 = 0.95 \qquad DW = 1.56$

$$h_t = 0.040 + 0.911\,r_t - 0.928\,s_t + 0.938\,\bar{K}_t - 0.894\,\bar{b}_{t-1}$$
$$(0.54)\ (30.86)^{**}\ (29.16)^{**}\ (28.08)^{**}\ (16.10)^{**}$$

$R^2 = 0.99 \qquad DW = 1.80$

$$\hat{p}_t = -0.002 + 1.471\,\hat{p}_{t-1} - 0.474\,\hat{p}_{t-2} - 0.224\,\bar{F}_{t-2} + 0.544\,\dot{\bar{P}}_{t-1}$$
$$(0.42)\ (22.02)^{**}\qquad (7.33)^{**}\qquad (4.55)^{**}\qquad (7.15)^{**}$$

$R^2 = 0.99 \qquad DW = 1.47$

Table 3.6 (continued)

$$\bar{x}_t = +0.114 + 1.144\,\bar{x}_{t-1} - 0.158\,\bar{x}_{t-2} - 0.002\,F_t + 0.040\,\dot{\bar{D}}_{t-1} + 0.143\,\dot{\bar{Y}}_{t-1}$$
$$(3.38)^{**}\ (10.74)^{**}\quad (1.51)\qquad (0.08)\qquad (0.85)\qquad (3.09)^{**}$$

$R^2 = 0.99$ $DW = 2.22$

$$\breve{P} = 0.013 + 1.570\,\breve{P}_{t-1} - 0.574\,\breve{P}_{t-2} - 0.082\,\breve{F}_{t-2} + 0.199\,\hat{P}_{t-1}$$
$$(2.58)^{**}\ (15.69)^{**}\quad (5.74)^{**}\qquad (1.31)^{**}\qquad (2.44)^{**}$$

$R^2 = 0.99$ $DW = 2.11$

$$F_t = -0.007 + 0.931\,F_{t-1} - 0.245\,F_{t-2} + 0.349\,P_{t-1} + 0.502\,\dot{G}\dot{D}P_{t-1}$$
$$(1.01)\ (9.14)^{**}\qquad (2.52)^*\qquad (2.47)^*\qquad (4.24)^{**}$$

$R^2 = 0.78$ $DW = 1.98$

$$d_t = -0.058 + 1.641\,d_{t-1} - 0.785\,d_{t-2} + 0.163\,gdp_{t-1} - 0.083\,F_{t-1}$$
$$(3.15)^{**}\ (24.14)^{**}\quad (13.67)^{**}\qquad (5.63)^{**}\qquad (1.73)^+$$

$R^2 = 0.99$ $DW = 1.57$

Notes: Figures in parentheses are t-values associated with estimated coefficients, where the superscripts **, *, and $^+$ denote significance at the 1, 5, and 10 percent levels, respectively. DW denotes the Durbin–Watson test for serial correlation. The variables are defined as follows: $k = $ log of deflated capital stocks in the business sector, $\bar{y} = $ log of real GDP in the business sector, $r = $ log of profit rate in the business sector, $s = $ log of profit margin in the business sector, $\dot{D} = $ growth rate of debt outstanding in the nonfinancial sector in real terms, $\dot{X} = $ growth rate of output of nonprofit sector in real terms, $F = $ nominal Federal funds rate, $\breve{z} = $ log of total profit of business sector in real terms, $h = $ log of hours of employment, $\bar{b} = $ log of labor productivity, $\hat{P} = $ log of price deflator for output in the business sector, $\breve{P} = $ inflation rate for output in the nonprofit sector, $\bar{F} = $ real Federal funds rate, $\bar{x} = $ log of real GDP in the nonprofit sector, $\dot{\bar{Y}} = $ growth rate of business sector output in real terms, $\breve{p} = $ log of price deflator for output in the nonprofit sector, $\dot{P} = $ inflation rate for output in the business sector, $\hat{P} = $ inflation rate of GDP, $\dot{G}\dot{D}P = $ real GDP growth rate, $d = $ log of debt outstanding in the nonfinancial sector in current dollars, and $gdp = $ log of GDP in nominal terms.

The goodness-of-fit of the estimated equations (other than the monetary policy rule) is quite high with adjusted R^2 values in the range of 0.90–0.99.[10] The adjusted R^2 values for the Federal fund rate equation are 0.78 for both OLS and SUR methods.

The business-sector-deflated capital stock equation was estimated with two lags of the focal variables. In the estimated equation using OLS in Table 3.5, the estimated coefficients of the first lags of $\bar{y}$, r, and s and second lags of r and s are significant at the 1 percent level, while the estimated coefficients of the second lag of $\bar{y}$ is significant at the 5 percent level. Originally, the capital stock equation included the Federal funds rate F, but the estimated coefficient was not found to be statistically significant and was dropped. When the growth rate of nonfinancial debt outstanding $\dot{D}$ was added to the capital stock equation, the estimated coefficient was statistically significant and improved out-of-sample forecasts of the focal variables. The estimated coefficient for $\dot{D}$ is significant at the 5 percent level. In the deflated capital stock equation using the SUR method in Table 3.6, the estimated coefficients for the first and second lags of $\bar{y}$, r, and s are all significant at the 1 percent level, while the estimated coefficient for $\dot{D}$ is significant at the 5 percent level.

The business sector real output equation was estimated with two lags of r, s, and $\bar{k}$, and then three variables were added to the equation – namely, the Federal funds rate, growth rate of nonprofit sector output, and growth rate of nonfinancial debt outstanding. In the real business output equation $\bar{y}$ in Table 3.5, the estimated OLS coefficients of the first lags of r, s, and $\bar{k}$ are all statistically significant at the 1 percent level. The estimated coefficient for $\dot{D}$ is significant at the 1 percent level. The estimated coefficients for F are statistically significant at the 10 percent level. In the real business output equation $\bar{y}$ in Table 3.6, the estimated SUR coefficients of the first lags of r, s, and $\bar{k}$ are all statistically significant at the 1 percent level. The estimated coefficient for $\dot{D}$ is statistically significant at the 1 percent level.

The business sector profit rate equation was estimated with the first lags of $\bar{y}$, s, and $\bar{k}$ and the Federal funds rate. The estimated coefficients of the lags were all significant at the 1 percent level in both OLS and SUR regressions in Tables 3.5 and 3.6.

The equation for total profit of the business sector in real terms was estimated with first lags of r and $\bar{k}$. The estimated coefficients of the lags were all significant at the 1 percent level in both OLS regressions and SUR in Tables 3.5 and 3.6.

The business sector employment equation uses the contemporaneous values of r, s, and $\bar{k}$ and the first lag of log of labor productivity. The estimated coefficients of the variables were all significant at the 1 percent level in both OLS and SUR regressions in Tables 3.5 and 3.6. When the estimated business sector employment

---

[10]The statistical significance of the lagged Federal funds rate in the estimated equations is consistent with the notion that a lag exists between a monetary policy shock and its impact on inflation, as nominal and real GDP peak responses occur several quarters later. Previous research has shown that sticky prices and information can generate lagged and gradual responses of inflation and output to monetary policy shocks (e.g., see Friedman (1961), Leeper et al. (1996), Christiano et al. (1999), and Mankiw and Reis (2002)).

equation is used for forecasting employment in period t, it uses forecasts of r, s, and $\bar{k}$ from the model for period t and the first lag $\bar{b}$.

The first and second lags of the log of prices in the estimated price model for the business sector are statistically significant at the 1 percent level using the OLS and SUR methods (Tables 3.5 and 3.6). The estimated coefficients for the second lag of the real Federal funds rate in the price model for the business sector are negative and statistically significant at 1 percent level in the OLS and SUR regressions. This result is consistent with Wicksell (1898). The significance of a 2-year lag order confirms Friedman's view that there is a long lag between monetary policy actions and their resultant impact on the economy. The estimated coefficient of the nonprofit sector's inflation rate is statistically significant at the 1 percent level in OLS and SUR regressions (Tables 3.5 and 3.6), which implies that inflation in the business sector is affected by inflation in the nonprofit sector.

The estimated equations of real output in the nonprofit sector $\bar{x}$ in OLS regressions and SUR reveal that nonprofit sector output in real terms is driven by its first lag and the growth rate of the output of business sector. The estimated coefficient for the Federal funds rate is negative but statistically insignificant in the OLS regressions and SUR (Tables 3.5 and 3.6). The growth rate of nonfinancial debt outstanding has a positive impact on the real output of nonprofit sector but its estimated coefficients are not highly significant.

The estimated first and second lags of log of prices in the nonprofit sector are statistically significant at the 1 percent level in OLS and SUR regressions (Tables 3.5 and 3.6). The estimated coefficients of the real Federal funds rate in the nonprofit sector price model are negative but not statistically significant in the regressions. The estimated coefficient of the business sector's inflation rate is statistically significant at the 5 percent level in the OLS and SUR regressions (Tables 3.5 and 3.6). These results imply that inflation in the nonprofit sector is influenced by inflation in the business sector.

The Federal funds rate equation shows that the estimated coefficients for the lag of the inflation rate are statistically significant at the 1 percent level in the OLS regression and 5 percent level in the SUR regression (Tables 3.5 and 3.6). The estimated coefficients for the growth rate of GDP in real terms are statistically significant at the 1 percent level in OLS and SUR regressions (Tables 3.5 and 3.6). The moderately high R^2 of 0.78 percent is due to using annual data. When quarterly data are used the estimated R^2 increases to 0.99.

Finally, the estimated equation for nonfinancial debt outstanding in nominal terms shows that total debt is driven by its own lags and log of nominal GDP (Tables 3.5 and 3.6). The estimated coefficients of the lags are significant at the 1 percent level in OLS and SUR regressions. The estimated coefficients for log of nominal GDP are positive and significant at the 1 percent level in OLS and SUR regressions, which suggest that higher demand for debt in response to higher growth rates of nominal GDP. The estimated coefficients for the Federal funds rate are negative and significant at the 5 percent level in the OLS regression and 10 percent level in the SUR regression. Consistent with the theory of loanable funds, the negative coefficient for the Federal funds rate suggests that higher (lower) Federal funds rates are expected to decrease (increase) total debt in nominal terms.

According to the empirical results in Tables 3.5 and 3.6, the profit system models of the US economy have a strong statistical fit. High adjusted R^2 values and significant t statistics give support for the conclusion that the individual models are reliable. However, these results cannot be interpreted to mean that the system of equations as a whole performs well. To do this we must test whether it can be used to reproduce historical data and produce accurate forecasts.

3.2.3 Testing Model Reliability

It is well known that estimated macroeconometric models and their forecasts are subject to a variety of potential pitfalls, including errors in measuring endogenous and exogenous variables, the assumption of additive error terms in equations, uncertainty in estimated coefficients, and misspecifications of individual equations as well as the whole system of equations. The statistical significance of estimated coefficients of the variables in individual equations (as shown in Tables 3.5 and 3.6) is just one of several criteria for testing model reliability. Higher statistical significance may be spurious and does not necessarily imply in-sample ability of the estimated model to mimic actual movements of data series or more accurate out-of-sample forecast accuracy. Thus, we conducted two additional tests of the model to assess the estimated model's reliability. In the first test we compare trajectories of stochastically simulated values of the variables in the models during the sample period 1959–2008 with the actual paths of these variables. Also, we compare actual and simulated values of profit rate, profit margin, growth rates of GDPs, output, capital stocks, and employment in the business sector and nonprofit output generated from the static and dynamic simulation of the model over the sample period 1959–2008. In the second test we compare out-of-sample variable forecasts of the models with their actual values in the period 2006–2008. These tests seek to investigate the strengths and weaknesses of the estimated models.

3.2.3.1 Historical Simulation of the Estimated Macroeconomic Model

Comparisons of historical patterns of the time series of macroeconomic aggregates in the model and the stochastically simulated patterns of the same variables over the sample period provide useful information on the ability of the estimated model to reproduce actual movements in historical data. For each variable in the model, historical simulation of estimated models can give insight into the length of the forecast horizon (time period) over which the model can mimic the path of the actual time series of the variable (if at all). Moreover, results from historical simulations can be useful for determining the length of the out-of-sample forecast horizon within which the model is expected to generate more accurate forecasts.

Figure 3.1 shows the results of 1,000 trials generated by running a Monte Carlo simulation of the estimated model using the Broyden (1965) method, which solves the model each time assuming that all error terms in the estimated model are normally distributed. The simulation incorporates coefficient uncertainty, uses the actual values of the variables in 1959–1961 as initial values, and generates the trajectories of all variables in the model from 1962 to 2008.[11] The simulation employs the actual effective nominal and real Federal funds rates, actual inflation, and actual nonfinancial debt outstanding. In general, the simulation results demonstrate that the system of equations is successful in mimicking the historical paths of the focal variables.

As Fig. 3.1(a)–(c) illustrates, simulated values of $G\bar{D}P$ (real US GDP), $\bar{Y}$ (real GDP in the business sector), and $\bar{X}$ (real GDP in the nonprofit sector) closely mimic the actual movements of these variables over the sample period from 1959 to 1990. Slight differences between simulated and actual values emerge after 1991. Figure 3.1(d)–(f) shows similar results for nominal values of GDP, Y, and X, respectively. In general, comparison of the simulated and historical trajectories of outputs reveals that the model successfully mimics aggregate output paths in both real and nominal terms over the sample period.

The simulation results for nominal capital stock shown in Fig. 3.1(g) shows that the model can mimic the movements of actual time series of capital stock from 1959 to 2003, or a period of more than 40 years. Thereafter there is some divergence in the simulated and actual paths of capital stock. After 2003 actual capital stock overshoots and then begins to return back to the simulated path, which suggests that the excessive expansion of capital stock after 2003 could not be sustained.

The simulation results for profit rates and profit margins in the business sector are shown in Fig. 3.1(h) and (i), respectively. Despite their wide fluctuations over time, the results demonstrate the model's ability to mimic the general paths of these two profitability parameters over the sample period. Notice that the simulated paths for profit rates and profit margins are able to capture some of the long-run turning points.

Fig. 3.1 Macroeconomic profit system model: actual and simulated values of the variables in the model: 1959–2008: (**a**) real US GDP; (**b**) real GDP in the business sector; (**c**) real GDP in the nonprofit sector; (**d**) nominal US GDP; (**e**) nominal GDP in the business sector; (**f**) nominal GDP in the nonprofit sector; (**g**) nominal capital stock in the business sector; (**h**) business sector profit rate; (**i**) business sector profit margin; (**j**) business sector profits in real terms; (**k**) business sector profits in nominal terms; and (**l**) business sector employment index

---

[11] For each equation of the model, a probability distribution of each estimated coefficient and the error term is constructed using standard errors and a normal curve. Random values of the estimated coefficients and error terms are chosen for each simulation. In a static simulation the estimated coefficients are used in combination with actual lagged values of endogenous variables to compute simulated values of variables at each point in time. By contrast, in a dynamic simulation the estimated coefficients are used in combination with lagged endogenous variables from the solution computed in previous periods. The average of these simulated values of variables is plotted in Fig. 3.1. Standard textbooks on econometric models and forecasts can be consulted for further details on the subject of stochastic simulation known also as Monte Carlo simulation.

(a) Real U.S. GDP

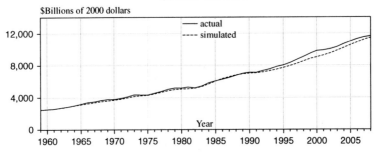

(b) Real *GDP* in the Business Sector

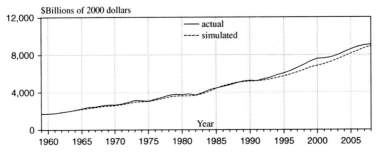

(c) Real *GDP* in the Nonprofit Sector

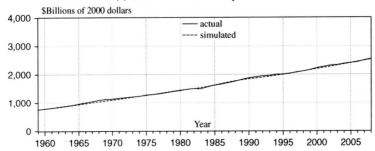

(d) Nominal U.S. *GDP*

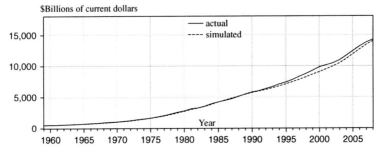

Fig. 3.1   (continued)

(e) Nominal *GDP* in the Business Sector

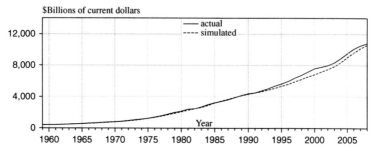

(f) Nominal *GDP* in the Nonprofit Sector

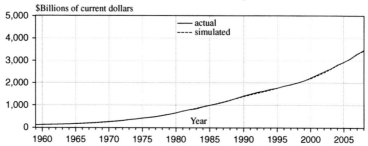

(g) Nominal Capital Stock in the Business Sector

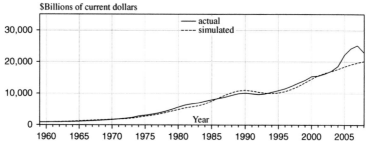

(h) Business Sector Profit Rate

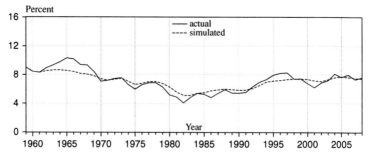

Fig. 3.1 (continued)

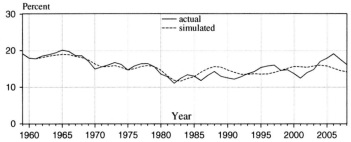

(i) Business Sector Profit Margin

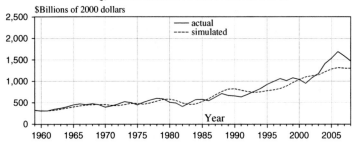

(j) Business Sector Profits in Real Terms

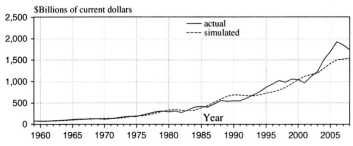

(k) Business Sector Profits in Nominal Terms

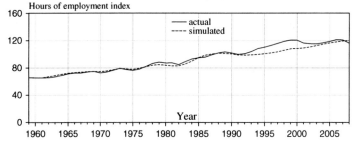

(l) Business Sector Employment Index

Fig. 3.1 (continued)

The simulation results for business sector profits in real and nominal terms are shown in Fig. 3.1(j) and (k), respectively. Despite their wide fluctuations over time, the results demonstrate the model's ability to closely mimic aggregate profits in the business sector. The simulated results also suggest that high growth rates of profits over the past few years are not sustainable in the long run.

The simulation results for hours of business employment in Fig. 3.1(l) show that the model can mimic actual values of employment for a decade and the general trend in employment over the long run.

The foregoing simulation results are based on the estimated model from the SUR method. Of course, other econometric methods would result in different estimates of the coefficients and different paths of simulated variables. Also, the simulation results depend on the chosen simulation algorithm (Bryoden, Gauss-Seidel, Newton, etc.) and various computing options in simulation, such as starting values, terminal conditions, maximum number of iterations, convergence limits, the use of analytic or numeric derivatives, and so on. In this regard, we should note that the simulation results based on OLS regression estimates are very similar to the SUR results in Fig. 3.1.

Table 3.7 compares the actual and simulated values of profit rate, profit margin, growth rates of GDPs (outputs), capital stocks, and employment in the business sector and nonprofit output generated from the static and dynamic simulations of the model over the sample period from 1959 to 2008. The first column reports the actual mean values. The second and third columns show the averages or expected values of one-period ahead forecasts, or $E_t(V_{t+1})$, from a static simulation of the

Table 3.7 Results from historical simulation of the estimated macroeconomic profit system model with comparisons of actual versus simulated values of the variables in the model using OLS and SUR regression methods in the sample period: 1959–2008

Variable		Static forecasts		Dynamic forecasts	
	Actual	OLS	SUR	OLS	SUR
$\dot{GDP}$ growth rate of GDP in nominal terms	7.1	7.1	7.0	7.1	7.0
$\dot{Y}$ growth rate of business sector GDP in nominal terms	7.0	7.1	6.9	7.0	7.0
$\dot{X}$ growth rate of nonprofit GDP in nominal terms	7.2	7.2	7.2	7.2	7.2
$\dot{K}$ growth rate of capital stock in the business sector in nominal terms	7.1	7.2	7.1	7.1	6.9
$\dot{Z}$ growth rate of business sector profit in nominal terms	7.2	7.1	6.8	7.0	7.1
$\ddot{GDP}$ growth rate of GDP in real terms	3.3	3.3	3.2	3.3	3.2
$\ddot{Y}$ growth rate of business sector GDP in real terms	3.5	3.6	3.4	3.5	3.5
$\ddot{X}$ growth rate of nonprofit sector GDP in real terms	2.5	2.5	2.5	2.5	2.5
$\ddot{Z}$ growth rate of business sector profit in real terms	3.6	3.4	3.2	3.9	3.6
R profit rate in the business sector	7.2	7.1	7.1	7.1	7.1
S profit margin in the business sector	15.5	15.5	15.5	15.5	15.4
$\dot{H}$ growth rate of business sector employment	1.2	1.3	1.1	1.3	1.3
$\dot{B}$ growth rate of business sector labor productivity	2.3	2.3	2.3	2.2	2.2

model (i.e., the actual values of lags of the variables are used to generate forecasts). The fourth and fifth columns report averages or expected values of the variables, or $E_{1959}(V_{t+j})$, generated from a dynamic simulation of the model (i.e., the model uses the actual values of the variables in 1959–1961 and generates forecasts of all variables in the period from 1962 onward using the simulated values). These results tend to confirm that the endogenous simulated variables closely track the original data series.

Finally, Fig. 3.2 shows the inflation rates for the business sector and nonprofit sector in the period 1959–2008. Here we see that at times there appear to be substantial differences between inflation rates in these two sectors. We infer that analyzing inflation in business and nonprofit sectors may lend additional insights into inflation forces within the economy that are not evident in national inflation rates.

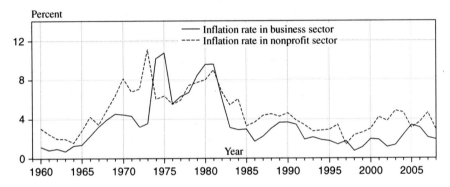

Fig. 3.2 Inflation rates in the business and nonprofit sectors

In general, these simulation experiments lend support for the ability of the system of equations that together encompass our profit system model to reproduce the historical paths of key variables in the US economy. In series with strong long-run trends, such as output and capital stock variables, the ability of the model to closely mimic the time paths of these variables is very good and appears to be stable within the sample period. Additionally, the profit rate and profit margin simulations suggest that general trends in these fairly volatile series can be identified. We infer from these favorable empirical findings that the model is able to explain the underlying process that generates time-varying profit rates and profit margins as well as long-run trends in US output measures and capital stock.

3.2.3.2 Out-of-Sample Forecasts of the Estimated Macroeconomic Model

A common problem in forecasting macroeconomic variables is frequent data revisions. The BEA releases the first "advance" estimates of the national accounts about a month after the end of a quarter, which are revised a month later when "preliminary" estimates are available and then revised again a month later when "final" estimates are available. The GDP data for the previous 3 years are revised every July, and historical revisions are made every 5 years. Some of the revisions can be significant; for instance, the BEA in February 2007 revised downward its estimate of the annual growth rate of the US GDP in the fourth quarter of 2006 from 3.5 to 2.0 percent and then 1 month later to 2.2 percent.

The impact of data revisions and data vintages on macroeconomic forecasting and policy analyses has been extensively studied. Several results from these studies are relevant for the empirical application of our model. First, data revisions and the choice of data vintage have important effects on macroeconomic forecasting and coincident policy analysis. For example, the use of preliminary data can lead to modest to large forecast errors.[12] Second, for evaluation of ex ante or out-of-sample forecasts, the data sets that were available to economic agents or forecasters at the time of forecasting must be used.[13] Third, data revisions have much more impact on the level of aggregate output than on its growth rates.[14] Fourth, and last, rather than using the latest vintage of historical data for estimation of models and forecasting purposes, which was standard practice in the past, an increasing number of macroeconomic researchers and forecasters use real-time data for model selection as well as for forecasting.[15]

In view of this previous research, for purposes of model estimation and out-of-sample forecasting of growth rates of macroeconomic aggregates, we used the data sets that were available at the time of forecast. For our model this point in time is the second week of each quarter when the Fed releases data and the "final" estimates of NIPA are provided by the BEA. Also, we used the latest available published data for comparing the actual and forecast values.

Given past research, studies find that data revisions have less impact on growth rates than levels; it is more informative to compare the growth rates of actual variables versus forecasted variables.

Table 3.8 reports the forecast results from estimating the model using OLS and SUR regression methods. The forecast date is September 2006 when the BEA completed its data revisions and capital stock data for the financial sector at the end

Table 3.8 Macroeconomic profit system model: out-of-sample forecasts of variables in the model using OLS and SUR regression methods compared to actual outcomes

	Forecast period		
Variable	2006	2007	2008
$\dot{GDP}$, growth rate of GDP in real terms			
OLS	2.9	1.8	1.5
SUR	2.9	2.0	1.5
Actual	**2.8**	**2.0**	**1.1**

---

[12] See Denton and Kuiper (1965) and Trivellato and Rettore (1986).

[13] See Fair and Shiller (1990).

[14] See Howrey (1996).

[15] For example, see Koenig and Dolmas (1997), Swanson and White (1997a, b), and Robertson and Tallman (1998).

Table 3.8 (continued)

Variable	Forecast period		
	2006	2007	2008
$\dot{Y}$, growth rate of business sector GDP in real terms			
OLS	3.2	1.9	1.6
SUR	3.2	2.2	1.5
Actual	**3.2**	**2.0**	**0.8**
$\dot{X}$, growth rate of nonprofit sector GDP in real terms			
OLS	1.6	1.4	1.2
SUR	1.6	1.5	1.2
Actual	**1.4**	**2.3**	**2.2**
$\dot{GDP}$, growth rate of GDP in nominal terms			
OLS	6.3	5.4	5.1
SUR	6.2	5.4	4.8
Actual	**6.1**	**4.8**	**3.3**
$\dot{Y}$, growth rate of business sector GDP in nominal terms			
OLS	6.7	5.4	5.0
SUR	6.6	5.4	4.7
Actual	**6.4**	**4.1**	**2.7**
$\dot{X}$, growth rate of nonprofit sector GDP in nominal terms			
OLS	5.2	5.4	5.2
SUR	5.2	5.3	5.1
Actual	**5.2**	**7.0**	**5.2**
$\dot{K}$, growth rate of capital stock in the business sector in nominal terms			
OLS	8.9	7.1	5.5
SUR	9.6	8.5	7.1
Actual	**9.2**	**4.1**	**−9.0**
$\dot{Z}$, growth rate of total profit in the business sector in nominal terms			
OLS	7.0	−0.6	−0.4
SUR	8.6	1.7	1.3
Actual	**13.7**	**−4.2**	**−5.7**
R, profit rate in the business sector			
OLS	7.4	6.8	6.5
SUR	7.5	7.0	6.6
Actual	**8.0**	**7.3**	**7.6**
S, profit margin in the business sector			
OLS	15.8	14.9	14.4
SUR	16.2	15.6	15.1
Actual	**19.1**	**17.6**	**16.1**

Table 3.8 (continued)

| | Forecast period | | |
Variable	2006	2007	2008
$\dot{H}$, growth rate of business sector employment			
OLS	1.7	0.6	0.4
SUR	1.3	0.5	0.1
Actual	**2.1**	**−0.3**	**−3.9**
$\dot{B}$, growth rate of business sector labor productivity			
OLS	1.6	1.3	1.2
SUR	1.9	1.7	1.4
Actual	**1.0**	**2.3**	**4.9**
$\dot{W}$, growth rate of nominal wage rate			
OLS	4.5	6.1	5.9
SUR	4.1	5.4	5.1
Actual	**1.6**	**7.1**	**11.7**
$\dot{P}$, GDP inflation rate			
OLS	3.4	3.5	3.5
SUR	3.3	3.3	3.3
Actual	**3.2**	**2.7**	**2.2**
$\dot{\hat{P}}$, business sector GDP inflation rate			
OLS	3.3	3.4	3.4
SUR	3.2	3.2	3.1
Actual	**3.1**	**2.1**	**1.9**
$\dot{\check{P}}$, nonprofit sector inflation rate			
OLS	3.6	3.9	4.0
SUR	3.6	3.8	3.9
Actual	**3.7**	**4.6**	**2.9**
$\dot{D}$, growth rate of nonfinancial debt outstanding in nominal terms			
OLS	8.0	6.5	5.4
SUR	7.7	6.1	5.0
Actual	**8.9**	**8.6**	**5.8**

Actual (bold face) figures are as of April 2009 releases by the BEA.

of previous year (or 2005) is released. Forecasts are estimated for 2006, 2007, and 2008 using actual Federal funds rates over time. The actual data are the vintage released by the BEA in April 2009 and will be revised in July 2009 when the BEA releases the results of its 13th comprehensive (or benchmark) revision of the NIPA. As shown in Table 3.8, the forecasted values of the growth rates of aggregate real GDP and real GDP in the business sector in 2006 and 2007 using the two regression methods are quite accurate. Although forecasts of the growth rate of real GDP in

2008 based on forecasts in 2006 are not accurate, the forecasts nonetheless show cooling of the economy from 2006. Forecasts of the growth rate of GDPs in nominal terms are accurate for the first year in the forecast horizon but less accurate thereafter due to overestimation of inflation rates in 2007 and 2008 and adding the estimated inflation rates to the growth rates of GDPs in real terms. Forecasts of profit rate and growth rate of capital stocks in nominal terms in 2006 and 2007 are the quite accurate. Forecasts of the growth rate of hours of business employment are accurate for a 1-year forecast horizon. Forecasts of the growth rate of profit shows an expected sharp decline in 2007 and 2008. Although the absolute magnitudes of the forecasts are not highly accurate, the model accurately predicts the direction of trends in the macroeconomic aggregates – that is, the economy was cooling from 2006 and that the signs of the slowdown could be found in several variables such as profit rate, profit margin, growth rates of GDPs in real and nominal terms, growth rate of total profit, and the growth rate of capital stock. Because detecting the direction of trends in macroeconomic variables in earlier stages can be important to the success of monetary policy, our profit system model results appear to be potentially useful for monetary policy analysis. In sum, our macroeconomic profit system model provides out-of-sample forecasts of the national economy and business sector that are fairly reasonable in view of actual outcomes, especially with respect to general trends in macroeconomic variables.

3.3 Monetary Policy Analysis and the Impacts of Economic Stimulus Plans

3.3.1 Monetary Policy Analysis

There have been two macroeconomic modeling approaches for the study of monetary policy transmission analysis – namely, dynamic simultaneous equation (DSE) models and structural VAR (SVAR) models.[16] Both modeling approaches must address the issue of identification of the empirical model. In the DSE modeling approach, identification is normally attained by using economic theory for imposing zero restrictions on the coefficients of the variables in the simultaneous equations (i.e., the Cowles Commission approach). By contrast, the SVAR approach focuses on the role of shocks to variables for attaining the identification of the estimated model. This approach avoids some of the difficulties inherent in the Cowles Commission approach. However, SVARs are less suitable for the analysis of the systematic part of monetary policy simulation (i.e., quantifying the impacts on the macroeconomic aggregates of changes in monetary policy instruments). The strength of the DSE modeling approach lies in its ability to use both economic theory and econometric methods for policy simulation. In particular, the DSE approach

---

[16]See Sims (1980, 1986, 1992, 1998, 1999), Bernanke (1986), Cooley and LeRoy (1985), Hood and Koopmans (1953), Koopmans (1950), and Laidler (1999).

can provide the estimates of dynamic multipliers for the study and analysis of the impact of changes in monetary policy instruments on nominal and real output.[17] Since dynamic multipliers do not distinguish between anticipated and unanticipated monetary policy, the estimates of dynamic multipliers are useful and necessary to determine the magnitudes of changes in monetary policy instruments to attain target growth rates of nominal output and real output as well as the inflation rate.

While the SVAR approach is more suited for the study of monetary policy shocks (i.e., the unsystematic part of monetary policy), there are some doubts and criticisms about the existence and meaning of these shocks. It has been argued that monetary authorities do not operate as random number generators.[18] In the US the Fed's open market committee convenes meetings every 6 weeks, and any policy error is likely to be quickly reversed.[19]

The channels of transmission of inflation and monetary policy in our profit system model are reflected in the recursive and simultaneous equations discussed in Section 3.1.7. Our modeling strategy for the study of monetary policy was guided by theory (i.e., Wicksellian models of inflation and loanable funds). The lag structures of focal variables and other variables for output, capital stock, profit rate, and profit margin were determined empirically to obtain the most statistically significant estimated coefficients or generate the most accurate out-of-sample forecasts.

3.3.2 Fiscal Policy Analysis

As mentioned earlier, the most effective monetary policy instrument on an everyday basis is changing the Federal funds rate. In normal circumstances the profit system model can be used for monetary policy analysis by conducting simulation of the estimated model assuming different trajectories of the Federal funds rate. However, since 2007, the USA and other major industrialized economies have been caught up in a credit crunch due to the collapse of residential real estate markets (house prices), rising defaults on subprime mortgages, the spread of defaults to the financial system, and the resultant massive deleveraging of industrialized economies. The collapse of the financial system spread to the "real" economy as US GDP in real terms shrank by 5.4 percent in the fourth quarter of 2008 following a decline rate of 2.7 percent in the third quarter of 2008. In the first quarter of 2009, the US real GDP decreased by 6.4 percent according to the second estimate by the BEA. To stimulate the economy, in a series of rate adjustments, the Fed cut the Federal funds rate from 5.25 in July 2007 to the current 0 to 0.25 percent target range. The sharp decline of the US economy in the fourth quarter of 2008 and the first quarter of 2009, the collapse of the stock market, and the financial crisis that began with the declining housing market in 2006

---

[17]See Cochrane (1998).
[18]See Bernanke and Mihov (1998).
[19]See Rudebusch (1998) and Gottschalk (2001).

are historic events that mark the most severe economic downturn since the Great Depression. Other major industrial countries also have fallen into a deep recession. In these turbulent times, to quote a popular phrase, "we are all Keynesians again." In February 2008 the Economic Stimulus Act of 2008 was passed by the US Congress in an effort to stimulate the economy by means of mainly tax cuts and rebates to US citizens and firms. One year later in February 2009 the US government embarked on a more ambitious stimulus plan to guide the economy to long-run growth with a stimulus package of $789 billion under the American Recovery and Reinvestment Act of 2009.

3.3.3 Macroeconomic Policy Analyses: A Scenario Approach

In this time of unprecedented twin economic and financial crises, the assessment of the impact of changes in the effective Federal funds rate on key macroeconomic variables should be carried out in the context of all macroeconomic policies implemented to overcome the crises. For this reason we utilize a scenario approach for the study of the impact of alternative macroeconomic policies. We use the estimated macroeconomic profit system model for macroeconomic policy analysis by simulating the model for the following five economic scenarios over the period 2009–2012:

Scenario A. The highest monthly average of the Federal funds rate in 2008 was 3.9 percent. Here we assume that the Fed maintained the Federal funds rate at this level for the period 2009–2012 and nonfinancial debt outstanding in nominal terms stayed at its level in 2008. This scenario is for analyzing the macroeconomic impact of a zero debt growth rate.

Scenario B. The debt growth rate is allowed to follow its normal path, while the Federal funds rate stays at 3.9 percent from 2009 to 2012. The estimated equation for nonfinancial debt outstanding is used to model the debt growth rate.

Scenario C. Normal debt growth is assumed but the Fed maintains the Federal funds rate at its year-end 2008 level of 0.2 percent over the period 2009–2012.

Scenario D. Scenario C plus increasing government spending due to the implementation of the American Recovery and Reinvestment Act of 2009. We assume $200 billion in government spending in each year from 2009 to 2012.

Scenario E. Scenario D and increasing the Federal funds rate from 0.2 percent in 2009 to 1 percent in 2010, 2 percent in 2011, and 3 percent in 2012.

Table 3.9 presents the comparative out-of-sample projections of the macroeconomic variables in the model for these five scenarios from 2009 to 2012. These results are based on SUR estimates of the profit system equations. Our findings are summarized below.

Table 3.9 Macroeconomic profit system model: comparative out-of-sample forecasts for five economic scenarios based on 1959–2008 data series

	Forecast period			
Variable	2009	2010	2011	2012
$\dot{GDP}$, growth rate of GDP in real terms				
Scenario A	−0.7	−0.3	0.4	1.0
Scenario B	0.9	0.7	1.0	1.3
Scenario C	1.3	1.3	1.3	1.5
Scenario D	2.0	2.1	2.2	2.5
Scenario E	2.0	2.1	2.1	2.3
$\dot{Y}$, growth rate of business GDP in real terms				
Scenario A	−1.2	−0.6	0.3	1.0
Scenario B	0.8	0.6	1.0	1.4
Scenario C	1.4	1.4	1.4	1.6
Scenario D	1.8	1.9	2.1	2.4
Scenario E	1.8	1.9	1.9	2.2
$\dot{X}$, growth rate of nonprofit GDP in real terms				
Scenario A	1.0	0.5	0.5	0.7
Scenario B	1.2	0.9	0.8	0.8
Scenario C	1.2	1.1	1.0	0.9
Scenario D	2.8	2.8	2.8	2.8
Scenario E	2.8	2.8	2.8	2.8
$\dot{GDP}$, growth rate of GDP in nominal terms				
Scenario A	1.4	1.9	2.6	3.2
Scenario B	2.9	2.9	3.2	3.6
Scenario C	3.4	3.5	4.3	5.1
Scenario D	4.1	4.3	5.3	6.2
Scenario E	4.1	4.3	5.1	5.8
$\dot{Y}$, growth rate of business GDP in nominal terms				
Scenario A	0.5	1.3	2.2	3.0
Scenario B	2.5	2.5	2.9	3.4
Scenario C	3.1	3.3	4.2	5.1
Scenario D	3.5	3.8	4.9	6.0
Scenario E	3.5	3.7	4.7	5.5
$\dot{X}$, growth rate of nonprofit GDP in nominal terms				
Scenario A	4.1	3.6	3.7	3.9
Scenario B	4.2	4.1	4.0	4.0
Scenario C	4.3	4.2	4.5	4.8
Scenario D	5.9	6.0	6.4	6.8
Scenario E	5.9	6.0	6.4	6.7
R, profit rate in the business sector				
Scenario A	7.5	7.6	7.8	8.1
Scenario B	7.5	7.6	7.8	8.0
Scenario C	7.9	8.2	8.7	9.1
Scenario D	7.9	8.2	8.7	9.1
Scenario E	7.9	8.2	8.5	8.7
S, profit margin in the business sector				
Scenario A	14.0	12.6	11.8	11.7
Scenario B	14.0	12.6	12.0	11.9
Scenario C	14.6	13.6	13.1	13.2
Scenario D	14.5	13.4	12.9	13.0
Scenario E	14.5	13.4	12.7	12.6

Table 3.9 (continued)

Variable	2009	2010	2011	2012
$\dot{Z}$, growth rate of total profit of business sector in nominal terms				
Scenario A	4.4	−12.3	−9.1	−4.1
Scenario B	4.4	−11.0	−7.3	−2.5
Scenario C	4.4	−6.9	−2.9	1.4
Scenario D	4.3	−6.8	−2.9	1.6
Scenario E	4.4	−6.9	−3.5	0.1
$\dot{K}$, growth rate of capital stock of business sector in nominal terms				
Scenario A	−11.3	−10.1	−6.5	−1.2
Scenario B	−11.4	−10.2	−6.8	−2.0
Scenario C	−9.8	−8.2	−4.1	1.0
Scenario D	−9.8	−8.2	−4.0	1.4
Scenario E	−9.8	−8.2	−4.0	1.2
$\dot{H}$, growth rate of business sector employment				
Scenario A	−2.5	−1.9	−1.1	−0.3
Scenario B	−0.7	−0.9	−0.6	−0.2
Scenario C	−0.3	−0.3	−0.4	−0.2
Scenario D	0.1	0.1	0.1	0.4
Scenario E	0.1	0.1	0.0	0.3
$\dot{P}$, GDP inflation rate				
Scenario A	2.1	2.2	2.2	2.2
Scenario B	2.0	2.1	2.2	2.3
Scenario C	2.0	2.1	2.9	3.5
Scenario D	2.0	2.2	3.0	3.6
Scenario E	2.0	2.2	3.0	3.4
$\acute{P}$, business sector GDP inflation rate				
Scenario A	1.7	1.8	1.9	2.0
Scenario B	1.7	1.8	1.9	2.0
Scenario C	1.7	1.8	2.8	3.5
Scenario D	1.7	1.8	2.8	3.5
Scenario E	1.7	1.8	2.8	3.3
$\breve{P}$, nonprofit sector GDP inflation rate				
Scenario A	3.0	3.1	3.1	3.2
Scenario B	3.0	3.1	3.1	3.2
Scenario C	3.0	3.1	3.5	3.9
Scenario D	3.0	3.1	3.5	3.9
Scenario E	3.0	3.1	3.5	3.8
$\dot{D}$, growth rate of debt outstanding in nominal terms				
Scenario A	0.0	0.0	0.0	0.0
Scenario B	4.0	2.6	1.5	1.0
Scenario C	4.3	3.2	2.5	2.4
Scenario D	4.4	3.3	2.6	2.6
Scenario E	4.4	3.3	2.6	2.4
F, Federal funds rate in nominal terms				
Scenario A	3.9	3.9	3.9	3.9
Scenario B	3.9	3.9	3.9	3.9
Scenario C	0.2	0.2	0.2	0.2
Scenario D	0.2	0.2	0.2	0.2
Scenario E	0.2	1.0	2.0	3.0

GḊP, *Growth Rate of GDP in Real Terms.* The availability of credit has played an important role in expanding the US economy since 1959, as the ratio of nonfinancial debt outstanding to nominal GDP grew from 1.4 in 1959 to 2.4 in 2008 (see Fig. 3.3). As defined in the data section, the total debt outstanding of the nonfinancial sector is the sum of household debt (consumer credit plus home mortgages), business debt (corporate and noncorporate businesses), and state, local, and federal government debt. Some economists blame the current financial and economic crises on excessive expansion of credit over the past three decades that enabled US households and firms to spend and live beyond their means. If credit levels remain at their 2008 level under Scenario A, US GDP in real terms is projected to decrease by 0.7 percent in 2009 and 0.3 percent in 2010, and then grow by 0.4 percent in 2011 and 1 percent in 2012 (Table 3.9). If credit levels continue to grow along their historical path under Scenario B, US GDP in real terms is projected to increase by 0.9 percent in 2009, 0.7 percent in 2010, 1 percent in 2011, and 1.3 percent in 2012. In this case the nonfinancial debt outstanding in nominal terms is expected to grow by 4 percent in 2009, 2.6 percent in 2010, 1.5 percent in 2011, and 1 percent in 2012. These growth rates are moderated by keeping the influential Federal funds rate at 3.9 percent from 2009 to 2012 and related negative impact of the Federal funds rate on debt (i.e., the negative coefficient for this rate in the estimated debt equation).

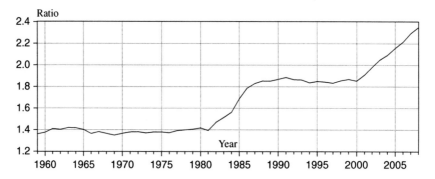

Fig. 3.3 Ratio of total debt in the nonfinancial sector in nominal terms to GDP in nominal terms

To reduce the negative impact of higher Federal funds rates on the US economy, the Fed reduced the rate to 0.2 percent at the end of 2008. Assuming that the Fed will maintain this rate from 2009 to 2012 under Scenario C, US GDP in real terms is projected to grow by 1.3 percent from 2009 to 2011 and 1.5 percent in 2012. This projected path of real GDP growth is rather anemic by historical standards.

As shown in Scenario D, the economic stimulus plan is projected to boost the growth rate of US GDP in real terms to 2.0 percent in 2009, 2.1 percent in 2010, 2.2 percent in 2011, and 2.5 percent in 2012. Since it is unlikely that the Fed will keep the Federal funds rate at close to zero in the years ahead, we provide projected results under Scenario E, with gradually increasing Federal funds rates over time.

When this rate is raised to 1 percent in 2010, 2 percent in 2011, and 3 percent in 2012, we obtain growth rates of real US GDP of 2.0 percent in 2009, 2.1 percent in 2010 and 2011, and 2.3 percent in 2012.

$\dot{Y}$, *Growth Rate of Business GDP in Real Terms.* Under Scenario A, the output of the business sector in real terms is projected to decrease by 1.2 percent in 2009, 0.6 percent in 2010 but increase by 0.3 percent in 2011 and 1 percent in 2012. For Scenario B these growth rates improve somewhat to 0.8 percent in 2009, 0.6 percent in 2010, 1 percent in 2011, and 1.4 percent in 2012. In Scenario C with the Federal funds rate reduced to 0.2 percent from 2009 the growth rates of business sector real output improve somewhat to 1.4 percent in 2009, 2010, and 2011 and 1.6 percent 2012. With fiscal stimulus Scenario D shows that real business sector output is projected to increase by 1.8 percent in 2009, 1.9 percent in 2010, 2.1 percent in 2011, and 2.4 percent in 2012. Scenario E's increases in the Federal funds rate have no impact on the growth rate of the output of business sector in 2009 and 2010 but reduce growth rates to 1.9 percent in 2011 and 2.2 percent in 2012.

$\dot{X}$, *Growth Rate of Nonprofit GDP in Real Terms.* Under Scenario A, the output of the nonprofit sector in real terms is projected to increase by 1 percent in 2009, 0.5 percent in 2010 and 2011, and 0.7 percent in 2012. For Scenario B these growth rates improve somewhat to 1.2 percent in 2009, 0.9 percent in 2010, and 0.8 percent in 2011 and 2012. In Scenario C with the Federal funds rate reduced to 0.2 percent from 2009 the growth rates of nonprofit sector real output improve somewhat to 1.1 percent in 2010, 1 percent in 2011, and 0.9 percent 2012. In Scenario D real output in the nonprofit sector is expected to grow at an annual rate of 2.8 percent per year from 2009 to 2012, which is more than twice their growth rates under Scenarios A, B, and C over 2009–2012. This growth rate is projected to remain at 2.8 percent even if the Federal funds rate is increased under Scenario E.

$G\dot{D}P$, *Growth Rate of GDP in Nominal Terms.* Unlike the real GDP results that projected declining or flat economic growth in the years ahead, US GDP in nominal terms is projected to trend upward from 2009 to 2012 under all five scenarios. As before, the economic stimulus plan is anticipated to boost output growth in the future. Under Scenario D, the US GDP in nominal terms is projected to increase by 4.1 percent in 2009, 4.3 percent in 2010, 5.3 percent in 2011, and 6.2 percent in 2012. Higher Federal funds rates under Scenario E are expected to reduce the growth rates in 2011 and 2012 to 5.1 and 5.8 percent, respectively. As we will see, the rising trend in nominal output is due to higher expected inflation rates from 2009 to 2012.

$\dot{Y}$, *Growth Rate of Business GDP in Nominal Terms.* The results for output growth in the business sector in nominal terms are similar to those for US GDP growth from 2009 to 2012. Low Federal funds rates and fiscal stimulus tend to increase output growth.

$\dot{X}$, *Growth Rate of Nonprofit GDP in Nominal Terms.* As in the case of nonprofit sector output in real terms, lower Federal funds rates and especially higher government spending are forecasted to boost output growth from 2009 to 2012.

R, Profit Rate in the Business Sector. Under all five scenarios, profit rates are projected to increase from 2009 to 2012. Interestingly, lower Federal funds rates are more influential in this respect than increased government spending. In Scenario C, when Federal funds rates are maintained at 0.2 percent over time, we see that profit rates increase from 7.9 percent in 2009 to 9.1 percent in 2012. These profit rates are unchanged for the most part by the economic stimulus plan under Scenarios D and E. As we will see, higher profit rates from 2009 to 2012 are attributable to lower capital stocks in the denominator, rather than higher total profits in the numerator.

S, Profit Margin in the Business Sector. Unlike profit rates that trend upward from 2009 to 2012, profit margins tend to decline under all five scenarios. Again, lower interest rates under Scenario C boost profit margins, and government spending under Scenarios D and E has little or no effect on profit margins.

$\dot{Z}$, Growth Rate of Total Profit in Nominal Terms. Under Scenarios A and B, total profits in the business sector are projected to contract sharply from 2010 to 2012. Lower Federal funds rates under Scenario C substantially increase total profits, which return to a positive growth rate in 2012. Fiscal stimulus under Scenarios D and E does not greatly change profit projections. In 2009 total profits are projected to grow by about 4.4 percent but these short-term gains are anticipated to be reversed in 2010. We interpret the negative growth rates of profit in 2010 and 2011 to downsizing by business firms due to relatively slow economic growth in these years.

$\dot{K}$, Growth Rate of Capital Stock of Business GDP in Nominal Terms. The pattern of the growth rate of business sector capital stocks in nominal terms to a great extent reflects the pattern of the growth rate of nominal total profits, as nominal capital stocks are the discounted values of nominal profits. The negative growth rates of business capital stock from 2009 to 2012 suggest the existence of a significant number of unprofitable activities in the US economy, which are projected to be trimmed to make the economy leaner and more efficient by 2012.

$\dot{H}$, Growth Rate of Business Employment. The negative growth rates of employment in the business sector in Scenarios A, B, and C suggest a pattern of jobless recovery in the US economy from 2009 to 2012. The economic stimulus plan improves the employment picture to some extent but the results appear to be weak in general. Nonetheless, higher growth rates of employment in the government sector due to the economic stimulus plan should help the overall labor market.

$\dot{P}$, GDP Inflation Rate. Under Scenarios A and B, assuming the Fed maintained the Federal funds rate at 3.9 percent, annual GDP inflation rates remain at less than 2.3 percent from 2009 to 2012. The reduction of the Federal funds rate from 3.9 percent to 0.2 percent under Scenarios C and D is expected to increase the annual GDP inflation rate to about 3.5 percent by 2012. In Scenario E we model a gradual increase in the Federal funds rate over time, but increased government spending apparently offsets this tighter monetary policy with projected inflation rising from

2.0 percent in 2009 to 3.4 percent in 2012. This inflation level appears to be moderate, which means that the threat of inflation as fiscal stimulus proceeds in the years to come is not significant.

$\hat{P}$, *Business GDP Inflation Rate.* For the five different scenarios annual inflation rates in the business sector are projected to be similar to those for the national economy.

$\tilde{P}$, *Nonprofit Sector Inflation Rate.* For the five scenarios annual inflation rates in nonprofit sector are projected to be somewhat higher than those in the business sector and national economy.

$\dot{D}$, *Growth Rate of Nonfinancial Debt Outstanding in Nominal Terms.* Scenarios D and E show that the growth rate of nonfinancial debt outstanding is projected to decrease from 4.4 percent in 2009 to around 2.5 percent in 2012. Credit markets in the years ahead are projected to be improved by the lower Federal funds rate and economic stimulus plan.

As shown in Table 3.9, the scenario approach helps to reveal the sensitivity of economic activity to different monetary and fiscal policy choices.[20] Other policy scenarios can be investigated in this way. In this regard, as the US economy recovers from the current crises, future policy choices can be studied for their potential effects on the economy.

3.4 Business Cycle Analysis

The central role of profit in the business cycle in market economies has been discussed and emphasized by prominent business cycle theorists. Consolidating a number of business cycle theories proposed between 1825 and 1913, Mitchell (1913) proposed a theory that was appropriately dubbed "the profit theory of business cycles" (see Persons 1914). Mitchell incorporated a wide variety of theories in his work.[21] In psychological and lead/lag theories of business cycles, waves of optimism and pessimism concerning profit expectations drive business investment

---

[20]We should note that the forecasts based on OLS regression estimates of the profit system equations are more optimistic than those generated from the SUR models. For example, the growth rate of real GDP is projected to be around 3 percent for all years from 2009 to 2012 under Scenarios D and E. We chose to report the SUR forecast results shown in Table 3.9 that are more conservative and, therefore, error on the side of under-estimation as opposed to over-estimation.

[21]For example, the theory of the unbalanced production of industrial equipment and complementary goods by Spiethoff (1902, 1903, 1909), the theory of severe fall in investment demand due to the high costs of construction by Hull (1911), the theory of variation in prospective profits by Lescure (1906), the theory of discrepancy between prospective profits and current capital utilization by Veblen (1904), the theory of discrepancy between organic and inorganic production by Sombart (1902, 1904, 1930), the theory of unbalanced volatility between prices of producers' and consumers' goods by Carver (1903), the theory of slow adjustment in interest rates to inflation rates by Fisher (1911), and the theory of impaired savings by Johannsen (1908).

decisions and, in turn, business cycles.[22] In overinvestment theories of business cycles, the business cycle is linked to the credit cycle, and the credit cycle is associated with an increase in the profitability of industry.[23] In monetary theories of the business cycle, credit expansion and contraction lead to changes in market interest rates and demands for consumer and capital goods that subsequently cause changes in profit-driven investment and generate business cycles.[24] Business cycles in the Austrian school of the business cycle are produced by firms' responses to changing profit rates across economic sectors due to monetary shocks disturbing relative prices and the term structure of interest rates.[25]

Closely related to our profit system model, profit fluctuation theories of business cycles focus on changes in revenues or costs as the initial cause of business cycles. Potential sources of changes in revenues and costs are the costs of land[26] and rising productivity that lowers labor costs after mergers and consolidation (Veblen 1904, 1923), innovations (Schumpeter 1927, 1939), and technology (Kydland and Prescott 1982, Plosser 1989, King et al. 1988).

Among nine factors that cause depressions cited by Fisher (1932), a reduction in profits and lower net worth was a salient determinant. According to Keynes (1930), who was keenly interested in how to get out of depressions, "... profits (or losses) having once come into existence, become ... a cause of what subsequently ensues; indeed (they are) the mainspring of change in the existing economic system." He also noted that, "As a rule, the existence of profit will provoke a tendency towards a higher rate of employment and of remuneration for the factors of production and vice versa." The gap between the marginal efficiency of capital – more specifically, the marginal efficiency of investment per Lerner (1953) – and the long-term interest rate causes investment fluctuations which when amplified by the multiplier generate trade cycles. As Keynes (1936) observed: "The trade cycle is best regarded, I think, as being occasioned by a cyclical change in the marginal efficiency of capital, though complicated, and often aggravated by associated changes in the other significant short-term period variables of economic system." In this regard, Hicks (1950) commented that Keynes himself did not develop a theory of business cycle asserting that "... this thesis would occupy a book rather than a chapter, and require close examination of facts."

Profit expectations are the primary cause of economic fluctuations in the accelerator theories of business cycle proposed by Aftalion (1913), Clark (1917), and Pigou (1920, 1927). Despite the key role of the internal rate of return (or marginal efficiency of capital) in the Keynesian theory of investment and trade cycle, the profit

---

[22]See Marshal (1879), Fisher (1907), Beveridge (1909), and Mill (1948).

[23]See Juglar (1862), Tugan-Baranovsky (1894), Spiethoff (1902, 1925), Cassel (1918), and Robertson (1915).

[24]See Wicksell (1907b), Hawtrey (1913, 1919, 1932), Hayek (1929, 1931, 1939, 1942), and Kaldor (1939, 1940a, b, 1942).

[25]See Menger (1871), Boehm-Bawerk (1895, 1921), Mises (1912, 1959), Haberler (1932, 1937a, b), and Hayek (1941).

[26]See George (1879).

rate or profit margin was ignored in the linear and nonlinear accelerator–multiplier theories of business cycle.[27] But in Kalecki's (1935, 1937, 1939) distribution model of the business cycle, the accelerator is replaced with profit. Also, in Goodwin's (1967) class struggle model of business cycle, changes in the shares of profits and wages in national income generate business cycles.

Economic historians have documented the relationship between profit fluctuations and macroeconomic fluctuations. Renowned and controversial economic historian Hamilton (1929) presented empirical evidence that profit inflation – that is, the widening gap between growth rates of prices and wage rates in sixteenth and seventeenth centuries England – played a key role in the industrialization of the UK. Hamilton's thesis was that industrial entrepreneurs reinvested windfall profits in capital intensive industries leading to higher industrial output and industrial wages. Consistent with this thesis, Keynes (1920) asserted that the large-scale industrial expansion of the UK in the sixteenth and seventeenth centuries could not be solely attributed to thrift or higher savings.

Profit maximization behavior of firms in classical and new-classical macroeconomics determines output levels.[28] The business cycle in real business cycle (RBC) theory is caused by random exogenous fluctuations in total factor productivity (TFP).[29] According to RBC theorists, changes in TFP bring about profit opportunities, and changes in macroeconomic aggregates are the responses of economic agents with rational expectations to profit opportunities that lead to cyclical fluctuations in macroeconomic aggregates.[30]

If changes in TFP shocks result in new profit opportunities, then it is reasonable to expect that changes in profit opportunities are reflected in profit rates and profit margins and that changes in these two profit parameters lead to changes in macroeconomic aggregates of output, capital stock, and employment.

As discussed in Chapter 2, in our profit system model the interaction between firms' output and capital stocks caused by changes in profit can generate business cycle effects. An increase (decrease) in profit affects both output and capital stock but in opposite ways. An increase (decrease) in total profit for a given level of output and capital stock increases (decreases) both profit rate and profit margin. These changes can happen, for instance, when the price of imported oil drops, all else the same. The higher profit rate in the numerator of the output equation increases output, but in the denominator of the capital stock equation a higher profit rate decreases capital stock. The higher profit margin in the numerator of the capital stock increases capital stock, while in the denominator of the output equation it decreases output. Thus, a change in profit induces a series of fluctuations in output

---

[27] See Aftalion (1913), Clark (1917), Hansen (1927, 1937, 1938), Harrod (1936, 1948), Samuelson (1939a, b), Metzler (1941), Hicks (1950), Duesenberry (1949), Smithies (1957), Pasinetti (1960), Kaldor (1940a, b), and Goodwin (1951).

[28] See Blanchard and Watson (1986), Caporale (1993), Friedman (1993), Gabisch and Lorenz (1987), and Lucas (1977, 1981, 1987).

[29] See Slutsky (1927), Frisch (1933), and Kydland and Prescott (1982).

[30] See Prescott (1986), Long and Plosser (1983), and King et al. (1988).

and capital stock given that both profit rate and profit margin are also determined by output and capital stock.

To see how a change in profit generates fluctuations in macroeconomic aggregates, the estimated US macroeconomic model in the period 1959–2008 is simulated to generate out-of-sample forecasts of the key variables when the aggregate profit in 2007 falls by 10 percent.

Figure 3.4(a)–(q) shows changes in the fundamental variables in response to this profit decline. All figures show a pattern of initial increasing or decreasing of growth rates followed by decreasing or increasing rates – that is, a pattern of overreaction to the fall in profit which later subsides resulting in the generation of a cyclical pattern in the economic time series. The patterns depend on the initial conditions, the magnitudes of the profit decline or surge, and the lead–lag relationships among the variables in the model as well as their estimated coefficients. Comparisons of the trajectories of forecasts show that a decline by 10 percent in the total profit of the business sector results in the following estimated impacts:

> The annual growth rate of the US GDP in real terms initially increases by about 0.3 percent in 2009 and then later decreases by 0.1 percent in real terms in 2013 (Fig. 3.4(a)).
>
> Figure 3.4(b)–(d) shows similar patterns of rise and fall in the annual growth rates of nominal GDP as well as real and nominal GDPs in the business sector.
>
> Output and profit fluctuations in the business sector generate output cycles in real and nominal GDPs of the nonprofit sector (Fig. 3.4(e) and (f)).
>
> The annual growth rate of business sector profit in nominal terms increases by more than 1 percent but later decreases by 1 percent (Fig. 3.4(g)).
>
> The annual growth rate of capital stock in nominal terms is increased by 1.1 percent in 2009 and then decreases by 1 percent in 2015 (Fig. 3.4(h))
>
> The pattern of changes in the annual growth rate of business sector employment is similar to the pattern of changes in the growth rates of business sector output (Fig. 3.4(i))
>
> A debt cycle is generated with its peak in 2011 and trough in 2018 (Fig. 3.4(j)).
>
> Changes in profit rate and profit margin display similar cycles with troughs in 2013 (Fig. 3.4(k) and (l))

Fig. 3.4 Response of macroeconomic aggregates to a 10 percent decrease in aggregate profits in 2007: (**a**) changes in real GDP growth rates; (**b**) changes in nominal GDP growth rates; (**c**) changes in real GDP growth rates in the business sector; (**d**) changes in nominal GDP growth rates in the business sector; (**e**) changes in real GDP growth rates in the nonprofit sector; (**f**) changes in nominal GDP growth rates in the nonprofit sector; (**g**) changes in the growth rates of business sector nominal profit; (**h**) changes in the growth rate of nominal capital stock in the business sector; (**i**) changes in the growth rate of business sector employment; (**j**) changes in the growth rate of nonfinancial debt outstanding; (**k**) changes in business sector profit rate; (**l**) changes in business sector profit margin; (**m**) changes in the GDP inflation rate; (**n**) changes in business sector inflation rate; (**o**) changes in nonprofit sector inflation rate; (**p**) changes in the federal funds rate; and (**q**) changes in the real federal funds rate

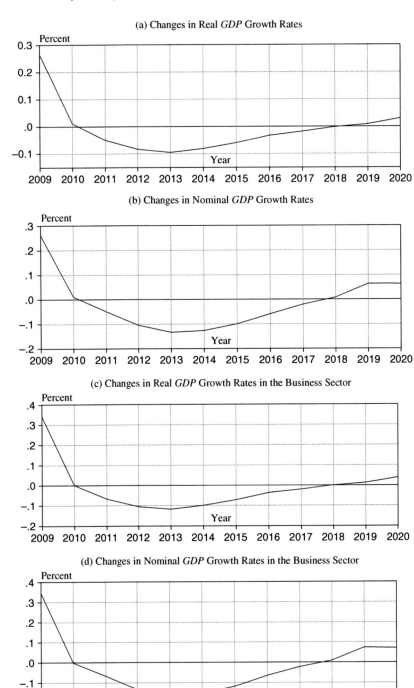

Fig. 3.4 (continued)

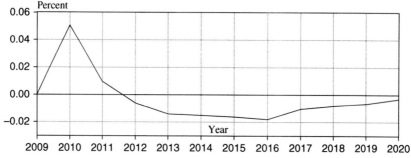

(e) Changes in Real *GDP* Growth Rates in the Nonprofit Sector.

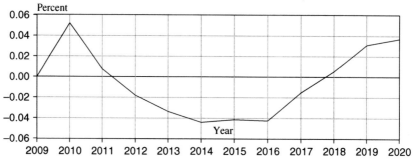

(f) Changes in Nominal GDP Growth Rates in the Nonprofit Sector

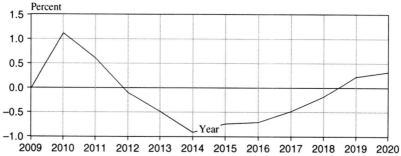

(g) Changes in the Growth Rates of Business Sector Nominal Profit

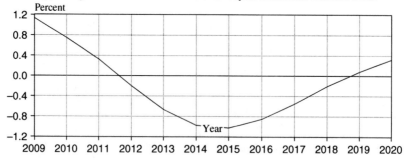

(h) Changes in the Growth Rate of Nominal Capital Stock in the Business Sector

Fig. 3.4 (continued)

(i) Changes in the Growth Rate of Business Sector Employment

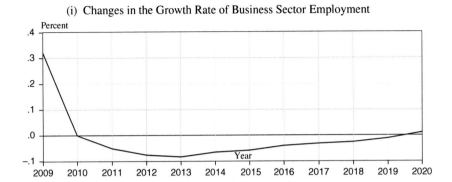

(j) Changes in the Growth Rate of Nonfinancial Debt Outstanding

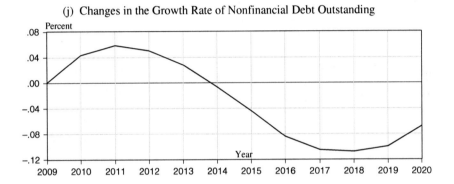

(k) Changes in Business Sector Profit Rate

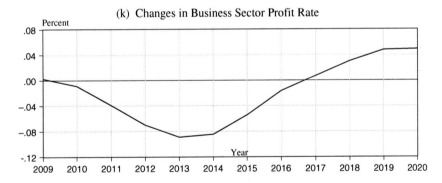

Fig. 3.4 (continued)

Changes in GDP inflation rate and business sector inflation rate show a cyclical pattern with troughs in 2014 (Fig. 3.4(m) and (n)). Changes in nonprofit sector inflation rate display a similar cycle (Fig. 3.4(o)).

Changes in nominal and real Federal funds rate have similar cyclical patterns with troughs in 2015 (Fig. 3.4(p) and (q)).

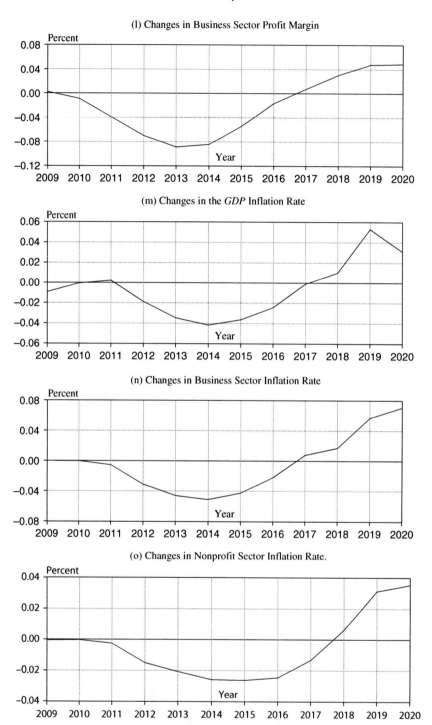

Fig. 3.4 (continued)

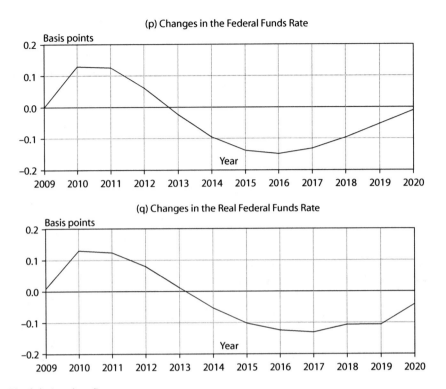

Fig. 3.4 (continued)

We infer from these findings that the profit system model can generate fluctuations in macroeconomic variables in response to changes in profit. Hence, profit is an important variable in business cycle analysis.

3.5 Conclusion

In this chapter the profit system model of the firm presented in Chapter 2 was expanded into a macroeconometric model of the business sector. We augmented the profit system by adding a model of the nonprofit sector. Together, the business sector and nonprofit sector models comprise a macroeconometric model of the national economy. This model was applied to the US economy, tested for model reliability, and used for macroeconomic forecasting, monetary policy analysis, and business cycle analysis. The empirical model results confirm the theoretical model proposed in Chapter 2 in terms of the pervasive roles that profit plays in the economy. The fit of individual equations was quite strong, and the system of equations could successfully mimic in-sample data series for the focal variables in the period 1959–2008. Out-of-sample forecasts for the period 2006–2008 using 1959–2005 data series indicated that the model performed well, especially with respect to growth rates of US

GDP and business sector as well as nonprofit sector GDPs. The estimated model was simulated to examine five different scenarios encompassing the macroeconomic impacts of different assumptions concerning monetary policy as reflected by Federal funds rates and fiscal policy as quantified by recent economic stimulus plans. Lastly, we considered how changes in profits affect the business cycle by showing how they can generate fluctuations in economic activity.

At this point it is worthwhile to overview and highlight some of the main characteristics of our profit system model of the economy:

1. *A Supply-Side-Oriented Macroeconomic Model.* Our profit system macroeconomic model views the macroeconomy from the supply side and thus directly estimates aggregate GDP as the sum of the GDPs of business and nonprofit sectors. This approach departs from a long tradition of modeling aggregate demand in macroeconomic modeling that began with Keynes (1936). Our new model does not require the estimation of several components of demand (e.g., consumers' expenditures, investment expenditures by firms, government expenditures, net exports, and inventory), which must be added to get aggregate GDP. Modern macroeconomics became demand-side-oriented when Keynes laid its foundations in the aftermath of the Great Depression with the publication of the *General Theory of Employment, Interest, and Money* in 1936. In Keynesian macroeconomics changes in the supply side were not considered to be important in the short run. According to Keynes, aggregate national output is determined from the sum of the aforementioned components of demand. Based on this foundation, several areas of theoretical and empirical macroeconomics emerged for estimating consumption, investment, government expenditure, net export, and inventory functions. Modeling these functions required the inclusion of numerous variables in the right hand sides of the model equations and necessitated the development of more equations for modeling some variables. Indeed, large-scale macroeconomic models consisting of hundreds of equations were developed in the 1960s and 1970s. The predictive failure of large-scale macroeconometric models (e.g., the 1974–1975 and 1979–1981 recessions), the poor performance of estimated consumption functions, and the Lucas (1976) criticism of static expectations led to the development of new classical macroeconomic, RBC, and vector autoregressive schemes. The latter new classical macroeconomics is based on a number of assumptions including the following: (1) macroeconomics should be grounded upon microfoundations wherein market supply and demand decisions are made by rational households and firms, (2) continuous market clearing occurs in general equilibrium of all markets and there is balance of aggregate supply and demand, and (3) the importance of supply side in the short run. In this regard, it is notable that Keynes' influence lingers in the recent generation of macroeconometric models (including RBC models), as the consumption function remains an important equation in these models.

2. *Microeconomic Foundations.* Our macroeconomic profit system model is based on the microfoundations of profit rate, profit margin, total profit, output, and capital stock of firms. In Chapter 2 related equations were derived from both

the Cobb–Douglas production function for the firm and accounting definitions of profit rate and profit margin. The business sector macroeconomic model presented in this chapter is an aggregate of all business firms. The aggregate output of the business sector is the sum of the value added generated by all firms. The aggregate capital stock of the business sector is the sum of the capital stocks of all firms. Similarly, the aggregate profit of the business sector is the sum of profits of all firms in the sector. Since there is no aggregation problem, there is no dichotomy between the microfoundation of firms and macrofoundation of the aggregate business sector model. When the model is applied to some sectors of the economy – for example, we apply it to the corporate sector in the next chapter – aggregate profits, outputs, and capital stocks are again the sum of these variables for all firms in a particular sector.

3. *No Restrictive Assumptions.* In Chapter 2 we combined the profit rate equation and profit margin equation to derive the production equation defining output as the product of profit rate and capital stock divided by profit margin. We argued that the output equation is a behavioral equation but no assumptions are made in deriving this equation. No matter how profit is defined, combining the profit rate and profit margin equations results in the derived output and capital stock equations. Importantly, it is not necessary to assume profit-maximizing behavior. By comparison, Keynesian macroeconomics requires two behavioral equations: (1) a consumption function specifying current aggregate consumption as a function of current aggregate output, and (2) an investment function where investment is determined by interest rates. Neoclassical and RBC macroeconomists derived their consumption functions from utility maximizing behavior of consumers and derived investment functions from profit-maximizing behavior firms.

4. *Relationships Between Macroeconomics and Macrofinance.* In view of Keynes, it has been a tradition in macroeconomic modeling to specify an investment model (I_t), add investment to the capital stock existing at the beginning of a period (K_t), and then deduct depreciation ($G_t = g_t K_t$) to obtain the value of capital stock at the end of the period (K_{t+1}): $K_{t+1} = K_t + I_{t+1} - g_t K_t$, where g_t is the depreciation rate. By contrast, the aggregate capital stock in the profit system model is directly estimated from aggregate output, profit rate, and profit margin as the discounted value of aggregate profits. Since the market value of capital stock is used, there is no need for deducting depreciation. Importantly, the models of aggregate profit, profit rate, and profit margin enable us to directly link the macroeconomic model to macrofinance. For example, the application of the profit system model in Chapter 4 to the corporate sector is later utilized in Chapter 6 to estimate stock market values based on estimated corporate sector profits and profit rates.

5. *Accounting Foundations.* The relationships between the profit rate, profit margin, profits, output, and capital stock are all derived from their accounting definitions. The contemporaneous regressions of the logarithm of one of the five variables on the logarithms of the other four variables result in plus or minus values of coefficients. The estimated equations of the contemporaneous relationships are

complete in the sense that no other variables are needed in the equations. When lags of profit rate, profit margin, profit, output, and capital stock are used for forecasting these variables, the equations have forecast errors. To minimize the errors or improve out-of-sample forecast accuracy, other variables can be added to the equations for these fundamental variables.

6. *Small Number of Variables.* Our macroeconomic profit system model has a small number of variables. The parsimonious use of variables in our model reflects the shift from large- to small-scale macroeonomic models that has taken place over the past five decades (Zellner (2001)). Unlike widely used atheoretical VAR models, our use of a small number of the variables is grounded in economic theory.

7. *Deep Parameters Are Variables.* The discount rate is the time-varying profit rate, and the impact of TFP due to technology is incorporated in the profit rate.

Recently, the US economy and major industrial economies were plunged into a deep recession, and firms (banks) became unwilling to borrow (lend) due to a sudden fall in expected profit rates. An important part of the US economic recovery plan is to increase the expected profit rate by reducing the Federal funds rate and increase the availability of credit in the financial system. Another part of the plan is to increase government spending. In this chapter we showed that our macroeconomic profit system model can be employed as a tool for monetary and fiscal policy analyses of these variables. We did not include world output or exchange rates in our analyses. However, the profit system models for the US business and nonprofit sectors can be expanded to include the growth rate of world GDP in real terms. Economic growth in China, India, and other developing countries should have a positive impact on the US economy in the future. Also, the exchange rate of the US dollar to a basket of world currencies could be added to our profit system equations to take into account potential effects of currency fluctuations on the US economy.

In closing we believe that our macroeconomic profit system model could help to explain the underlying forces involved in economic expansions and contractions. For example, the stock market crash of October 1929 dramatically decreased the expected rate of return on capital or profit rate. According to our output equation, the fall of output in the Great Depression was due to falling expected profit rates given that the physical capital stock in the numerator remained fixed and profit margins declined but not as dramatically as profit rates. The Great Depression was not due to lack of effective demand because people were seeking jobs and wanted to purchase goods and services. Nor was the collapse due to any technological shock. Instead, a precipitous drop in expected business profit rates instigated a sharp output contraction. Hence, extremely low expected profit rates were a primary culprit in the Great Depression. Likewise, we conjecture that falling profits is a major determinant in less severe and shorter-term economic contractions, including the current 2008–2009 recession. Future research is recommended to more fully document how profit rates and profit margins affect economic growth throughout the business cycle.

Chapter 4
Profit System Models of the Corporate Sector

This chapter applies the profit system model to the US corporate sector. The US corporate sector produced more than 75 percent of the output of the US business sector and about 60 percent of the US GDP in recent years. Like the aggregate business sector model in Chapter 3, estimated corporate sector models can be used for (1) forecasting the volumes of output and capital stock as well as profit rates, profit margins, and aggregate profits in the corporate sector; (2) macroeconomic policy analysis; and (3) business cycle analysis. However, here we focus on the aggregate profit of the corporate sector. The aggregate profit of the corporate sector is a crucial variable because its level and growth rate have important implications for market economies. Higher growth rates of aggregate corporate profits suggest that more business investments are passing the market tests of profitability. The historical simulation of aggregate corporate profit provides insights into its long-run path based on the values of fundamental variables, such as sales, capital stocks, profit rates, and profit margins. When aggregate corporate profit is discounted using an appropriate capitalization rate, the result is the total market valuation of aggregate corporate stocks. Chapter 6 extends the analyses to this stock market application.

For estimating corporate models we use data on aggregate output, aggregate profit, and aggregate capital stock of the US corporate sector available in National Income and Product accounts of the BEA and Z1 series of the Fed. There is a subtle difference between the aggregate profits of corporations supplied by the BEA and Fed compared to the aggregate corporate data supplied by Standard and Poor's (S&P's) and other financial institutions for computing profit per share of the S&P Composite Index. Profit data compiled by the BEA and Fed are estimated from federal tax returns of corporations, whereas S&P uses financial returns for estimating total corporate profit. We utilize the tax-based profit data of the BEA and the Fed. Importantly, the estimated fundamental models of the corporate sector are used for out-of-sample forecasting of output, capital stock, profit rate, profit margin, aggregate profit, and market valuation. Analyses are repeated for the nonfinancial corporate sector, which excludes the financial corporate sector. Based on our forecasted out-of-sample results, the nonfinancial corporate sector is expected to grow faster than the total business

A. Anari, J.W. Kolari, *The Power of Profit*, DOI 10.1007/978-1-4419-0649-6_4,
© Springer Science+Business Media, LLC 2010

sector, due to forecasted slower growth in the nonfinancial sector over the next few years.

4.1 Corporate Models

Publicly available time series data sets from the Fed and the BEA allow the application of our profit system model to the US corporate sector as well as to the US nonfinancial corporate sector.

4.1.1 The Corporate Model

Panel A of Table 4.1 presents the profit system model for the corporate sector. The corporate model is comprised of equations (4.1.1), (4.1.2), (4.1.3), (4.1.4), and (4.1.5), where capital stock and output are in current dollars due to the absence of a price deflator for output in the corporate sector. These equations are counterparts of the corresponding equations in Table 2.1. The equations for capital stock and output in the corporate sectors are estimated with two lags of the fundamental variables as suggested by empirical results. In the corporate capital stock equation (4.1.1) the log of capital stock in current dollars (k) is determined by lags of logarithms of corporate sector output in current dollars (y), profit rate (r), profit margin (s), and the growth rate of nonfinancial debt outstanding ($\dot{D}$). For the growth rate of nonfinancial debt outstanding in nominal terms ($\dot{D}$), we use its contemporaneous values as suggested by empirical results. In the corporate sector output equation (4.1.2) corporate output (y) is determined by the fundamental variables of profit rate (r), profit margin (s), capital stock (k), and growth rate of GDP in current dollars (GDP). Because the corporate sector is a segment of the aggregate economy and is influenced by the broader economy, the growth rate of GDP in nominal terms is added to output equation (4.1.2). Since the growth rate of nominal GDP is based on the macroeconomic profit system model in Chapter 3 containing information about the Federal funds rate, it is not necessary to include this rate in the output equation for the corporate sector. In the profit rate equation (4.1.3) the log of profit rate (r) is determined by lags of logarithms of output (y), profit margin (s), and capital stock (k). A lag order of 1 is specified for the Federal funds rate (F) per empirical results. In the profit margin equation (4.1.4) forecasts of logarithms of profit rate (r), capital stock (k), and output (y) are used for estimating forecasts of log profit margin (s). In the total profit equation (4.1.5) the log of total profit (z) in current dollars is determined by the lags of logarithms of capital stock in current dollars (k) and profit rate (r).

Since aggregate corporate profits are to be used in Chapter 6 for the study of aggregate stock market valuation, we use after-tax corporate profits in these analyses. The macroeconomic model in Chapter 3 is used to obtain forecasts of the Federal funds rate, the growth rate of total debt outstanding in the nonfinancial sector, and the growth rate of nominal GDP. These variables are utilized in the corporate sector model.

Table 4.1 Corporate and nonfinancial corporate profit system models

---

Goods and services market equations

Capital stock model

$$k_t = \alpha_0 + \alpha_1 y_{t-1} + \alpha_2 y_{t-2} + \alpha_3 r_{t-1} + \alpha_4 r_{t-2} + \alpha_5 s_{t-1} + \alpha_6 s_{t-2} + \alpha_7 \dot{D}_t \qquad (4.1.1)$$

Output model

$$y_t = \beta_0 + \beta_1 r_{t-1} + \beta_2 r_{t-2} + \beta_3 s_{t-1} + \beta_4 s_{t-2} + \beta_5 k_{t-1} + \beta_6 k_{t-2} + \beta_7 G\dot{D}P_t \qquad (4.1.2)$$

Profit rate model

$$r_t = \theta_0 + \theta_1 y_{t-1} + \theta_2 s_{t-1} + \theta_3 k_{t-1} + \theta_4 F_{t-l} \qquad (4.1.3)$$

Profit margin model

$$s_t = r_t + k_t - y_t \qquad (4.1.4)$$

Total profit model

$$z_t = \upsilon_0 + \upsilon_1 r_{t-1} + \upsilon_2 k_{t-1} \qquad (4.1.5)$$

Additional goods and services market equations in the nonfinancial corporate sector model:

Price model

$$\widehat{p}_t = \varphi_0 + \varphi_1 \widehat{p}_{t-1} + \varphi_2 \widehat{p}_{t-2} + \varphi_3 \bar{F}_{t-2} + \varphi_4 \dot{P}_{t-1} \qquad (4.1.6)$$

Deflated (real) output model

$$\bar{y}_t = y_t - \widehat{p}_t \qquad (4.1.7)$$

Deflated total profit model

$$\bar{z}_t = z_t - \widehat{p}_t \qquad (4.1.8)$$

Bold-numbered equations are empirically estimated (see Tables 4.2 and 4.3), and other
  equations are derived from their forecasts. All equations are solved simultaneously and
  recursively in forecasting and simulation analyses (see Table 4.4 as well as Figs. 4.1 and 4.2).

Variables are defined as follows:
$K(k)$ = nominal capital stock (log) in billions of dollars
$Y(y)$ = nominal output (log) in billions of dollars
$R(r)$ = profit rate (log) in percent
$S(s)$ = profit margin (log) in percent
$Z(z)$ = after-tax profit in billions of dollars
$\dot{D}$ = growth rate of total debt outstanding of nonfinancial sector in nominal terms (financial
  sector variable)
F = Federal funds rate in percent (financial sector variable)
$G\dot{D}P$ = growth rate of GDP in nominal terms,
  where K_t = antilog k_t, Y_t = antilog y_t, R_t = antilog r_t, S_t = antilog s_t, and Z_t = antilog z_t.

Additional variables in the nonfinancial corporate model are defined as follows:

$\widehat{P}(\widehat{p})$ = price deflator (log) equal to output in nominal terms divided by output in real terms
$\bar{F}$ = real Federal funds rate in percent (financial sector variable)
$\dot{P}$ = GDP inflation rate
$\bar{Z}(\bar{z})$ = after-tax deflated profit in billions of 2000 dollars
$\bar{Y}(\bar{y})$ = output (log) in billions of 2000 dollars,
  where $\bar{Y}_t$ = antilog$(\bar{y}_t)$ and $\bar{Z}_t$ = antilog$(\bar{z}_t)$.

4.1.2 The Nonfinancial Corporate Model

The NIPA data from the BEA contain time series of outputs in the nonfinancial corporate sector in current and 2,000 dollars. These times series can be used to compute a price index (price deflator) for the nonfinancial corporate sector by dividing the time series of nominal output by the time series of output in 2000 constant dollars. Thus, in Table 4.1 we specify price equation (4.1.6) for the nonfinancial corporate sector where the logarithm of the price index $(\widehat{P})$ is determined by its own lags, the Federal funds rate in real terms $(\bar{F})$ per Wicksell (1898), and the general inflation rate for the aggregate economy represented by the GDP inflation rate $(\dot{P})$. In equation (4.1.7) the log of the price deflator $(\widehat{P})$ in the nonfinancial corporate sector is deducted from log nominal output (y) in this sector to compute the log of real output $(\bar{y})$ in the sector. Similarly, in equation (4.1.8) the log of the price deflator $(\widehat{P})$ in the nonfinancial corporate sector is deducted from log nominal total profit (z) to compute the log of real total profit $(\bar{z})$. It may also be justified to use the price deflator for the whole corporate sector, as nonfinancial corporate sector output accounted for about 90 percent of corporate sector output from 1959 to 2008. However, the share of nonfinancial sector output in the whole corporate sector decreased from 94.3 percent in 1959 to 86.1 percent in 2008, although this proportion no doubt will increase in 2009 to some extent due to recent shrinkage in the financial sector.

4.2 Data for Estimating Corporate and Nonfinancial Corporate Sector Models

For the application of our profit system model to the US corporate and US nonfinancial corporate sectors, we use the corporate components of the business sector data series for the period 1959–2008 employed in Chapter 3. The time series data for corporate profits and corporate capital stock are from the Fed's Z1 series, and corporate output data time series are from the NIPA of the BEA. The output of the corporate sector is measured in terms of gross value added by the BEA, such that they are GDPs of the corporate sector. As already noted, the price deflator for nonfinancial corporate sector output equals nonfinancial corporate output in nominal terms divided by nonfinancial corporate output in 2000 dollars (Table 1.14 of the BEA).

4.3 The Estimated Corporate Profit System Model

Table 4.2 shows the estimated equations for the corporate profit system model based on OLS and SUR methods, which are shown in panels A and B, respectively. Again, the corporate capital stock and output equations are estimated with two lags of the fundamental variables. The goodness-of-fit of the estimated equations is quite high with adjusted R^2 values of 0.99 for the capital stock and output equations, 0.98 for the profit equation, and a range of 0.78–0.81 for the profit rate equation. The lag structures for nominal Federal funds rate (F), the growth rate of debt outstanding in

Table 4.2 Estimated corporate profit system model: 1958–2008

A. OLS regression estimates

$k_t = 0.115 + 1.882\, y_{t-1} - 0.895\, y_{t-2} - 1.425\, r_{t-1} + 0.699\, r_{t-2} +$ $R^2 = 0.99$ $DW = 2.09$
   (1.62)   (9.16)**   (4.58)**   (8.68)**   (4.17)**

   $1.448\, s_{t-1} - 0.768\, s_{t-2} + 0.766\, \dot{D}_t$
   (8.02)**   (3.93)**   (3.12)**

$y_t = 0.008 + 1.078\, r_{t-1} - 0.031\, r_{t-2} - 1.072\, s_{t-1} + 0.017\, s_{t-2} +$ $R^2 = 0.99$ $DW = 1.40$
   (0.34)   (13.29)**   (0.40)   (12.23)**   (0.20)

   $1.025\, k_{t-1} - 0.026\, k_{t-2} + 1.172 \dot{GDP}_{t-1}$
   (15.66)**   (0.40)   (14.97)**

$r_t = -1.037 + 0.656\, y_{t-1} + 0.522\, s_{t-1} - 0.676\, k_{t-1} - 2.584\, F_{t-1}$ $R^2 = 0.81$ $DW = 1.94$
   (4.33)**   (3.15)**   (5.52)**   (3.18)**   (4.67)**

$z_t = -0.199 + 0.989\, k_{t-1} + 0.885\, r_{t-1}$ $R^2 = 0.98$ $DW = 1.85$
   (0.79)   (54.07)**   (11.08)**

B. Seemingly unrelated regression estimates

$k_t = 0.114 + 1.913\, y_{t-1} - 0.924\, y_{t-2} - 1.441\, r_{t-1} + 0.668\, r_{t-2} +$ $R^2 = 0.99$ $DW = 2.08$
   (1.81)+   (11.52)**   (5.58)**   (10.41)**   (4.72)**

   $1.462\, s_{t-1} - 0.718\, s_{t-2} + 0.617 \dot{D}_t$
   (9.61)**   (4.37)**   (3.08)**

$y_t = 0.009 + 1.113\, r_{t-1} - 0.075\, r_{t-2} - 1.108\, s_{t-1} + 0.062\, s_{t-2} +$ $R^2 = 0.99$ $DW = 1.47$
   (0.44)   (15.56)**   (1.11)   (14.33)**   (0.84)

   $1.084\, k_{t-1} - 0.086\, k_{t-2} + 1.062 \dot{GDP}_{t-1}$
   (18.87)**   (1.50)   (15.85)**

$r_t = -0.743 + 0.761\, y_{t-1} + 0.681\, s_{t-1} - 0.773\, k_{t-1} - 1.276\, F_{t-1}$ $R^2 = 0.78$ $DW = 1.96$
   (3.63)**(5.94)**   (9.34)**   (5.96)**   (4.11)**

$z_t = -0.203 + 0.989\, k_{t-1} + 0.885\, r_{t-1}$ $R^2 = 0.98$ $DW = 1.85$
   (0.84)   (56.02)**   (11.43)**

Notes: Figures in parentheses are *t*-values associated with estimated coefficients with superscripts **, *, and + denoting significance at the 1, 5, and 10% levels, respectively. *DW* denotes the Durbin–Watson test for serial correlation. The variables are defined as follows: $k =$ log capital stock in the corporate sector in current dollars, $y =$ log output in the corporate sector in current dollars, $r =$ log profit rate in the corporate sector, $s =$ log profit margin in the corporate sector, $z =$ log total profit in the corporate sector, $\dot{D} =$ growth rate of nonfinancial debt outstanding (financial sector variable), $\dot{GDP} =$ nominal *GDP* growth rate, and $F =$ nominal Federal funds rate (financial sector variable).

the nonfinancial sector $(\dot{D})$, and the growth rate of GDP in nominal terms $(\dot{GDP})$ in the equations were determined empirically. In this regard, zero to two-period lags are tested and the most statistically significant lag lengths selected.

In the corporate capital stock equation (k) the estimated coefficients for the first and second lags of logarithms of output (y), profit rate (r), and profit margin (s) are significant at the 1 percent level in OLS and SUR regressions. The estimated coefficients for the growth rate of nonfinancial debt outstanding ($\dot{D}$) are significant at the 1 percent level in OLS and SUR regressions.

In the corporate output equation (y) the estimated coefficients for the first lags of profit rate (r), profit margin (s), and capital stock (k) are significant at the 1 percent level in OLS and SUR regressions. The estimated coefficients for the second lags of the same variables are not significant but were not dropped to correct potential serial correlation problems. Also, the estimated coefficient for the growth rate of GDP in nominal terms ($\dot{GDP}$) is statistically significant at the 1 percent level. By contrast, the estimated coefficients for the Federal funds rate (F) are not significant and, therefore, were dropped for this reason as well as the fact that the growth rate of $\dot{GDP}$ contains Federal funds rate information.

For the corporate profit rate (r) equation the estimated coefficients for the first lags of logarithms of profit margin (s), output (y), capital stock (k), and the nominal Federal funds rate (F) are significant at the 1 percent level in OLS and SUR regressions.

Lastly, in the total profit equation the estimated coefficients for first lags of logarithms of capital stock (k) and profit rate (r) are significant at the 1 percent level in OLS and SUR regressions.

4.4 The Estimated Nonfinancial Corporate Sector Profit System Model

Table 4.3 gives the estimated equations for the nonfinancial corporate profit system model based on OLS and SUR regression methods, which are shown in panels A and B, respectively. The statistical significance of the estimated coefficients for the variables in the equations for logarithms of capital stock, output, profit rate, and total profit in nonfinancial corporate sector is similar to their corresponding variables for the whole corporate sector reported in Section 4.3. In the equation for logarithm price deflator ($\hat{p}$) in the nonfinancial corporate sector, the estimated coefficients for the first lag of the price deflator are statistically significant at the 1 percent level in OLS and SUR regressions. The estimated coefficients for the second lag of the Federal funds rate in real terms are negative and significant at the 1 percent significance level in OLS and SUR regressions. Hence, there is a negative relationship between the real interest rate and the inflation in line with Wicksell (1898). The estimated coefficient for the lagged GDP inflation rate in the output equation is positive and statistically significant at the 10 percent level in the SUR.

4.5 Stochastic Simulations of the Estimated Corporate Models

As discussed in Section 3.2.3, stochastic simulations are performed to determine the ability of the equations that comprise the corporate profit system models to track the historical path of the variables over time. Despite the good statistical fit of individual equations in the system, it is possible that the model as a whole does not work in

Table 4.3 Estimated nonfinancial corporate profit system model: 1958–2008

A. OLS regression estimates

$k_t = 0.105 + 1.887\, y_{t-1} - 0.903\, y_{t-2} - 1.436\, r_{t-1} + 0.710\, r_{t-2} +$ $R^2 = 0.99$ $DW = 2.25$
        (1.30) (8.92)**   (4.26)**   (9.67)**   (4.79)**

$\quad 1.446\, s_{t-1} - 0.776\, s_{t-2} + 0.816\, \dot{D}_t$
        (9.12)**   (4.62)**   (3.24)**

$y_t = 0.030 + 0.976\, r_{t-1} + 0.053 r_{t-2} - 0.952\, s_{t-1} - 0.069 s_{t-2} +$ $R^2 = 0.99$ $DW = 1.71$
        (1.19) (12.32)**   (0.71)   (10.95)**   (0.87)

$\quad 0.927\, k_{t-1} + 0.071\, k_{t-2} + 1.210\, \dot{GDP}_{t-1}$
        (13.38)**   (1.02)   (15.78)**

$r_t = -1.020 + 0.596\, y_{t-1} + 0.522\, s_{t-1} - 0.635\, k_{t-1} - 2.188\, F_{t-1}$ $R^2 = 0.70$ $DW = 1.75$
        (3.66)** (2.61)**   (4.76)**   (2.71)**   (3.57)**

$z_t = -0.361 + 0.973\, k_{t-1} + 0.801\, r_{t-1}$ $R^2 = 0.91$ $DW = 1.77$
        (1.19)   (42.09)**   (7.89)**

$\hat{p}_t = -0.000 + 1.134\, \hat{p}_{t-1} - 0.140\, \hat{p}_{t-2} - 0.212\, \bar{F}_{t-2} + 0.790\, \dot{P}_{t-1}$ $R^2 = 0.99$ $DW = 1.48$
        (0.01)   (2.39)**   (0.29)   (2.95)**   (1.54)

B. Seemingly unrelated regression estimates

$k_t = 0.139 + 1.819\, y_{t-1} - 0.830\, y_{t-2} - 1.353\, r_{t-1} + 0.575\, r_{t-2} +$ $R^2 = 0.99$ $DW = 1.98$
        (2.02)$^+$ (10.83)**   (4.93)**   (11.44)**   (4.92)**

$\quad 1.358\, s_{t-1} - 0.598\, s_{t-2} + 0.722 \dot{D}_t$
        (10.82)**   (4.53)**   (3.73)**

$y_t = 0.023 + 1.038\, r_{t-1} - 0.015 r_{t-2} - 1.021\, s_{t-1} - 0.002\, s_{t-2} +$ $R^2 = 0.99$ $DW = 1.71$
        (1.03) (15.79)**   (0.24)   (14.17)**   (0.03)

$\quad 1.024\, k_{t-1} - 0.025\, k_{t-2} + 1.093\, \dot{GDP}_{t-1}$
        (17.85)**   (1.43)   (17.57)**

$r_t = -0.804 + 0.714\, y_{t-1} + 0.644\, s_{t-1} - 0.743\, k_{t-1} - 0.840\, F_{t-1}$ $R^2 = 0.66$ $DW = 1.79$
        (3.27)** (5.38)**   (7.38)**   (5.59)**   (2.77)**

$z_t = -0.375 + 0.975\, k_{t-1} + 0.802\, r_{t-1}$ $R^2 = 0.97$ $DW = 1.77$
        (1.28)   (44.00)**   (8.20)**

$\hat{p}_t = 0.001 + 1.063\, \hat{p}_{t-1} - 0.071\, \hat{p}_{t-2} - 0.186\, \bar{F}_{t-2} + 0.790\, \dot{P}_{t-1}$ $R^2 = 0.99$ $DW = 1.40$
        (0.12)   (2.58)**   (0.17)   (2.96)**   (1.77)$^+$

Notes: Figures in parentheses are t-values associated with estimated coefficients with superscripts ** and $^+$ denoting significance at the 1% and 10% levels, respectively. DW denotes the Durbin–Watson test for serial correlation. The variables are defined as follows: $k =$ log capital stock in the nonfinancial corporate sector in current dollars, $y =$ log output in the nonfinancial corporate sector in current dollars, $r =$ log profit rate in the nonfinancial corporate sector, $s =$ log profit margin in the nonfinancial corporate sector, $z =$ log total profit in the nonfinancial corporate sector, $\dot{D} =$ growth rate of nonfinancial sector debt outstanding (financial sector variable), $\dot{GDP} =$ nominal GDP growth rate, and $F =$ nominal Federal funds rate (financial sector variable).

(a) GDP in Current Dollars in the Corporate Sector

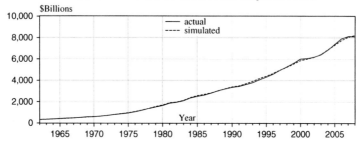

(b) Capital Stock in Current Dollars in the Corporate Sector

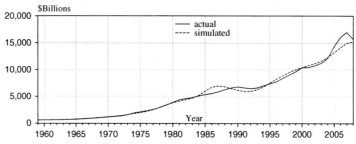

(c) Corporate Sector Profit Rates

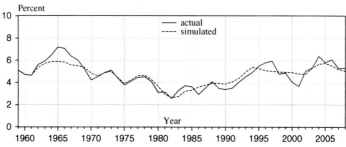

(d) Corporate Sector Profit Margins

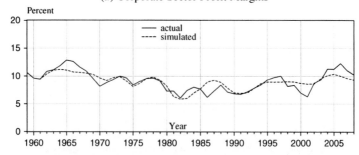

Fig. 4.1 (continued) (Actual and simulated values of the variables in the corporate sector model: 1959–2008: (**a**) *GDP* in current dollars in the corporate sector; (**b**) capital stock in current dollars in the corporate sector; (**c**) corporate sector profit rates; (**d**) corporate sector profit margins; and (**e**) corporate sector profit in current dollars

(*e*) Corporate Sector Profit in Current Dollars

terms of reproducing the actual data series for the variables. Figures 4.1 and 4.2 provide the corporate sector and nonfinancial corporate sector simulation results for the period 1962–2008. The dynamic simulations shown there utilize the initial values of the variables from 1959 to 1961 and then forecast the variables from 1962 to 2008 to compute their values.

Like the business sector simulation results in Chapter 3, the graphs in Figs. 4.1 and 4.2 for the corporate sector and nonfinancial corporate sector are promising. Actual output, capital stock, profit margin, profit rate, and total profit data series are closely mimicked by the stochastically generated trajectories of the variables in both the corporate sector and the nonfinancial corporate sector models. A very close relationship between actual and simulated paths is achieved over the sample period. Also, the profit rate and profit margin graphs suggest that the models can capture turning points (to some extent) in the cyclic movements of these variables over time. For example, Fig. 4.2(d) shows that turning points for simulated profit rates in a number of cases coincide with actual profit rates. The simulated paths of aggregate profits of corporate sector and nonfinancial corporate sector in Fig. 4.1(e) and 4.2(f), respectively, suggest that recent high growth rates of corporate profits may not be sustainable in the future. In general, we infer that our corporate models can success-fully estimate the paths of GDP, capital stock, profit rates, profit margins, and aggre-gate profits in the corporate and nonfinancial corporate sectors of the US economy.

4.6 Out-of-Sample Forecasts of Corporate Profit System Models

Table 4.4 presents out-of-sample forecasts of the variables in the corporate mod-els. The forecast results show that a corporate sector recovery is expected after 2010. Comparison of forecast results for the aggregate corporate sector in panel A and forecast results for the nonfinancial corporate sector in panel B shows that the nonfinancial corporate sector is expected to recover more strongly and earlier than the aggregate corporate sector. Notice that the growth rate of nonfinancial sec-tor *GDP* in real terms in panel B reaches 3.2 percent in 2011 and 3.5 percent in

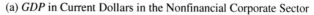

(a) *GDP* in Current Dollars in the Nonfinancial Corporate Sector

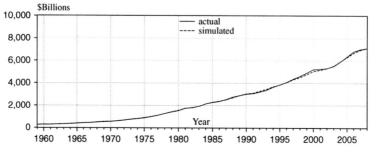

(b) *GDP* in $2000 Dollars in the Nonfinancial Corporate Sector

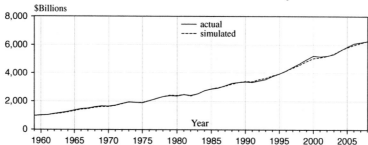

(c) Capital Stock in Current Dollars in the Nonfinancial Corporate Sector

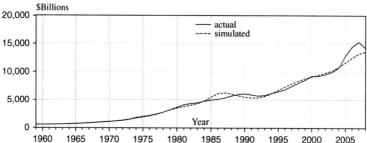

(d) Nonfinancial Corporate Sector Profit Rates

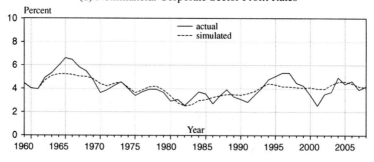

Fig. 4.2 (continued)

(e) Nonfinancial Corporate Sector Profit Margins

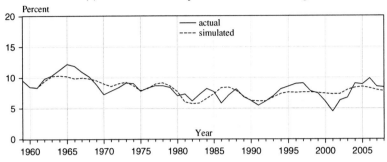

(f) Nonfinancial Corporate Sector Profit in Current Dollars

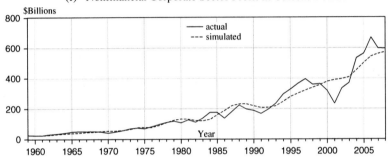

Fig. 4.2 (continued) Actual and simulated values of the variables in the nonfinancial corporate sector model: 1959–2008: (**a**) *GDP* in current dollars in the nonfinancial corporate sector; (**b**) *GDP* in $2000 constant dollars in the nonfinancial corporate sector; (**c**) capital stock in current dollars in the nonfinancial corporate sector; (**d**) nonfinancial corporate sector profit rates; (**e**) nonfinancial corporate sector profit margins; and (**f**) nonfinancial corporate sector profit in current dollars

2012, which is about 1 percent higher than the real growth rate in the total business sector (see Table 3.9). We infer that the projected weakness in the corporate sector is attributable to the troubled financial corporate sector. Our forecast results point to a diminishing financial sector in terms of its share of aggregate *GDP* in the corporate sector in the years ahead.

4.7 A Quarterly Profit System Model of the Nonfinancial Corporate Sector

The availability of profit, output, and capital stock data for the nonfinancial corporate sector on a quarterly basis from the BEA and Fed allowed us to develop and estimate a quarterly model of this sector. The Appendix contains the estimated quarterly models using OLS and SUR methods. Unlike the annual data series version of this model in Table 4.3, the estimated equations for profit rate have much

Table 4.4 Out-of-sample forecasts of the estimated corporate sector and nonfinancial corporate sector models

	2009	2010	2011	2012
A. Corporate sector				
$\dot{Y}$, growth rate of output in nominal terms	2.5	3.5	5.1	6.5
R, after-tax profit rate	5.2	5.4	5.6	5.7
S, after-tax profit margin	8.9	8.3	7.8	7.5
$\dot{Z}$, growth rate of after-tax profit in nominal terms	4.4	−10.8	−4.3	−1.3
$\dot{K}$, growth rate of capital stock in nominal terms	−9.3	−7.9	−4.0	1.3
B. Nonfinancial corporate sector				
$\dot{Y}$, growth rate of output in nominal terms	3.7	3.9	5.5	6.5
R, after-tax profit rate	4.2	4.6	4.8	4.8
S, after-tax profit margin	7.2	6.9	6.5	6.3
$\dot{Z}$, growth rate of after-tax profit in nominal terms	2.8	−10.5	−2.0	−0.9
$\dot{K}$, growth rate of capital stock in nominal terms	−10.2	−9.2	−4.6	2.1
$\dot{P}$, inflation rate	1.1	1.3	2.2	2.9
$\dot{Y}$, growth rate of output in real terms	2.6	2.7	3.2	3.5
$\dot{Z}$, growth rate of after-tax profit in real terms	1.7	−11.6	−4.1	−3.6

higher R^2 values. Of course, the estimated quarterly model can be used in conjunction with the estimated annual models presented in this chapter. However, the time series data for profit and capital stocks of the corporate sector are originally compiled by the BEA on an annual basis and subsequently converted to quarterly data by the Fed.

4.8 Conclusion

This chapter is built upon earlier chapters by developing profit system models of the corporate and nonfinancial corporate sectors of the US economy. Data were collected for the period 1959–2008 from the BEA and the Fed. The models employed the same setup as in the aggregate business sector model in Chapter 3. Inputs from the business sector model included the total GDP growth rate in nominal terms, growth rate of nonfinancial debt outstanding, and nominal and real Federal funds rates. In this regard, when used for forecasting purposes, the macroeconomic model of the US economy in Chapter 3 was needed to estimate these variables. Empirical analyses demonstrated the reliability of the models. Also, stochastic simulations within the sample period showed that the models can accurately mimic output, capital stock, profit rates, profit margins, and aggregate profits in the corporate and nonfinancial corporate sectors. We interpret this evidence to mean that our profit system approach to modeling the corporate business sector captures the real world dynamics between the focal variables.

Consequently, we used the estimated models for out-of-sample forecasts of the variables. Our forecast results projected that output in the nonfinancial corporate sector will grow faster than the corporate sector or total business sector due to slower growth in the financial sector in coming years. These results seem reasonable in view of the severe problems in the financial sector in recent years.

An important application of the corporate sector profit system models is the valuation of the aggregate stock market. In Chapter 6 we use these models in a discounted cash flow (DCF) framework for this purpose.

Appendix: Estimated Nonfinancial Corporate Profit System Model Using Quarterly Data Series: 1958Q1–2008Q4

A. OLS regression estimates

$$k_t = 0.027 + 1.757\, y_{t-1} - 0.758\, y_{t-2} - 1.604\, r_{t-1} + 0.637\, r_{t-2} +$$
$$(2.77)^{**} \ (21.82)^{**} \ (9.43)^{**} \quad (27.28)^{**} \ \ (11.05)^{**}$$
$$1.599\, s_{t-1} - 0.630\, s_{t-2} + 0.136\, \dot{D}_{t-1}$$
$$(25.78)^{**} \ \ (10.17)^{**} \ \ (3.80)^{**}$$
$R^2 = 0.99 \ DW = 2.41$

$$y_t = 0.029 + 1.214\, r_{t-1} - 0.216 r_{t-2} - 1.198\, s_{t-1} + 0.203\, s_{t-2} +$$
$$(2.28)^* \ (13.58)^{**} \ (2.44)^* \quad (12.05)^{**} \quad (2.09)^*$$
$$1.184 K_{t-1} - 0.186 K_{t-2} + 0.517 GDP_{t-1}$$
$$(10.27)^{**} \ \ (1.61) \qquad (2.63)^*$$
$R^2 = 0.99 \ DW = 2.01$

$$r_t = -0.223 + 1.392\, y_{t-1} - 0.493\, y_{t-2} + 1.004\, s_{t-1} - 0.117\, s_{t-2} -$$
$$(2.58)^* \ (2.42)^* \quad (0.86) \qquad (10.01)^{**} \quad (1.23)$$
$$1.648\, k_{t-1} + 0.739\, k_{t-2} - 0.676\, F_{t-1}$$
$$(3.39)^{**} \ \ (1.53) \qquad (3.40)^{**}$$
$R^2 = 0.99 \ DW = 1.62$

$$z_t = -0.074 + 0.991\, k_{t-1} + 0.951\, r_{t-1}$$
$$(1.00) \ \ (171.44)^{**} \ (38.60)^{**}$$
$R^2 = 0.99 \ DW = 1.61$

$$\hat{p}_t = -0.002 + 1.086 \hat{p}_{t-1} - 0.087 \hat{p}_{t-2} - 0.020 \bar{F}_{t-2} + 0.237 \dot{P}_{t-1}$$
$$(3.36)^{**} \ (13.73)^{**} \ (1.10) \qquad (2.09)^* \qquad (10.12)^{**}$$
$R^2 = 0.99 \ DW = 1.62$

B. Seemingly unrelated regression (SUR) estimates

$$k_t = 0.026 + 1.779\, y_{t-1} - 0.779\, y_{t-2} - 1.627\, r_{t-1} + 0.654\, r_{t-2} +$$
$$(2.71)^{**} \ (23.14)^{**} \ (10.15)^{**} \quad (28.97)^{**} \ (11.87)$$
$$1.617\, s_{t-1} - 0.642\, s_{t-2} + 0.117\, \dot{D}_{t-1}$$
$$(27.31)^{**} \ \ (10.84)^{**} \ \ (3.50)^{**}$$
$R^2 = 0.99 \ DW = 2.41$

$$y_t = 0.029 + 1.187\, r_{t-1} - 0.196 r_{t-2} - 1.187\, s_{t-1} + 0.203\, s_{t-2} +$$
$$(2.50)^* \ (18.95)^{**} \ (3.17)^* \quad (17.05)^{**} \quad (2.97)^{**}$$
$$1.251\, k_{t-1} - 0.252\, k_{t-2} + 0.433 G\dot{D}P_{t-1}$$
$$(15.54)^{**} \ \ (3.13)^{**} \ \ (3.18)^{**}$$
$R^2 = 0.99 \ DW = 2.01$

Appendix (continued)

$r_t = -0.106 + 0.852y_{t-1} + 0.083y_{t-2} + 0.967s_{t-1} - 0.024\,s_{t-2} -$ $\qquad\qquad R^2 = 0.99\ DW = 1.62$
$\quad\ (1.51)\ \ (4.36)^{**}\quad\ (0.43)\qquad (24.26)^{**}\ \ (0.76)$

$\quad 1.640\,k_{t-1} + 0.696\,k_{t-2} - 0.107\,F_{t-1}$
$\quad (9.95)^{**}\quad\ (4.30)^{**}\quad\ (1.63)$

$z_t = -0.063 + 0.992\,k_{t-1} + 0.955\,r_{t-1}$ $\qquad\qquad\qquad\qquad R^2 = 0.99\ DW = 1.61$
$\quad\ (0.86)\ \ (172.93)^{**}\ \ (39.23)^{**}$

$\hat{p}_t = -0.002 + 1.076\hat{p}_{t-1} - 0.076\hat{p}_{t-2} - 0.022\bar{F}_{t-2} + 0.237\dot{P}_{t-1}$ $\qquad R^2 = 0.99\ DW =1.62$
$\quad\ (3.18)^{**}\ (13.89)^{**}\ \ (0.99)\qquad (2.31)^*\qquad (10.32)^{**}$

Notes: Figures in parentheses are t-values associated with estimated coefficients with superscripts ** and * denoting significance at the 1% and 5% levels, respectively. DW denotes the Durbin–Watson test for serial correlation. The variables are defined as follows: k = log capital stock in the nonfinancial corporate sector in current dollars, y = log output in the nonfinancial corporate sector in current dollars, r = log profit rate in the nonfinancial corporate sector, s = log profit margin in the nonfinancial corporate sector, z = log total profit in the nonfinancial corporate sector, $\dot{D}$ = growth rate of nonfinancial debt outstanding (financial sector variable), $G\dot{D}P$ = nominal GDP growth rate, and F = nominal Federal funds rate (financial sector variable).

Chapter 5
Profit System Models for Industries

In this chapter profit system models are developed for US industries. Our purpose is to estimate profit system models for different industries and use the estimated models for out-of-sample forecasts of key business variables. Industry analyses are popular in benchmarking exercises that compare individual firms' performance to its industry. Also, industry analyses can reveal important trends that will affect individual firms. We report profit system results for the following industries: Mining, Quarrying, and Oil and Gas Extraction (NAICS 21), Utilities (NAICS 22), Construction (NAICS 23), Manufacturing (NAICS 31–33), Wholesale Trade (NAICS 42), Retail Trade (NAICS 44–45), Transportation and Warehousing (NAICS 48–49), Information (NAICS 51), Finance and Insurance (NAICS 52), Professional and Business Services (NAICS 54–56), Education and Health Services (NAICS 61–62), and Leisure and Hospitality (NAICS 71–72). Due to data restrictions, the scope of our analyses is limited to the period 1987–2007, with forecasts covering the period 2008–2011.

5.1 The Empirical Representation of the Model for Industries

Using the available data on output, profit, and capital stock of US industries, we estimated different empirical profit system models discussed in Chapter 2. The profit system model shown in Table 5.1 proved to be the most suitable model for empirical application to US industrial data in terms of the significance of estimated coefficients and out-of-sample forecast accuracy. This model is presented in Table 2.2 (i.e., the alternative basic profit system model of the goods and services market with output and capital stock in current dollars). In this model the capital stocks and outputs of industries are in current (nominal) values. The logarithm of capital stock (k) in the capital stock equation (5.1.1) is determined by lags of logarithms of output (y), profit rate (r), and profit margin (s). The forecast of the logarithm of capital stock (k) from equation (5.1.1) and lags of logarithms of profit rate (r) and profit margin (s) are used in output equation (5.1.2) for forecasting the logarithm of output (y). Equation (5.1.3) uses the forecast of the logarithm of capital stock (k) from equation (5.1.1), forecast of output (y) from equation (5.1.2), and lag of profit margin (s) for forecasting the profit rate (r). Equation (5.1.4) uses forecasts of capital

A. Anari, J.W. Kolari, *The Power of Profit*, DOI 10.1007/978-1-4419-0649-6_5,
© Springer Science+Business Media, LLC 2010

Table 5.1 Empirical representation of industry profit system model

---

Capital stock model
$$k_t = \alpha_0 + \alpha_1 y_{t-1} + \alpha_2 r_{t-1} + \alpha_3 s_{t-1} + \alpha_5 \dot{D}_{t-L} + \alpha_6 F_{t-L} \tag{5.1.1}$$
Output model
$$y_t = \beta_0 + \beta_2 r_{t-1} + \beta_3 s_{t-1} + k_t + \beta_5 \dot{D}_{t-L} + \beta_6 F_{t-L} \tag{5.1.2}$$
Profit rate model
$$r_t = \theta_0 + y_t + \theta_3 s_{t-1} - k_t + \theta_5 \dot{D}_{t-L} + \theta_6 F_{t-L} \tag{5.1.3}$$
Profit margin model
$$s_t = r_t + k_t - y_t \tag{5.1.4}$$
Total profit model
$$Z_t = Y_t \times S_t \tag{5.1.5}$$
Variables are defined as follows:
$Y(y)$ = output in current dollars (log)
$K(k)$ = capital stock in current dollars (log)
$R(r)$ = profit rate (log)
$S(s)$ = profit margin (log)
Z = total profit
F = Federal funds rate in percent (financial sector variable)
$\dot{D}$ = growth rate of nonfinancial debt outstanding in percent (financial sector variable),
where K_t = antilog k_t, Y_t = antilog y_t, R_t = antilog r_t, S_t = antilog s_t, and $L = 0, 1, \ldots, n$ generic number of lags to be determined empirically.

---

stock (k), output (y), and profit rate (r) from equations (5.1.1), (5.1.2), and (5.1.3) to estimate the forecast of the profit margin (s). These four equations generate forecasts of capital stock, output, profit rate, and profit margin in log terms, such that the antilogarithm gives the levels of the variables (K, Y, R, and S). Lastly, equation (5.1.5) uses the forecasts of output (Y) and profit margin (S) to forecast profit.

The main advantage of this model is the smaller number of coefficients of the variables to be estimated. In output equation (5.1.2) the number of coefficients to be estimated is reduced by one via using the forecast of the logarithm of capital stock (k) generated from the capital stock equation (5.1.1) with its coefficient assumed to be +1. In the profit rate equation (5.1.3) the number of coefficients to be estimated is reduced by two through using (1) the forecast of the logarithm of capital stock (k) generated from the capital stock equation (5.1.1) with its coefficient set equal to −1 and (2) the forecast of the logarithm of output (y) generated from the output equation (5.1.2) with its coefficient set equal to +1. Reducing the number of coefficients to be estimated is important when the number of observations is not large. For forecasting purposes the main disadvantage or limitation of the model is that, in the first period in the forecast horizon, using forecasts of the logarithm of capital (k) in equation (5.1.2) may affect forecasts of logarithm of output (y) and using forecasts of the logarithms of capital stock (k) and output (y) may influence forecasts of log profit rate (r).

Due to the small number of observations in our time series of profit, output, and capital stock for industries, we employ the nominal values of the fundamental variables and specify a lag order of one in the empirical profit system model.

As noted in previous chapters, the cost and availability of credit play important roles in the determination of profit, output, and capital stock. For this reason equations (5.1.1), (5.1.2), and (5.1.3) include the Federal funds rate (F) and the growth rate of total nonfinancial debt outstanding ($\dot{D}$). The lag orders for these financial sector variables are empirically determined. The estimated coefficients of $\dot{D}$ in equations (5.1.1), (5.1.2), and (5.1.3) are expected to be positive reflecting the positive (negative) impact of higher (lower) growth rates of debts on k, y, and r. The estimated coefficients for F in equations (5.1.1), (5.1.2), and (5.1.3) are expected to be negative due to the negative (positive) impact of higher (lower) F on k, y, and r. The financial variables (F and $\dot{D}$) are dropped from equations for k, y, and r when their estimated coefficients are not statistically significant or do not improve out-of-sample forecasts.

5.2 Industry Data

Time series data are collected from the US BEA and the Bureau of Labor Statistics (BLS). The BEA measures the outputs of industries in terms of value added and reports the following components of value added: (1) compensation of employees, (2) taxes on production and imports less subsidies, and (3) gross operating surplus.[1] For each industry group the BEA reports fixed capital assets data consisting of equipment and software as well as the value of structures excluding the value of land. In BLS studies of total factor productivities for US industries, estimates of the land component of capital stocks of industries are provided. For each industry we add the time series of the value of the land components of fixed assets from the BLS to the time series of the total tangible assets of industries from the BEA to estimate the time series of capital stocks of industries (K). We use gross value added of output to measure output (Y) and gross operating surplus to measure total profits (Z) of an industry. Dividing gross operating surplus (Z) for each industry by output measured in terms of total gross value added (Y) gives estimates of profit margins (S). Likewise, dividing the gross operating surplus (Z) by fixed assets provides estimates of profit rates (R) for industries.

Of course, there are always data issues, and the BEA industry data are no exception. Due to a transition from the standard industrial classification (SIC) system to NAICS, data are only available on an annual basis from 1987. As of March 2009, data are available for 21 annual observations from 1987 to 2007. This relatively short data series may be alleviated later when the BEA completes its transition from SIC to NAICS. It should be recognized that all estimates of economic variables are proxies for their true values, and error terms in estimated models include errors in the measurement of variables. For these reasons we emphasize trends in the data and forecasts generated from the model rather than their levels in this chapter.

---

[1] Gross operating surplus is sales minus the cost of intermediate goods and services minus the compensation of employees with no allowance for depreciation of capital.

5.3 Empirical Results

Tables 5.2–5.25 report the estimated equations for 12 industry groups in the period 1987–2007, in addition to forecasts generated from the estimated equations for profit rate, profit margin, total profit, output, and capital stock over the future time horizon 2008–2011. Again, due to the small number of observations, we only estimate the equations for capital stock, output, and profit rates, with all variables in nominal terms. Also, only the first lags of the variables are included in the equations. We employ two regression methods – namely, OLS and Zellner's (1962) SUR. For future projections of the variables, the simulations of the model use the initial values of the variables in 2007 and thereafter generate lagged values of the variables to produce forecasts of the variables in each year from 2008 to 2011. Since simulations of the estimated industrial models require forecasts of the Federal funds rates and the growth rate of nonfinancial debt outstanding for 2008 onward, we use actual annual 2008 data and annual 2009–2011 forecasts of these variables generated from the simulations of the macroeconomic model in Scenario E presented in Chapter 3 (i.e., Federal funds rates gradually increase over time from 0.2 percent in 2009 to 1 percent in 2010 and 2 percent in 2011, in addition to government stimulus spending of \$200 billion per year from 2009 to 2011).

Table 5.2 Mining, quarrying, and oil and gas extraction (NAICS 21): estimated profit system equations

---

A. OLS regression estimates

$k_t = 1.208 + 0.867\, y_{t-1} - 0.892\, r_{t-1} + 1.292\, s_{t-1} - 1.448\, F_{t-1}$ $R^2 = 0.97$ $DW = 1.97$
      $(1.90)^+ \; (8.68)^{**} \quad (4.66)^{**} \quad (3.16)^{**} \quad (2.37)^*$

$y_t = -0.652 + 0.613\, r_{t-1} - 0.529\, s_{t-1} + k_t + 0.399\, op_t$ $R^2 = 0.98$ $DW = 2.49$
      $(1.90)^+ \; (2.38)^* \quad (1.23) \qquad\qquad (5.20)^{**}$

$r_t = -0.028 + y_t + 0.774\, s_{t-1} - k_t - 1.951\, F_{t-1}$ $R^2 = 0.88$ $DW = 2.02$
      $(0.27) \quad (5.22)^{**} \qquad (1.71)^+$

B. SUR regression estimates

$k_t = 1.654 + 0.835\, y_{t-1} - 0.714\, r_{t-1} + 1.061\, s_{t-1} - 1.788\, F_{t-1}$ $R^2 = 0.97$ $DW = 1.89$
      $(3.69)^{**} \; (12.09)^{**} \quad (4.88)^{**} \quad (3.51)^{**} \quad (3.58)^{**}$

$y_t = -0.547 + 0.686\, r_{t-1} - 0.642\, s_{t-1} + k_t + 0.366\, op_t$ $R^2 = 0.97$ $DW = 2.58$
      $(1.89)^+ \; (3.19)^{**} \quad (1.78)^+ \qquad\qquad (6.23)^{**}$

$r_t = -0.034 + y_t + 0.787\, s_{t-1} - k_t - 1.672\, F_{t-1}$ $R^2 = 0.88$ $DW = 2.04$
      $(0.37) \quad (5.79)^{**} \qquad (1.65)^+$

Notes: Figures in parentheses are t-values associated with estimated coefficients with superscripts **, *, and + denoting significance at the 1, 5, and 10 percent levels, respectively. The variables are defined as follows: k = log of capital stock, y = log of output, r = log of profit rate, s = log of profit margin, F = Federal funds rate (financial sector variable), and op = log of oil price.

When reporting estimated profit system model results, capital stock (k), output (y), profit rate (r), and profit margin (s) are all in logarithms. However, forecasts of capital stock (K), output (Y), and total profit (Z) are shown in levels. And, the profit rate and profit margin variables are in percentage.

The following overviews give brief discussions of the estimation and forecast results.

5.3.1 Mining, Quarrying, and Oil and Gas Extraction (NAICS 21)

Estimated Profit System Models (Table 5.2). The estimated coefficients for lags of output, profit rate, and profit margin in the capital stock equation for this industry are all significant at the 1 percent level in OLS and SUR regressions. The estimated coefficient for the Federal funds rate in the capital stock equation is statistically significant at the 5 percent level in the OLS regression and 1 percent level in the SUR. The estimated coefficient for the profit rate in the output equation is statistically significant at the 5 percent level in the OLS regression and 1 percent level in the SUR. The estimated coefficient of profit margin in this equation is significant at the 10 percent level in the SUR. Since crude oil and natural gas extraction comprise an important part of the US mining industry, and oil and gas extraction industry is highly influenced by crude oil prices, we include crude oil prices in the output equation and find that the estimated coefficients for the logarithm of West Texas intermediary crude oil prices are statistically significant at the 1 percent level in OLS and SUR regressions. In the profit rate equation the estimated coefficients for the profit margin are significant at the 1 percent level in OLS and SUR regressions. Lastly, the estimated coefficients for the Federal funds rate in the profit rate equation are negative and statistically significant at the 10 percent level in OLS and SUR regressions.

Projections of Fundamental Variables (Table 5.3). The high profit rate of 14.2 percent in 2008 was mainly due to the record historical high prices of crude

Table 5.3 Mining, quarrying, and oil and gas extraction (NAICS 21): projections of fundamental variables

	OLS					SUR				
Year	R %	S %	Z $billion	Y $billion	K $billion	R %	S %	Z $billion	Y $billion	K $billion
2008	14.2	65.3	200.2	306.9	1,407.9	14.2	65.5	197.3	301.4	1,388.6
2009	10.6	64.7	158.3	244.7	1,494.3	10.9	64.8	159.9	246.8	1,473.4
2010	11.4	69.1	190.7	275.9	1,666.4	11.4	68.4	182.0	266.1	1,598.1
2011	12.0	71.6	223.2	311.7	1,859.0	11.7	70.4	201.1	285.5	1,717.3

Notes: The variables are defined as follows: R = profit rate, S = profit margin, Z = total profit in the industry, Y = output in the industry, and K = capital stock in the industry.

oil that climbed in July 2008 to more than $140 per barrel. If we assume that price of crude oil will be $50 per barrel in the near future, projections of profit rates suggest a decline from 14.2 percent in 2008 to a range of 10.6–10.9 percent in 2009 and then later improvement to 11.7–12.0 percent in 2011. At this price profit margins are also expected to decrease from a range of 65.3–65.5 percent in 2008 to 64.7–64.8 percent in 2009 and then later improve to 70.4–71.6 percent if the economic stimulus succeeds. Total industry profit is projected to decrease from a range of $197.3–$200.2 billion in 2008 to $158.3–$159.9 billion in 2009 and then increase to $201.1–$223.2 billion in 2011. Output measured in terms of value added is forecasted to decrease from $301.4–$306.9 billion in 2008 to $244.7–$246.8 billion in 2009 and then recover to $285.5–$311.7 billion in 2011. Finally, capital stock is anticipated to grow from $1,388.6–$1,407.9 billion in 2009 to $1,717.3–$1,859.0 billion by 2011. Together, these results forecast some degree of recovery in this sector in the years ahead.

5.3.2 Utilities Industry (NAICS 22)

Estimated Profit System Models (Table 5.4). In the capital stock equation for the utilities industry, the estimated coefficients for lags of output and profit rate are significant at the 1 percent level in the OLS and SUR regressions. The estimated

Table 5.4 Utilities industry (NAICS 22): estimated profit system equations

A. OLS regression estimates

$k_t = -0.056 + 1.021\ y_{t-1} -0.860\ r_{t-1} +0.510\ s_{t-1} + 0.766\ \dot{D}_{t-2}$ $R^2 = 0.99$ $DW = 2.90$
      (0.15)   (38.59)** (4.16)**   (1.36)   (1.85)$^+$

$y_t = -0.786 + 0.567\ r_{t-1} - 0.674\ s_{t-1} + k_t - 0.192\ F_t$ $R^2 = 0.97$ $DW = 1.83$
      (2.11)* (2.09)*   (1.10)   (0.45)

$r_t = -0.365 + y_t + 0.241\ s_{t-1} - k_t - 0.057\ F_{t-2}$ $R^2 = 0.72$ $DW = 2.03$
      (2.73)**   (0.92)   (0.20)

B. SUR regression estimates

$k_t = -0.021 + 1.014\ y_{t-1} -0.859\ r_{t-1} +0.504\ s_{t-1} + 0.778\ \dot{D}_{t-2}$ $R^2 = 0.99$ $DW = 2.89$
      (0.06)   (45.18)** (4.90)**   (1.58)   (2.22)*

$y_t = -0.817 + 0.494\ r_{t-1} - 0.460\ s_{t-1} + k_t - 0.679\ F_t$ $R^2 = 0.97$ $DW = 1.88$
      (2.77)**(2.37)*   (0.94)   (2.14)*

$r_t = -0.338 + y_t + 0.276\ s_{t-1} - k_t - 0.273\ F_{t-2}$ $R^2 = 0.71$ $DW = 1.97$
      (2.84)**   (1.17)   (1.21)

Notes: Figures in parentheses are *t*-values associated with estimated coefficients with superscripts **, *, and $^+$ denoting significance at the 1, 5, and 10 percent levels, respectively. The variables are defined as follows: k = log of capital stock, y = log of output, r = log of profit rate, s = log of profit margin, F = Federal funds rate (financial sector variable), and $\dot{D}$ = growth rate of nonfinancial debt outstanding (financial sector variable).

Table 5.5 Utilities industry (NAICS 22): projections of fundamental variables

	OLS					SUR				
Year	R %	S %	Z $billion	Y $billion	K $billion	R %	S %	Z $billion	Y $billion	K $billion
2008	10.9	61.7	186.2	301.8	1,702.5	11.0	61.6	187.3	304.0	1,698.2
2009	11.1	61.5	200.7	326.2	1,812.6	11.4	61.4	205.7	334.8	1,805.7
2010	11.2	61.5	211.7	344.0	1,898.0	11.6	61.6	218.9	355.3	1,893.2
2011	11.2	61.7	220.6	357.6	1,969.0	11.7	62.3	229.6	368.6	1,965.1

Notes: The variables are defined as follows: R = profit rate, S = profit margin, Z= total profit in the industry, Y = output in the industry, and K = capital stock in the industry.

coefficient for the growth rate of nonfinancial debt outstanding is statistically significant at the 10 percent level in the OLS regression and 5 percent level in the SUR regression. The estimated coefficient for lagged profit rate in the utilities output equation is significant at the 5 percent level in OLS and SUR regressions. The statistical insignificance of profit margin in the utilities output equation means that the expected capital stock and lagged profit rate contain most information for predicting the logarithm of output. No variables are significant in the profit rate equation, which may be attributable to industry regulation.

Projections of Fundamental Variables (Table 5.5). Profit rates and profit margins in the regulated utility industry are expected to remain around their corresponding levels in 2008 over the forecast horizon from 2009 to 2011. Total utilities industry profit is forecasted to increase to more than $220 billion by 2011 when the value added of utilities industry is anticipated to exceed more than $357 billion. Also, the capital stock in the utilities industry is expected to exceed $1,965 billion by 2011. These results suggest that the utilities industry is predicted to experience healthy growth and profit trends in the years ahead.

5.3.3 Construction Industry (NAICS 23)

Estimated Profit System Models (Table 5.6). The estimated coefficients for lags of output and profit rate in the capital stock equation in the construction industry are statistically significant at the 1 percent level in OLS and SUR regressions. In this equation the estimated coefficient for profit margin is statistically significant at the 10 percent level in the OLS regression and 5 percent level in the SUR regression. The estimated coefficient for the Federal funds rate is negative and statistically significant at the 5 percent level in the OLS regression and 1 percent level in the SUR. The estimated coefficients of lagged profit rate in the output equation are significant at the 1 percent level for both regression methods. In this equation the estimated coefficients for profit margin are significant at the 5 percent level in OLS and SUR regressions. In the profit rate equation the Federal funds rate has a

Table 5.6 Construction industry (NAICS 23): estimated profit system equations

A. OLS regression estimates

$k_t = 0.165 + 0.974\ y_{t-1} - 0.620\ r_{t-1} + 0.598\ s_{t-1} - 1.447\ F_{t-2}$ $R^2 = 0.99$ $DW = 2.36$

    (0.50)   (28.80)**   (2.87)**   (1.70)$^+$ (2.29)*

$y_t = -0.182 + 0.630\ r_{t-1} - 0.834\ s_{t-1} + k_t + 0.510\ \dot{D}_t$ $R^2 = 0.98$ $DW = 2.28$

    (0.54)   (2.94)**   (2.45)*   (0.69)

$r_t = -0.751 + y_t + 0.326\ s_{t-1} - k_t - 0.924\ F_{t-1}$ $R^2 = 0.64$ $DW = 1.28$

       (2.42)*   (1.23)   (1.61)

B. SUR regression estimates

$k_t = 0.238 + 0.964\ y_{t-1} - 0.746\ r_{t-1} + 0.714\ s_{t-1} - 1.364\ F_{t-2}$ $R^2 = 0.98$ $DW = 2.64$

    (0.85)   (35.42)**   (4.15)**   (2.46)*   (2.78)**

$y_t = -0.142 + 0.531\ r_{t-1} - 0.721\ s_{t-1} + k_t + 0.573\ \dot{D}_t$ $R^2 = 0.98$ $DW = 2.00$

    (0.49)   (3.01)**   (2.51)*   (1.00)

$r_t = -0.757 + y_t + 0.310\ s_{t-1} - k_t - 1.177\ F_{t-1}$ $R^2 = 0.63$ $DW = 1.27$

    (2.65)**   (1.27)   (2.41)*

Notes: Figures in parentheses are t-values associated with estimated coefficients with superscripts **, *, and $^+$ denoting significance at the 1, 5, and 10 percent levels, respectively. The variables are defined as follows: k = log of capital stock, y = log of output, r = log of profit rate, s = log of profit margin, F = Federal funds rate (financial sector variable), and $\dot{D}$ = growth rate of nonfinancial debt outstanding (financial sector variable).

negative impact on construction industry profit rate, and its estimated coefficient is statistically significant at the 5 percent level in the SUR.

Projections of Fundamental Variables (Table 5.7). Both OLS regression and SUR regression estimates of construction industry profit rates suggest increasing profit rates and profit margins from 2008 to 2011. Total construction profit is expected to increase to more than $252 billion by 2011 when the value added of construction industry is forecasted to exceed more than $785 billion. Also, construction industry capital stock is projected to exceed $641 billion by 2011. Of course, these

Table 5.7 Construction industry (NAICS 23): projections of fundamental variables

	OLS					SUR				
	R	S	Z	Y	K	R	S	Z	Y	K
Year	%	%	$billion	$billion	$billion	%	%	$billion	$billion	$billion
2008	35.8	29.0	191.1	658.8	533.2	36.4	29.1	195.7	672.5	538.3
2009	38.0	30.3	208.9	688.4	549.8	38.6	30.5	214.6	703.2	555.9
2010	39.7	31.9	229.9	721.2	579.5	40.6	32.4	237.3	733.2	584.5
2011	39.4	32.2	252.6	785.4	641.7	40.2	32.7	258.5	791.7	643.1

Notes: The variables are defined as follows: R = profit rate, S = profit margin, Z = total profit in the industry, Y = output in the industry, and K = capital stock in the industry.

trends have been severely disrupted by global economic and financial crises in 2008 and 2009. In view of recent events, we interpret this evidence to suggest that the construction industry will return to its long-run growth and profit paths as economic recovery and government infrastructure investment under the 2009 economic stimulus plan takes place in the future.

5.3.4 Manufacturing Industry (NAICS 31–33)

Estimated Profit System Models (Table 5.8). The estimated coefficients for lags of output, profit rate, and profit margin in the capital stock equation in the manufacturing industry are all significant at the 1 percent level in OLS and SUR regressions. The estimated coefficient of the growth rate of nonfinancial debt outstanding is statistically significant at the 10 percent level in the OLS regression and 5 percent level in the SUR regression. The estimated coefficients for lagged profit rate and profit margin in the manufacturing output equations are both significant at the 1 percent level in OLS and SUR regressions. The Federal funds rate has a negative but not significant impact on manufacturing output. The estimated coefficients for lagged profit margin in the profit rate equation are significant at the 1 percent level in OLS and SUR regressions. The estimated coefficients for the Federal funds rate in the

Table 5.8 Manufacturing industry (NAICS 31–33): estimated profit system equations

A. OLS regression estimates

$k_t = 0.282 + 0.984\ y_{t-1} -0.781\ r_{t-1} +0.855\ s_{t-1} + 0.332\ \dot{D}_{t-1}$ $R^2 = 0.99$ $DW = 1.45$
  (0.86) (26.07)**   (6.48)**   (4.46)**   (1.87)$^+$

$y_t = -0.116 + 0.984\ r_{t-1} -1.099\ s_{t-1} + k_t -0.386\ F_{t-1}$ $R^2 = 0.98$ $DW = 2.06$
  (1.05) (5.69)**   (5.43)**   (1.12)

$r_t = -0.273 + y_t + 0.694\ s_{t-1} - k_t - 1.015\ F_{t-2}$ $R^2 = 0.87$ $DW = 1.09$
  (2.42)*   (6.54)**   (3.47)**

B. SUR regression estimates

$k_t = 0.037 + 1.012\ y_{t-1} -0.729\ r_{t-1} +0.741\ s_{t-1} + 0.306\ \dot{D}_{t-1}$ $R^2 = 0.99$ $DW = 1.32$
  (0.14) (33.99)**   (7.77)**   (4.91)**   (2.21)*

$y_t = -0.136 + 0.956\ r_{t-1} -1.080\ s_{t-1} + k_t -0.364\ F_{t-1}$ $R^2 = 0.98$ $DW = 2.01$
  (1.45) (6.80)**   (6.47)**   (1.27)

$r_t = -0.285 + y_t + 0.695\ s_{t-1} - k_t - 0.766\ F_{t-2}$ $R^2 = 0.87$ $DW = 1.08$
  (2.86)**   (7.47)**   (3.19)**

Notes: Figures in parentheses are t-values associated with estimated coefficients with superscripts **, *, and $^+$ denoting significance at the 1, 5, and 10 percent levels, respectively. The variables are defined as follows: k = log of capital stock, y = log of output, r = log of profit rate, s = log of profit margin, F = Federal funds rate (financial sector variable), and $\dot{D}$ = growth rate of nonfinancial debt outstanding (financial sector variable).

Table 5.9 Manufacturing industry (NAICS 31–33): projections of fundamental variables

	OLS					SUR				
Year	R %	S %	Z $billion	Y $billion	K $billion	R %	S %	Z $billion	Y $billion	K $billion
2008	23.8	35.8	591.3	1,650.9	2,482.9	23.8	35.8	591.3	1,649.8	2,479.3
2009	23.3	35.3	592.0	1,674.7	2,536.2	23.4	35.4	593.0	1,676.0	2,533.7
2010	23.7	35.5	608.1	1,713.0	2,570.7	23.7	35.4	608.7	1,718.5	2,573.4
2011	24.8	37.0	644.5	1,743.2	2,601.7	24.5	36.5	640.3	1,755.5	2,612.9

Notes: The variables are defined as follows: R = profit rate, S = profit margin, Z = total profit in the industry, Y = output in the industry, and K = capital stock in the industry.

manufacturing profit rate equations are negative and statistically significant at the 1 percent level in OLS and SUR regressions.

Projections of Fundamental Variables (Table 5.9). Since World War II, the US manufacturing industry has been declining in terms of its share of the nation's GDP. The value added by the manufacturing industry as a percentage of US GDP declined from 21.3 percent in 1978 to 11.7 percent in 2007. Manufacturing profit rates and profit margins are expected to slightly increase from their corresponding levels in 2008 over the forecast horizon to 2011. Total manufacturing profit is projected to increase from $591.3 billion in 2008 to more than $640 billion in 2011. This growth is mainly due to inflation in these years. Manufacturing gross value added is forecast to increase from about $1,650 billion in 2008 to more than $1,743 billion in 2011. And, manufacturing capital stock is expected to increase from a range of $2,479.3–$2,482.9 billion in 2008 to more than $2,601 billion in 2011. As in the case of the construction industry, the 2008 and 2009 economic and financial crises have severely disrupted these moderate long-run trends. However, as economic recovery occurs, the results suggest that the manufacturing industry will return to at least modest growth and profit trends.

5.3.5 Wholesale Trade Industry (NAICS 42)

Estimated Profit System Models (Table 5.10). In the capital stock equation for the wholesale trade industry, the estimated coefficients for lags of output and profit rate are statistically significant at the 1 percent level in OLS regression and SUR regression estimates, and the estimated coefficient for profit margin is significant at the 1 percent level in SUR. The estimated coefficients of the growth rate of nonfinancial debt outstanding are statistically significant at the 1 percent significance level using both methods. The estimated coefficients for lagged profit rate and profit margin in the wholesale trade output equation are significant at the 1 percent level in OLS and SUR regressions. The estimated coefficients for the Federal funds rate in the wholesale output equation are negative and statistically significant at the 10 percent level in the OLS regression and 1 percent level in the SUR regression. The estimated coefficients for profit margin in the profit rate equation are statistically

Table 5.10 Wholesale trade industry (NAICS 42): estimated profit system equations

A. OLS regression estimates

$k_t = -0.105 + 0.973\ y_{t-1} - 0.437\ r_{t-1} + 0.359\ s_{t-1} + 1.216\ \dot{D}_{t-2}$ $R^2 = 0.99$ $DW = 2.22$

    (0.42) $(40.01)^{**}$ $(2.79)^{**}$ (1.62) $(3.46)^{**}$

$y_t = 0.019 + 0.681\ r_{t-1} - 0.736\ s_{t-1} + k_t - 0.579\ F_{t-1}$ $R^2 = 0.99$ $DW = 2.10$

    (0.09) $(4.37)^{**}$ $(2.96)^{**}$ $(1.85)^{+}$

$r_t = -0.565 + y_t + 0.576\ s_{t-1} - k_t - 1.027\ F_{t-1}$ $R^2 = 0.83$ $DW = 2.12$

    $(2.52)^{*}$ $(3.68)^{**}$ $(2.41)^{*}$

B. SUR regression estimates

$k_t = 0.156 + 0.948\ y_{t-1} - 0.449\ r_{t-1} + 0.440\ s_{t-1} + 1.186\ \dot{D}_{t-2}$ $R^2 = 0.99$ $DW = 2.16$

    (0.87) $(54.47)^{**}$ $(4.00)^{**}$ $(2.71)^{**}$ $(4.93)^{**}$

$y_t = 0.007 + 0.674\ r_{t-1} - 0.744\ s_{t-1} + k_t - 0.744\ F_{t-1}$ $R^2 = 0.99$ $DW = 1.99$

    (0.04) $(5.04)^{**}$ $(3.43)^{**}$ $(2.80)^{**}$

$r_t = -0.533 + y_t + 0.608\ s_{t-1} - k_t - 0.735\ F_{t-1}$ $R^2 = 0.83$ $DW = 2.07$

    $(2.60)^{**}$ $(4.27)^{**}$ $(2.02)^{*}$

Notes: Figures in parentheses are *t*-values associated with estimated coefficients with superscripts **, *, and + denoting significance at the 1, 5, and 10 percent levels, respectively. The variables are defined as follows: k = log of capital stock, y = log of output, r = log of profit rate, s = log of profit margin, F = Federal funds rate (financial sector variable), and $\dot{D}$ = growth rate of nonfinancial debt outstanding (financial sector variable).

significant at the 1 percent level in OLS and SUR regressions. Also, the estimated coefficients for the Federal funds rate in the profit rate equation are negative and statistically significant at the 5 percent level in OLS and SUR regressions.

Projections of Fundamental Variables (Table 5.11). Wholesale trade industry profit rates are expected to increase from 28.6 percent in 2008 to a range of 32.1–32.3 percent in 2011. Wholesale trade profit margins are projected to increase from

Table 5.11 Wholesale trade industry (NAICS 42): projections of fundamental variables

	OLS					SUR				
Year	R %	S %	Z $billion	Y $billion	K $billion	R %	S %	Z $billion	Y $billion	K $billion
2008	28.6	23.5	199.7	848.3	698.5	28.6	23.6	198.2	840.6	692.6
2009	29.2	23.7	212.9	899.1	729.9	29.2	23.6	208.8	883.1	716.2
2010	31.4	24.7	232.6	942.6	742.0	31.2	24.3	224.8	923.7	721.1
2011	32.3	25.1	242.4	966.8	750.2	32.1	24.6	233.3	947.5	726.5

Notes: The variables are defined as follows: R = profit rate, S = profit margin, Z = total profit in the industry, Y = output in the industry, and K = capital stock in the industry.

23.5–23.6 percent in 2008 to 24.6–25.1 percent in 2011. Total profit in the wholesale trade industry is forecasted to increase from \$198.2–\$199.7 billion in 2008 to \$233.3–\$242.4 billion in 2011. The gross value added of the wholesale trade industry is expected to increase from a range of \$840.6–\$848.3 billion in 2008 to \$947.5–\$966.8 billion in 2011. Also, capital stock is anticipated to increase from a range of \$692.6–\$698.5 billion in 2008 to \$726.5–\$750.2 billion in 2011. These trends indicate good growth and profit prospects in this industry, which have been recently disrupted by global economic and financial crises in 2008 and 2009.

5.3.6 Retail Trade Industry (NAICS 44–45)

Estimated Profit System Models (Table 5.12). In the capital stock equation for the retail trade industry, the estimated coefficients for lags of output, profit rate, and profit margin are significant at the 1 percent level in OLS and SUR regressions. The growth rate of nonfinancial debt has a positive impact on the capital stock equation and is significant at the 10 percent level in the OLS regression. The estimated coefficients for profit rate and profit margin in the retail trade output equation are statistically significant at the 1 percent level in OLS and SUR regressions. The Federal

Table 5.12 Retail trade industry (NAICS 44–45): estimated profit system equations

---

A. OLS regression estimates

$$k_t = -0.118 + 1.042\ y_{t-1} - 0.729\ r_{t-1} + 0.752\ s_{t-1} + 0.720\ \dot{D}_{t-2} \qquad R^2 = 0.99 \qquad DW = 2.60$$
$$\quad\ (0.53)\quad (35.00)^{**}\quad (3.99)^{**}\quad (3.49)^{**}\quad (1.68)^+$$

$$y_t = 0.006 + 0.873\ r_t - 0.830\ s_{t-1} + k_t - 0.057\ F_t \qquad\qquad R^2 = 0.98 \qquad DW = 2.48$$
$$\quad\ (0.02)\quad (4.59)^{**}\quad (3.39)^{**}\qquad\ (0.13)$$

$$r_t = -0.515 + y_t + 0.646\ s_{t-1} - k_t - 0.399\ F_t \qquad\qquad R^2 = 0.65 \qquad DW = 1.76$$
$$\quad\ (1.62)\qquad\quad (3.19)^{**}\qquad (0.81)$$

B. SUR regression estimates

$$k_t = -0.004 + 1.020\ y_{t-1} - 0.780\ r_{t-1} + 0.779\ s_{t-1} + 0.319\ \dot{D}_{t-2} \qquad R^2 = 0.99 \qquad DW = 2.64$$
$$\quad\ (0.02)\quad (49.74)^{**}\quad (5.58)^{**}\quad (4.45)^{**}\quad (1.03)$$

$$y_t = 0.075 + 0.949\ r_{t-1} - 0.888\ s_{t-1} + k_t - 0.302\ F_t \qquad\qquad R^2 = 0.98 \qquad DW = 2.69$$
$$\quad\ (0.32)\quad (6.33)^{**}\quad (4.32)^{**}\qquad\ (0.88)$$

$$r_t = -0.511 + y_t + 0.648\ s_{t-1} - k_t - 0.422\ F_t \qquad\qquad R^2 = 0.65 \qquad DW = 1.76$$
$$\quad\ (1.74)^+\qquad\ (3.47)^{**}\qquad (0.93)$$

Notes: Figures in parentheses are *t*-values associated with estimated coefficients with superscripts **, and + denoting significance at the 1, and 10 percent levels, respectively. The variables are defined as follows: k = log of capital stock, y = log of output, r = log of profit rate, s = log of profit margin, F = Federal funds rate (financial sector variable), and $\dot{D}$ = growth rate of nonfinancial debt outstanding (financial sector variable).

Table 5.13   Retail trade industry (NAICS 44–45): projections of fundamental variables

	OLS					SUR				
Year	R %	S %	Z $billion	Y $billion	K $billion	R %	S %	Z $billion	Y $billion	K $billion
2008	13.1	22.4	213.2	951.3	1,626.7	13.0	22.4	209.1	932.7	1,608.1
2009	13.4	22.7	230.8	1,017.5	1,723.6	13.3	22.7	223.8	985.5	1,680.1
2010	13.6	22.8	244.3	1,071.8	1,800.4	13.5	22.8	236.0	1,033.5	1,746.0
2011	13.7	22.8	255.2	1,120.3	1,869.0	13.6	22.8	246.1	1,078.6	1,811.3

Notes: The variables are defined as follows: R = profit rate, S = profit margin, Z = total profit in the industry, Y = output in the industry, and K = capital stock in the industry.

funds rate has a negative effect on retail trade output in OLS and SUR regressions but is not statistically significant. The estimated coefficients for profit margin in the profit rate equation are statistically significant at the 1 percent level in OLS and SUR regressions, while the estimated coefficients for the Federal funds rate are negative but not significant.

Projections of Fundamental Variables (Table 5.13). Retail trade industry profit rates and profit margins are expected to rise only modestly from 2008 to 2011. Total profit in the retail trade industry is forecasted to increase from a range of $209.1–$213.2 billion in 2008 to $246.1–$255.2 billion in 2011. The gross value added of the retail trade industry is projected to increase from a range of $932.7–$951.3 billion in 2008 to $1,078.6–$1,120.3 billion in 2011. Total capital stock is expected to increase from $1,608.1–$1,626.7 billion in 2008 to $1,811.3–$1,869.0 billion in 2011. Again, the recent economic downturn in 2008 and 2009 changes these projections; nonetheless, as economic recovery takes hold, the retail trade industry should return to these long-run trends.

5.3.7 Transportation and Warehousing Industry (NAICS 48–49)

Estimated Profit System Models (Table 5.14). The estimated coefficients for lags of output, profit rate, and profit margin in the capital stock equation for the transportation and warehousing industry are all significant at the 1 percent level in OLS and SUR regressions. The estimated coefficient for the growth rate of nonfinancial debt outstanding is positive and statistically significant at the 5 percent level in the OLS regression and 10 percent in the SUR regression. The estimated coefficients for lagged profit rate and profit margin in the output equation are statistically significant at the 1 percent level in OLS and SUR regressions. The estimated coefficients for the Federal funds rate in the output equation are negative and statistically significant at the 1 percent level in OLS and SUR regressions. And, the estimated coefficients for profit margin and the Federal fund rate in the profit rate equation are statistically significant at the 1 percent level in OLS and SUR regressions.

Table 5.14 Transportation and warehousing industry (NAICS 48–49): estimated profit system equations

---

A. *OLS regression estimates*

$k_t = 1.156 + 0.883\, y_{t-1} - 0.578\, r_{t-1} + 0.611\, s_{t-1} + 0.490\, \dot{D}_t$ $\qquad R^2 = 0.99 \qquad DW = 2.09$

$\quad$ (3.42)** (22.00)** (4.39)** $\quad$ (3.77)** $\qquad$ (2.26)*

$y_t = -0.062 + 0.740\, r_{t-1} - 0.598\, s_{t-1} + k_t - 0.838\, F_{t-1}$ $\qquad R^2 = 0.99 \qquad DW = 1.92$

$\quad$ (0.57) (9.47)** (4.08)** $\qquad$ (3.05)**

$r_t = -0.292 + y_t + 0.698\, s_{t-1} - k_t - 1.158\, F_{t-1}$ $\qquad R^2 = 0.91 \qquad DW = 1.92$

$\quad$ (1.64) $\qquad$ (4.67)** $\qquad$ (3.18)**

B. *SUR regression estimates*

$k_t = 0.947 + 0.910\, y_{t-1} - 0.658\, r_{t-1} + 0.706\, s_{t-1} + 0.324\, \dot{D}_t$ $\qquad R^2 = 0.99 \qquad DW = 2.24$

$\quad$ (3.48)** (28.29)** (6.20)** $\quad$ (5.35)** $\qquad$ (1.86)+

$y_t = -0.068 + 0.726\, r_{t-1} - 0.580\, s_{t-1} + k_t - 0.922\, F_{t-1}$ $\qquad R^2 = 0.99 \qquad DW = 1.87$

$\quad$ (0.70) (10.68)** (4.48)** $\qquad$ (4.03)**

$r_t = -0.292 + y_t + 0.699\, s_{t-1} - k_t - 1.141\, F_{t-1}$ $\qquad R^2 = 0.91 \qquad DW = 1.93$

$\quad$ (1.78)+ $\qquad$ (5.08)** $\qquad$ (3.41)**

Notes: Figures in parentheses are *t*-values associated with estimated coefficients with superscripts **, *, and + denoting significance at the 1, 5, and 10 percent levels, respectively. The variables are defined as follows: k = log of capital stock, y = log of output, r = log of profit rate, s = log of profit margin, F = Federal funds rate (financial sector variable), and $\dot{D}$ = growth rate of nonfinancial debt outstanding (financial sector variable).

Projections of Fundamental Variables (Table 5.15). Profit rates in this industry are expected to increase from 11.9 percent in 2008 to 13.6 percent in 2011. Profit margin is projected to increase from 32.7 percent in 2008 to 34.7 percent in 2011. Total profit is forecasted to increase from a range of $136.2–$137.1 billion in 2008 to $161.2–$167.9 billion in 2011. Gross value added is anticipated to increase from

Table 5.15 Transportation and warehousing industry (NAICS 48–49): projections of fundamental variables

	OLS					SUR				
Year	R %	S %	Z $billion	Y $billion	K $billion	R %	S %	Z $billion	Y $billion	K $billion
2008	11.9	32.7	136.2	416.5	1,140.2	11.9	32.7	137.1	419.4	1,149.4
2009	12.0	32.7	138.7	424.7	1,154.2	12.0	32.6	141.1	432.0	1,175.0
2010	13.0	34.1	151.2	443.9	1,163.3	13.0	34.0	155.8	457.9	1,197.0
2011	13.6	34.8	161.2	463.5	1,183.1	13.7	34.7	167.9	483.6	1,230.0

Notes: The variables are defined as follows: R = profit rate, S = profit margin, Z = total profit in the industry, Y = output in the industry, and K = capital stock in the industry.

$416.5–$419.4 billion in 2008 to $463.5–$483.6 billion in 2011. And, capital stock in this industry is expected to increase from $1,140.2–$1,149.4 billion in 2008 to $1,183.1–$1,230.0 billion in 2011. Like a number of other industries, these optimistic trends were disrupted by the 2008 and 2009 economic and financial crises. The strong growth projected in our results suggests that the transportation and warehousing industry will return to health as the economy recovers.

5.3.8 Information Industry (NAICS 51)

Estimated Profit System Models (Table 5.16). The information industry is comprised of Internet service providers, web search portals, publishing industries, broadcasting, and telecommunications. The estimated coefficients for lagged output in the capital stock equation for this industry are significant at the 1 percent level in OLS and SUR regressions. The estimated coefficients for lagged profit rate and profit margin in the capital stock equation are statistically significant at the 5 percent level in the OLS regression and 1 percent level in the SUR regression. The estimated coefficients for the growth rate of nonfinancial debt outstanding in the capital stock equation are statistically significant at the 1 percent level in OLS and SUR regressions. The estimated coefficients for the profit rate and profit margin in the output equation are significant at the 1 percent for the two regression methods. The Federal

Table 5.16 Information industry (NAICS 51): estimated profit system equations

A. OLS regression estimates

$k_t = 1.201 + 0.879\, y_{t-1} - 0.314\, r_{t-1} + 0.327\, s_{t-1} + 1.077\, \dot{D}_{t-2}$ $R^2 = 0.99$ $DW = 1.27$
   (5.13)** (34.99)** (2.40)*   (2.29)*   (4.01)**

$y_t = -0.463 + 0.524\, r_{t-1} - 0.756\, s_{t-1} + k_t - 1.247\, F_{t-1}$ $R^2 = 0.99$ $DW = 1.72$
   (2.76)**(3.32)**   (4.78)**   (2.51)*

$r_t = -0.159 + y_t + 0.738\, s_{t-1} - k_t - 0.800\, F_t$ $R^2 = 0.74$ $DW = 1.87$
   (1.26)   (4.67)**   (1.74)⁺

B. SUR regression estimates

$k_t = 1.145 + 0.884\, y_{t-1} - 0.345\, r_{t-1} + 0.354\, s_{t-1} + 1.115\, \dot{D}_{t-2}$ $R^2 = 0.99$ $DW = 1.21$
   (5.76)** (41.45)** (3.11)**   (2.92)**   (4.89)**

$y_t = -0.448 + 0.543\, r_{t-1} - 0.774\, s_{t-1} + k_t - 1.251\, F_{t-1}$ $R^2 = 0.99$ $DW = 1.75$
   (3.00)**(3.88)**   (5.49)**   (2.84)**

$r_t = -0.163 + y_t + 0.739\, s_t - k_t - 0.712\, F_t$ $R^2 = 0.74$ $DW = 1.87$
   (1.40)   (5.07)**   (1.68)⁺

Notes: Figures in parentheses are *t*-values associated with estimated coefficients with superscripts **, *, and ⁺ denoting significance at the 1, 5, and 10 percent levels, respectively. The variables are defined as follows: k = log of capital stock, y = log of output, r = log of profit rate, s = log of profit margin, F = Federal funds rate (financial sector variable), and $\dot{D}$ = growth rate of nonfinancial debt outstanding (financial sector variable).

Table 5.17 Information industry (NAICS 51): projections of fundamental variables

	OLS					SUR				
Year	R %	S %	Z $billion	Y $billion	K $billion	R %	S %	Z $billion	Y $billion	K $billion
2008	23.0	48.7	285.9	587.0	1,244.4	23.0	48.7	286.5	588.9	1,248.4
2009	23.9	50.0	297.4	594.5	1,245.2	23.8	49.8	297.7	598.2	1,253.0
2010	25.4	50.7	308.8	609.1	1,217.9	25.2	50.3	309.3	614.7	1,227.1
2011	25.7	50.8	310.1	610.5	1,206.8	25.6	50.4	311.0	617.4	1,215.8

Notes: The variables are defined as follows: R = profit rate, S = profit margin, Z = total profit in the industry, Y = output in the industry, and K = capital stock in the industry.

funds rate has a negative impact on the information industry output, and its estimated coefficient is statistically significant at the 5 percent level in the OLS regression and 1 percent level in the SUR regression. The estimated coefficients for the profit margin in the profit rate equation are statistically significant at the 1 percent level in OLS and SUR regressions. Lastly, the estimated coefficients for the Federal funds rate in the profit rate equation are negative and statistically significant at the 10 percent level in OLS and SUR regressions.

Projections of Fundamental Variables (Table 5.17). The information industry contracted in the aftermath of the dotcom meltdown in 2000. However, profit rates in this industry are expected to improve from 23 percent in 2008 to 25.6–25.7 percent in 2011. Profit margins are projected to increase from about 48.7 percent in 2008 to 50.4–50.8 percent in 2011. Total profit for the industry is expected to increase from about $285.9–$286.5 billion in 2008 to more than $310 billion in 2011. Gross value added is projected to increase from about $587 billion in 2008 to $610.5–$617.4 billion in 2011. Unlike the other trends, total capital stock is expected to decrease from a range of $1,244.4–$1,248.4 billion in 2008 to $1,206.8–$1,215.8 billion in 2011. These results suggest some industry shrinkage due to overinvestment; however, profits and sales should continue to trend upward at a modest pace after recent economic troubles subside.

5.3.9 Finance and Insurance Industry (NAICS 52)

Estimated Profit System Models (Table 5.18). The finance and insurance industry experienced unprecedented post-Great Recession era turmoil in 2008 and 2009. Numerous large institutions either failed or were bailed out by the government, and many other distressed institutions were merged out with healthy organizations. Our results for this industry are based on data series ending in 2007 before this upheaval took place. As such, some degree of caution is warranted in the interpretation of our findings. The estimated coefficients for the lags of output, profit rate, and profit margin, as well as for the growth rate of nonfinancial debt in the capital stock equation

Table 5.18   Finance and insurance industry (NAICS 52): estimated profit system equations

A. OLS regression estimates

$k_t = 0.443 + 0.965\ y_{t-1} - 0.672\ r_{t-1} + 0.797\ s_{t-1} + 1.802\ \dot{D}_{t-1}$ $R^2 = 0.99$ $DW = 2.08$

(1.58)   (44.73)**   (5.05)**   (3.03)**   (3.12)**

$y_t = 0.204 + 0.580\ r_{t-1} - 0.119\ s_{t-1} + k_t$ $R^2 = 0.99$ $DW = 1.38$

(1.34)   (3.17)**   (0.34)

$r_t = -0.321 + y_t + 0.640\ s_{t-1} - k_t$ $R^2 = 0.89$ $DW = 1.93$

(2.52)*   (4.54)**

B. SUR regression estimates

$k_t = 0.417 + 0.963\ y_{t-1} - 0.635\ r_{t-1} + 0.670\ s_{t-1} + 1.448\ \dot{D}_{t-1}$ $R^2 = 0.99$ $DW = 1.85$

(2.46)*   (80.52)**   (5.94)**   (3.22)**   (4.53)**

$y_t = 0.197 + 0.647\ r_{t-1} - 0.230\ s_{t-1} + k_t$ $R^2 = 0.99$ $DW = 1.46$

(1.41)   (4.20)**   (0.77)

$r_t = -0.321 + y_t + 0.640\ s_{t-1} - k_t$ $R^2 = 0.89$ $DW = 1.93$

(2.65)**   (4.79)**

Notes: Figures in parentheses are t-values associated with estimated coefficients with superscripts **, *, and $^+$ denoting significance at the 1 and 5, percent levels, respectively. The variables are defined as follows: k = log of capital stock, y = log of output, r = log of profit rate, s = log of profit margin, and $\dot{D}$ = growth rate of nonfinancial debt outstanding (financial sector variable).

for the finance and insurance industry, are significant at the 1 percent level in OLS and SUR regressions. The estimated coefficients for the profit rate in the output equation are statistically significant at the 1 percent level in OLS and SUR regressions. The estimated coefficients for profit margin in the profit rate equation are significant at the 1 percent level using the two regression methods. The estimated coefficients for the Federal funds rate in the output and profit rate equations are not statistically significant and so are dropped from output and profit rate equations. This latter result suggests that the volume of credit activity (as represented by the growth rate of nonfinancial debt outstanding) is more important than the cost of credit in the financial services industry.

Projections of Fundamental Variables (Table 5.19). Little change is expected in profit rates and profit margins of this industry over the forecast horizon. Total profits of the finance and insurance industry are expected to increase somewhat from a range of \$458.2–\$464.8 billion in 2008 to \$473.9–\$478.1 billion in 2011. Gross value added is projected to increase somewhat also from a range of \$1,152.3–\$1,168.9 billion in 2008 to \$1,178.0–\$1,196.7 billion in 2010 and then fall to \$1,166.6–\$1,177.0 billion in 2011. And, total capital stock is forecasted to decrease from \$2,069.9–\$2,088.2 billion in 2008 to \$1,993.5–\$1,994.7 billion in 2011. Hence, the profit system model could discern at year-end 2007 that the finance and insurance industry was going to contract in the years ahead, albeit modestly. In this

Table 5.19 Finance and insurance industry (NAICS 52): projections of fundamental variables

	OLS					SUR				
Year	R %	S %	Z $billion	Y $billion	K $billion	R %	S %	Z $billion	Y $billion	K $billion
2008	22.3	39.8	464.8	1,168.9	2,088.2	22.1	39.8	458.2	1,152.3	2,069.9
2009	23.0	40.2	480.9	1,196.8	2,091.7	22.8	40.2	472.2	1,175.3	2,070.8
2010	23.6	40.4	484.0	1,196.7	2,055.1	23.3	40.4	476.5	1,178.0	2,040.7
2011	24.0	40.6	478.1	1,177.0	1,994.7	23.8	40.6	473.9	1,166.6	1,993.5

Notes: The variables are defined as follows: R = profit rate, S = profit margin, Z = total profit in the industry, Y = output in the industry, and K = capital stock in the industry.

regard, the collapse of numerous major banks and other financial institutions in 2008 and 2009 was not forecast, but these unprecedented events were unforeseen by most experts at that time. We interpret the results for this industry to suggest that the massive contraction in profits and sales of the financial services industry in recent years is transitory in nature and a moderate rebound is likely in the years ahead.

5.3.10 Professional and Business Services Industry (NAICS 54–56)

Estimated Profit System Models (Table 5.20). This industry is comprised of professional, scientific, and technical services (NAICS 54) plus management of companies and enterprises (NAICS 55) plus administrative and support and waste management and remediation services (NAICS 56). The estimated coefficients for lags of output, profit rate, and profit margin, as well as the growth rate of nonfinancial debt outstanding, in the capital stock equation in this industry are all significant at the 1 percent level in OLS and SUR regressions. The estimated coefficients for profit rate and profit margin are statistically significant at the 1 percent level in the output equation using both methods. The estimated coefficients for profit margin in the profit rate equation are statistically significant at the 1 percent level in OLS and SUR regressions. Since the estimated coefficients for the Federal funds rate in the output and profit rate equations are not statistically significant, this variable is dropped from output and profit rate equations. The significance of the growth rate of nonfinancial debt outstanding and insignificance of the Federal funds rate in the estimated models suggest that credit availability (rather than cost) is the main financial variable affecting this industry.

Projections of Fundamental Variables (Table 5.21). Little change in profit rates and profit margins is expected over the forecast horizon. Total profits, gross value added, and the stock of capital in this industry are projected to increase from 2008 to 2009 and then fall below their 2008 levels in 2011. Hence, this industry appears to be in a steady state with little or no growth expected in the near future.

Table 5.20 Professional and business service industry (NAICS 54–56): estimated profit system equations

---

A. *OLS regression estimates*

$k_t = 0.110 + 0.968\ y_{t-1} - 0.468\ r_{t-1} + 0.563\ s_{t-1} + 1.601\ \dot{D}_t$ $R^2 = 0.99$ $DW = 1.90$

    (1.99)* (74.93)** (2.60)**   (3.82)**   (3.90)**

$y_t = 0.226 + 0.848\ r_{t-1} - 0.713\ s_{t-1} + k_t$ $R^2 = 0.99$ $DW = 2.15$

    (3.41)** (7.77)**   (7.69)**

$r_t = -0.179 + y_t + 0.860\ s_{t-1} - k_t$ $R^2 = 0.66$ $DW = 1.26$

    (1.27)   (7.74)**

B. *SUR regression estimates*

$k_t = 0.105 + 0.970\ y_{t-1} - 0.517\ r_{t-1} + 0.604\ s_{t-1} + 1.543\ \dot{D}_t$ $R^2 = 0.99$ $DW = 1.81$

    (2.21)* (91.82)** (3.48)**   (4.95)**   (4.60)**

$y_t = 0.224 + 0.781\ r_{t-1} - 0.666\ s_{t-1} + k_t$ $R^2 = 0.99$ $DW = 1.97$

    (3.66)**(8.02)**   (7.97)**

$r_t = -0.179 + y_t + 0.860\ s_{t-1} - k_t$ $R^2 = 0.66$ $DW = 1.26$

    (1.34)   (8.16)**

Notes: Figures in parentheses are t-values associated with estimated coefficients with superscripts **, and *, denoting significance at the 1, and 5 percent levels, respectively. The variables are defined as follows: k = log of capital stock, y = log of output, r = log of profit rate, s = log of profit margin, and $\dot{D}$ = growth rate of nonfinancial debt outstanding (financial sector variable).

Table 5.21 Professional and business services industry (NAICS 54–56): projections of fundamental variables

	OLS					SUR				
Year	R %	S %	Z $billion	Y $billion	K $billion	R %	S %	Z $billion	Y $billion	K $billion
2008	39.2	28.0	488.8	1,747.2	1,246.1	39.2	28.0	490.3	1,752.5	1,249.3
2009	39.3	27.9	491.2	1,759.8	1,250.3	39.3	27.9	494.5	1,771.4	1,257.7
2010	39.3	27.9	486.0	1,744.3	1,235.6	39.4	27.9	491.0	1,762.4	1,247.7
2011	39.4	27.8	477.3	1,716.2	1,213.0	39.4	27.8	484.0	1,740.3	1,229.5

Notes: The variables are defined as follows: R = profit rate, S = profit margin, Z = total profit in the industry, Y = output in the industry, and K = capital stock in the industry.

5.3.11 Education and Health Services Industry (NAICS 61–62)

Estimated Profit System Models (Table 5.22). This industry is comprised of educational services (NAICS 61) plus health care and social assistance (NAICS 62). The estimated coefficients for lags of output, profit rate, and profit margin, as well as the

Table 5.22 Education and health services industry (NAICS 61–62): estimated profit system equations

---

A. OLS regression estimates

$k_t = 0.026 + 0.997\ y_{t-1} -0.916\ r_{t-1} +0.897\ s_{t-1} + 0.746\ \dot{D}_t$ $R^2 = 0.99$ $DW = 1.65$

  (0.46)   (81.84)** (12.17)**   (8.46)**   (3.09)**

$y_t = 0.191 + 0.823\ r_{t-1} - 0.671\ s_{t-1} + k_t$ $R^2 = 0.99$ $DW = 0.69$

  (1.60)   (7.42)**   (4.81)**

$r_t = -0.240 + y_t + 0.856\ s_{t-1} - k_t$ $R^2 = 0.89$ $DW = 1.91$

  (1.51)   (8.72)**

B. SUR regression estimates

$k_t = 0.017 + 0.998\ y_{t-1} -0.945\ r_{t-1} +0.920\ s_{t-1} + 0.568\ \dot{D}_t$ $R^2 = 0.99$ $DW = 1.49$

  (0.35)   (107.74)** (15.86)**   (10.99)**   (3.10)**

$y_t = 0.198 + 0.856\ r_{t-1} - 0.707\ s_{t-1} + k_t$ $R^2 = 0.99$ $DW = 0.69$

  (1.80)$^+$ (9.47)**   (6.00)**

$r_t = -0.240 + y_t + 0.856\ s_{t-1} - k_t$ $R^2 = 0.89$ $DW = 1.91$

  (1.59)   (9.19)**

Notes: Figures in parentheses are t-values associated with estimated coefficients with superscripts **, and + denoting significance at the 1, and 10, percent levels, respectively. The variables are defined as follows: k = log of capital stock, y = log of output, r = log of profit rate, s = log of profit margin, and $\dot{D}$ = growth rate of nonfinancial debt outstanding (financial sector variable).

growth rate of nonfinancial debt outstanding, in the capital stock equation are significant at the 1 percent level in OLS and SUR regressions. The estimated coefficients for profit rate and profit margin in the output equation are statistically significant at the 1 percent level in OLS and SUR regressions. The estimated coefficients for profit margin in the profit rate equation are significant at the 1 percent level in OLS and SUR regressions. Since the estimated coefficients for the Federal funds rate in the output and profit rate equations are not statistically significant, this variable is dropped from output and profit rate equations. In this regard, the significance of the growth rate of nonfinancial debt outstanding and insignificance of the Federal funds rate in the estimated models imply that credit availability (rather than cost) is the main financial variable affecting this industry.

Projections of Fundamental Variables (Table 5.23). Profit rates and profit margins are expected to remain around their 2008 levels in 2011. However, total profits are forecasted to increase from about $215 billion in 2008 to a range of $242.6–$247.9 billion in 2011. Gross value added is projected to increase from a range of $1,153.1–$1,155.2 billion in 2008 to $1,300.2–$1,328.2 billion in 2011. And, capital stocks are expected to increase from $1,699.7–$1,707.3 billion in 2008 to $1,891.3–$1,946.5 billion in 2011. These results indicate that the education and health industry is expected to enjoy steady growth and profits in the years ahead.

Table 5.23 Education and health service industry (NAICS 61–62): projections of fundamental variables

	OLS					SUR				
Year	R %	S %	Z $billion	Y $billion	K $billion	R %	S %	Z $billion	Y $billion	K $billion
2008	12.7	18.7	215.3	1,153.1	1,699.7	12.6	18.7	215.7	1,155.2	1,707.3
2009	12.7	18.7	225.6	1,208.7	1,772.2	12.7	18.7	227.1	1,216.7	1,792.3
2010	12.8	18.7	234.5	1,256.4	1,834.1	12.7	18.7	237.7	1,273.4	1,870.5
2011	12.8	18.7	242.6	1,300.2	1,891.3	12.7	18.7	247.9	1,328.2	1,946.5

Notes: The variables are defined as follows: R = profit rate, S = profit margin, Z = total profit in the industry, Y = output in the industry, and K = capital stock in the industry.

5.3.12 Leisure and Hospitality Services Industry (NAICS 71–72)

Estimated Profit System Models (Table 5.24). This industry is comprised of arts, entertainment, and recreation (NAICS 71) plus accommodation and food services (NAICS 72). The estimated coefficients for output in the capital stock equation are statistically significant at the 1 percent level in OLS and SUR regressions. In this equation the estimated coefficients for profit rate are statistically significant at the

Table 5.24 Leisure and hospitality industry (NAICS 71–72): estimated profit system equations

A. OLS regression estimates

$k_t = 0.825 + 0.977\, y_{t-1} - 0.320\, r_{t-1} + 0.471\, s_{t-1} + 1.193\, \dot{D}_{t-1}$ $R^2 = 0.99$ $DW = 1.61$
    (2.29)   (43.39)**   (1.78)$^+$ (1.57)   (3.16)**

$y_t = -0.694 + 0.330\, r_{t-1} - 0.488\, s_{t-1} + k_t - 0.436\, F_t$ $R^2 = 0.99$ $DW = 2.28$
    (2.87)**(1.68)$^+$ (1.57)   (1.36)

$r_t = -0.456 + y_t + 0.641\, s_{t-1} - k_t - 0.457\, F_t$ $R^2 = 0.76$ $DW = 1.90$
    (1.95)$^+$ (3.61)**   (1.44)

B. SUR regression estimates

$k_t = 1.023 + 0.961\, y_{t-1} - 0.451\, r_{t-1} + 0.739\, s_{t-1} + 0.846\, \dot{D}_{t-1}$ $R^2 = 0.99$ $DW = 2.08$
    (3.82)** (60.81)** (3.14)**   (3.09)**   (3.43)**

$y_t = -0.617 + 0.338\, r_{t-1} - 0.431\, s_{t-1} + k_t - 0.154\, F_t$ $R^2 = 0.99$ $DW = 2.32$
    (2.92)** (1.97)*   (1.57)   (0.63)

$r_t = -0.474 + y_t + 0.625\, s_{t-1} - k_t - 0.525\, F_t$ $R^2 = 0.76$ $DW = 1.87$
    (2.20)*   (3.82)**   (1.81)$^+$

Notes: Figures in parentheses are t-values associated with estimated coefficients with superscripts **, *, and $^+$ denoting significance at the 1, 5, and 10 percent levels, respectively. The variables are defined as follows: k = log of capital stock, y = log of output, r = log of profit rate, s = log of profit margin, F = Federal funds rate (financial sector variable), and $\dot{D}$ = growth rate of nonfinancial debt outstanding (financial sector variable).

10 percent level in the OLS regression and 1 percent significance level in the SUR regression. The estimated coefficients for profit margin in the capital stock equation are statistically significant at the 1 percent level in the SUR. The estimated coefficients for the growth rate of nonfinancial debt outstanding are positive and statistically significant at the 1 percent level in OLS and SUR regressions. The estimated coefficients for profit rate in the output equation are statistically significant at the 10 percent level in the OLS regression and the 5 percent level in the SUR regression. The estimated coefficients for profit margin in the profit rate equation are statistically significant at the 1 percent level in OLS and SUR regressions. The estimated coefficient for Federal funds rate in the profit rate equation is significant at the 10 percent significance level in the SUR. Like a number of other industries, the significance of the growth rate of nonfinancial debt outstanding and the much lower significance of the Federal funds rate in the estimated models for leisure and hospitality services suggest that credit availability (rather than cost) is the main financial variable affecting this industry.

Projections of Fundamental Variables (Table 5.25). Little change is expected in profit rates and profit margins in this industry over the forecast horizon. Total profits are expected to increase from about $148.6–$149.6 billion in 2008 to $166.0–$168.6 billion in 2011. Gross value added is projected to increase from $549.4–$553.2 billion in 2008 to $603.9–$615.7 billion in 2011. And, capital stock is projected to increase from $1,179.8–$1,187.3 billion in 2008 to $1,283.7–$1,295.8 billion in 2011. These trends predict steadily increasing profits and sales in the future.

Table 5.25 Leisure and hospitality industry (NAICS 71–72): projections of fundamental variables

	OLS					SUR				
Year	R %	S %	Z $billion	Y $billion	K $billion	R %	S %	Z $billion	Y $billion	K $billion
2008	12.6	27.0	149.6	553.2	1,187.3	12.6	27.0	148.6	549.4	1,179.8
2009	13.0	27.3	160.1	585.3	1,229.2	12.9	27.4	157.5	574.4	1,220.4
2010	13.1	27.4	166.2	605.6	1,269.2	13.0	27.5	163.1	592.2	1,256.8
2011	13.0	27.4	168.6	615.7	1,295.8	12.9	27.5	166.0	603.9	1,283.7

Notes: The variables are defined as follows: R = profit rate, S = profit margin, Z = total profit in the industry, Y = output in the industry, and K = capital stock in the industry.

5.4 Conclusion

Despite the small number of observations based on annual data series for the period 1987–2007, the results from the application of our profit system model to US industries are encouraging. A large proportion of the estimated coefficients for lags of output, profit rate, and profit margin in the capital stock, output, and profit rate equations for most industries were statistically significant at the 1 or 5 percent levels.

Also, the R^2 statistics of the estimated capital stock, output, and profit rate equations were quite high, with ranges of 0.97–0.99 for capital stock and output equations and 0.63–0.91 for profit rate equations. Re-estimating the model with two lags can increase the range of R^2 values and remedies the serial correlation problem in some equations, but due to the small number of observations, we reported the original results with the first lags of the logarithms of the fundamental variables.

Since the profit system models have strong goodness-of-fit to the actual data, we extended the analyses to forecasting industries' profit rates, profit margins, total profits, outputs, and capital stocks for the period 2008–2011 assuming that the US economy evolves as predicted by Scenario E discussed in Chapter 3. Of course, in late 2008 and 2009 a sharp and severe downturn in the economy took place, which our data in 2007 does not encompass and could not have predicted. Nonetheless, our analyses demonstrate how profit system models can be readily applied to forecast long-run trends in industry performance and activity measures. The significance of estimated coefficients for the growth rate of nonfinancial debt outstanding in most capital stock equations for industries implies that resolution of the current credit crunch is important to their future prosperity.

Chapter 6
A Profit System Model of Stock Market Valuation

As discussed in previous chapters, our profit system model provides estimates and forecasts of total profits for both individual firms and groups of firms. Here we consider its application to groups of firms with stock prices that are aggregated into a general stock market price index. First, we use our model to generate in-sample estimates and out-of-sample forecasts of the total profits of corporate firms in a stock market index. Second, since corporate firms' profits are available to shareholders, discounting these aggregate profits by an appropriate rate of return gives the present value of total profits. This present value represents an estimate of the intrinsic or underlying value of the stock market index. It is important to note that our stock market valuation model depends on profit system model estimates and forecasts of total profits. This approach is consistent with the long-standing and popular discounted cash flow(DCF) approach to stock market valuation.

For demonstration purposes we apply this standard DCF approach to two different stock market indices: the Standard and Poor's Industrial index (SPXI) and Center for Research in Security Prices (CRSP) index. The SPXI is comprised of industrial firms in the S&P 500 index of largest US firms. The CRSP index contains all firms trading their stock on the NYSE, AMEX, and NASDAQ exchanges. Our goal is to determine whether our profit system model can be utilized to specify a fundamental model of stock prices based on the focal variables of sales, profit, and capital stock. Upon estimating our fundamental stock valuation model, comparisons of the actual trajectories of the focal variables with their simulated trajectories generated from the estimated model are made. These comparisons provide useful information for potentially identifying when the actual stock market index may have been over- or undervalued. Also, out-of-sample projections of total profits can be discounted using proxies for the required rate of return on equity and growth rates of profits to yield estimates of potential future stock market values.

Section 6.1 applies the profit system model to the SPXI to develop a fundamental model of this stock market index. Section 6.2 applies the corporate sector profit system model in Chapter 4 to the CRSP index.

A. Anari, J.W. Kolari, *The Power of Profit*, DOI 10.1007/978-1-4419-0649-6_6,
© Springer Science+Business Media, LLC 2010

6.1 A Profit System Model of the Standard and Poor's Industrial Index

6.1.1 Stock Market Price Indexes

Stock market price indexes, such as Standard and Poor's 500 index (S&P 500), SPXI index, Dow Jones Industrial Average (DJIA), and many others, are used to measure and monitor the performance of the aggregate stock market. They are also used for (1) modeling stock prices of individual corporations or groups of stocks, (2) investment portfolio analysis, and (3) economic forecasting. Regarding individual firms' stock prices, the relationships between aggregate stock market returns and individual share returns are used in asset pricing models. Well-known models such as the Capital Asset Pricing Model (CAPM)[1] and Fama-French three-factor model[2] attempt to describe the return generating process for individual stocks or portfolios of stocks and their associated risk dimensions. With respect to economic forecasting, the S&P Composite index is included in the index of leading economic indicators by the Conference Board (a global organization with more than 2,000 member firms around the world). Due to these important uses of market stock price indexes, there has been extensive research[3] in financial economics on estimating models of stock market price indexes. These models relate aggregate stock price indexes to a wide variety of factors, including, for example, the valuation ratios of dividend/price, earnings/price, smoothed earnings/price, and book-equity/market-equity, in addition to interest rates, the level of consumption to wealth, high and low market risk stocks, and other macro-oriented variables. Unfortunately, there is tremendous controversy about the predictability of aggregate stock market returns using these different factors. Short-run predictability in terms of months is unimpressive. And, the long-run predictability over periods of 1 year or more of these variables is subject to question on statistical grounds.[4] A major limitation of these models is that, while they relate stock prices to earnings or dividends, they do not have a model of aggregate profits of the corporate sector to guide estimates of aggregate earnings and dividends.

Asset pricing models are based on the key assumption that there is a market rate of return derived from stock prices that reflects the intrinsic value of stock prices. Market stock prices or rates of return are used as an anchor for evaluating the risks associated with individual stock prices and rates of return. The search for the true, intrinsic, or fundamental value of stock prices is important because large stock price fluctuations and reversals in values of individual and aggregate market stock

---

[1] See Sharpe (1964).

[2] See Fama and French (1992, 1993, 1995).

[3] See Marsh and Merton (1987), Campbell and Shiller (1988a), Fama and French (1988), Lee (1996, 1998), Boudoukh et al. (2008), Campbell and Thompson (2008), Cochrane (2008), Welch and Goyal (2008), and many other studies referenced in these papers.

[4] See Boudoukh et al. (2008).

prices show that stock prices in any period might be grossly over- or undervalued. For instance, in the aftermath of a worldwide stock market crash that took place on Monday, October 19, 1987, known as Black Monday, the S&P 500 index lost 20.5 percent and the DJIA lost 22.6 percent of their values. As another example, in response to the bursting technology bubble, the NASDAQ index fell from almost 4,600 in early 2000 to less than 1,300 in late 2002 – a fall of over 70 percent! More recently, the S&P 500 index fell from around 1,250 in September 2008 to below 700 in March 2009. The DJIA fell from a peak of 14,164 on October 9, 2007, to less than 7,000 in March 2008, a drop of more than 50 percent! Fortunately, sharp market downturns have been reversed in subsequent months and years as stock prices returned to their long-run equilibrium path.

The difference between the market prices of stocks and their intrinsic values arises from two sources: (1) market psychology (e.g., crowd behavior) and (2) the lack of a satisfactory fundamental model of stock prices. According to modern finance theory, stock prices are assumed to be determined by fundamental factors such as expected future dividends.[5] An implication of the dividend discount model (DDM) is that stock market fluctuations are explained by fluctuations in dividends. Empirical volatility tests of DDM model with a constant discount rate showed that stock prices are too volatile to be explained by dividend volatility.[6] The failure of the DDM led to the development of several research efforts on the intrinsic values of stock prices. Numerous models of stock prices have been proposed attempting to explain stock values in terms of the fundamentals of expected future dividends, time-varying discount rates, expected future earnings, price/earning ratios, book values, expected future sales of underlying businesses, and accounting-based residual income methods.[7] Recent models incorporating market psychology have also been proposed.[8] Related to our profit system model in this chapter, McGratten and Prescott (2000) have proposed a model of stock prices linked to the macroeconomy. Similar in some ways to our approach, they utilized the Cobb–Douglas production function, allowed for time-varying profit margins and developed a growth model for the corporate sector. Their model estimated that the US stock market was fairly valued in 2000 before the tech bubble collapsed. However, the market declined about 40 percent from 2000 to 2003.

Here we apply the profit system model to the estimation of fundamental aggregate stock valuation. First, we estimate nominal profit per share for a group of

---

[5]See Williams (1938), Miller and Modigliani (1961), Gordon (1962), Campbell and Shiller (1988b), Brealey et al. (2008), and Jennegren (2008).

[6]See LeRoy and Porter (1981), Shiller (1981), Flavin (1983),Kleidon (1986a, b), Marsh and Merton (1986), West (1988), Campbell and Shiller (1987), Gilles and LeRoy (1991), Cochrane (1992), Fama and French (1993), and others.

[7]See Cutler et al. (1990), Delong et al.(1990), Daniel et al. (1998), Ohlson (1991, 1995), Feltham and Ohlson (1995), Pontiff and Schall (1998), Lee (1999), Lee et al. (1999), Francis et al. (2001), Ruback (2002), Dechow et al. (2001), and others.

[8]For example, Barberis et al. (1998) provide a model of overreaction by investors, while Odean (1998) presents a model of underreaction.

corporations. Profit is estimated in a system of dynamic equations representing our focal variables of sales, capital stock, profit rate, and profit margin, in addition to financial variables influencing these variables, including the Federal funds rate and the growth rate of debt outstanding. Second, we discount estimated nominal profits per share using a proxy for the required rate of return by shareholders minus the growth rate of profits per share in real terms. This widely accepted DCF approach is grounded in the simple logic that stock values represent the present value of future earnings available to shareholders. Interestingly, we know of no other studies that take this fundamental approach to stock valuation, due to the fact that no formal model of previous or future profits is specified in existing stock valuation models. This gap in the stock valuation literature is a major shortfall that the profit system model attempts to fill.

6.1.2 Data for Standard and Poor Industrial Index Firms

The 2008 edition of the *Analyst's Handbook* by S&P's offers annual data for the SPXI from 1967 to 2007 on sales per share, profit per share, and book value of equity per share, all in indexed dollar terms. These three fundamental variables are necessary for the empirical application of our profit system model. We use sales per share as a proxy for output per share, and book value of equity per share is a proxy for capital stock per share, as the *Analyst's Handbook* does not provide value added per share or physical capital stock per share. Table 6.1A in the Appendix provides the fundamental data for SPXI analyses.

To derive the time series of the fundamental values of the stock price index for SPXI, we divide profit per share by an appropriate discount factor to be discussed shortly.

6.1.3 A Profit System Model for Stock Market Index Valuation

Panel A of Table 6.1 presents a profit system model for a group of corporations, and panel B specifies an aggregate stock price index model based on profits. Using the available data on sales, profit, and book equity values for SPXI firms, we estimated different empirical representations of the profit system model discussed in Chapter 2. We found that the model presented in panel A is the most suitable for empirical application in terms of statistical significance of the estimated coefficients as well as out-of-sample forecast accuracy. This is the model presented in Table 2.2 (i.e., the alternative basic profit system model of the goods and services market with output and capital stock in current dollars). Equations (6.1.1), (6.1.2), (6.1.3), (6.1.4), and (6.1.5) are the same as equations (2.2.1), (2.2.2), (2.2.3), (2.2.4), and (2.2.5). The capital stock and output are in terms of their current (nominal) values. In this model the forecast of capital stock (k) from equation (6.1.1) is used in equation (6.1.2) to forecast output. And, the forecast of capital stock (k) from equation (6.1.1) and forecast of output (y) from equation (6.1.2) are used for forecasting profit

Table 6.1 Profit system model of Standard and Poor's industrial index firms and DCF stock valuation model

---

A. Profit system model based on goods and services market equations

Capital stock model

$$k_t = \alpha_0 + \alpha_1 y_{t-1} + \alpha_2 r_{t-1} + \alpha_3 s_{t-1} + \alpha_5 \dot{D}_{t-L} + \alpha_6 F_{t-L} \tag{6.1.1}$$

Output model

$$y_t = \beta_0 + \beta_2 r_{t-1} + \beta_3 s_{t-1} + k_t + \beta_5 \dot{D}_{t-L} + \beta_6 F_{t-L} \tag{6.1.2}$$

Profit rate model

$$r_t = \theta_0 + y_t + \theta_3 s_{t-1} - k_t + \theta_5 \dot{D}_{t-L} + \theta_6 F_{t-L} \tag{6.1.3}$$

Profit margin model

$$s_t = r_t + k_t - y_t \tag{6.1.4}$$

Total profit model

$$Z_t = Y_t \times S_t \tag{6.1.5}$$

B. DCF stock valuation model

$$V_t = \frac{Z_{t+1}}{\hat{R}_t - \dot{Z}} \tag{6.1.6}$$

$$\hat{R}_t = R_{ct} + \dot{P}_t + I_t \tag{6.1.7}$$

Bold numbered equations are empirically estimated (see Table 6.2) and other equations are derived from their forecasts. All equations are solved simultaneously and recursively in forecasting and simulation analyses (see Table 6.3 as well as Figs. 6.1 and 6.3).

Variables are defined as follows:

Panel A

$Y(y)$ = sales per share in current dollars to proxy output (log)
$K(k)$ = book value of equity per share to proxy capital stock (log)
$R(r)$ = after-tax profit rate (log)
$S(s)$ = after-tax profit margin (log)
Z = after-tax profit per share
F = Federal funds rate in percent
$\dot{D}$ = growth rate of total debt outstanding in the nonfinancial sector in nominal terms
L = 0, 1, 2 generic number of lags to be determined empirically,
where K_t = antilog k_t, Y_t = antilog y_t, R_t = antilog r_t, and S_t = antilog s_t

Panel B

V_t = stock price index in nominal terms at time t
Z_{t+1} = one-period-ahead after-tax profit per share estimated from the profit system model
$\hat{R}_t$ = required rate of return on equity in period t
$\dot{Z}$ = growth rate of after-tax profit per share in real terms (deflated by the *GDP* deflator)
R_{ct} = after-tax profit rate in period t from the corporate sector profit system model in Chapter 4
$\dot{P}_t$ = *GDP* inflation rate in period t from the macroeconomic profit system model in Chapter 3
I_t = average interest rate spread in period t between AAA and BAA rated corporate bonds.

---

rate in equation (6.1.3). Equation (6.1.4) uses the forecasts of capital stock (k), output (y), and profit rate (r) from equations (6.1.1), (6.1.2), and (6.1.3) to estimate the forecast of profit margin (s). These four equations generate forecasts of capital stock (k), output (y), profit rate (r), and profit margin (s) in log terms, and their antilogarithms give the levels of the variables. Equation (6.1.5) uses forecasts of output (Y) and profit margin (S) for forecasting profit (Z) in current (nominal) dollars.

Since the fundamental variables of sales, profit, and capital stock in the model are on a per share basis, the profit per share estimated from equation (6.1.5) is estimated on a per share basis also. When one-period-ahead profit is discounted in equation (6.1.6), the fundamental value of the S&P Industrial price index can be estimated. Equation (6.1.6) is a DCF valuation model, where $\hat{R}$ is the required rate of return on equity and $\overline{\overline{Z}}$ is the growth rate of after-tax profit per share in real terms (deflated by the *GDP* deflator). Finally, equation (6.1.7) shows the components of the required rate of return on equity.

Because the number of observations in our time series of profit, output, and capital stocks is not large, we specified a lag order of 1 in the empirical application of the profit system model to aggregated industrial sector data.

As discussed in Chapter 2, the cost and availability of credit play an important role in the determination of profit, output, and capital stock. As such, equations (6.1.1), (6.1.2), and (6.1.3) include the Federal funds rate (F) and the growth rate of total nonfinancial debt outstanding in nominal terms ($\dot{D}$). The lag orders of the Federal funds rate (F) and growth rate of total nonfinancial debt outstanding ($\dot{D}$) are empirically determined.

6.1.4 Estimated Profit System Model for the S&P
Industrial Index Firms

Table 6.2 presents the empirical results for the profit system model with respect to the firms in the SPXI. Panels A and B correspond to results based on the regression methods of OLS and SUR, respectively. The R^2 values of the estimated equations for capital stock, output, and profit rate equations range from 0.90 to 0.99, which suggests strong goodness-of-fit. Equations (6.1.1), (6.1.2), and (6.1.3) were initially estimated including both the Federal funds rate (F) and the debt growth rate ($\dot{D}$) but were dropped from the equations due to insignificance. The estimated coefficients for lags of output, profit rate, and profit margin in the regression models for capital stock, output, and profit rate are all statistically significant at the 1 percent level in OLS and SUR regressions. The estimated coefficient for the Federal funds rate in capital stock equation (6.1.1) is significant at the 5 percent significance level in the SUR. The estimated coefficients for the debt growth rate in output equation (6.1.2) are significant at the 10 percent level in the OLS regression and 1 percent in the SUR. The estimated coefficients for the Federal funds rate in the profit rate equation (6.1.3) are statistically significant at the 1 percent level in OLS and SUR regressions.

Figure 6.1 shows the results of 1,000 trials generated by running a Monte Carlo simulation of the estimated profit-based business model for SPXI firms using the Broyden algorithm. This algorithm solves the model each time assuming that all error terms in the estimated model are normally distributed. The simulation incorporates coefficient uncertainty, uses the actual values of the variables in 1967 as initial values, and generates the trajectories of all variables in the model from 1968 to 2007. In general, Fig. 6.1(a)–(e) shows that the model can mimic the in-sample

Table 6.2 Estimated profit system model for Standard and Poor's industrial index firms

A. OLS regression estimates	
$k_t = 0.262 + 0.980\ y_{t-1} -0.897\ r_{t-1} +0.953\ s_{t-1} -0.510\ F_{t-1}$	$R^2 = 0.99$ $DW = 2.11$
(0.70) (38.38)** (11.85)** (10.31)** (1.59)	
$y_t = -0.022 + 0.899\ r_{t-1} - 0.923\ s_{t-1} + k_t + 0.755\ \dot{D}_{t-1}$	$R^2 = 0.99$ $DW = 2.26$
(0.13) (15.68)** (11.88)** (1.78)$^+$	
$r_t = -0.599 + y_t + 0.742\ s_{t-1} - k_t - 1.351\ F_{t-1}$	$R^2 = 0.90$ $DW = 1.67$
(2.99)** (9.51)** (3.85)**	
B. SUR regression estimates	
$k_t = 0.763 + 0.942\ y_{t-1} -0.824\ r_{t-1} +1.007\ s_{t-1} -0.442\ F_{t-1}$	$R^2 = 0.99$ $DW = 1.84$
(3.09)** (62.06)** (13.76)** (13.41)** (2.29)*	
$y_t = 0.020 + 0.905\ r_{t-1} - 0.906\ s_{t-1} + k_t + 1.094\ \dot{D}_{t-1}$	$R^2 = 0.99$ $DW = 2.25$
(0.13) (16.80)** (12.65)** (4.23)**	
$r_t = -0.600 + y_t + 0.742\ s_{t-1} - k_t - 1.354\ F_{t-1}$	$R^2 = 0.90$ $DW = 1.66$
(3.11)** (9.89)** (4.02)**	

Notes: Figures in parentheses are t-values associated with estimated coefficients, where the superscripts **, *, and $^+$ denote significance at the 1, 5 and 10 percent levels, respectively. DW denotes the Durbin–Watson test for serial correlation. The variables are defined as follows: k = log of capital stocks, y = log of output, r = log of profit rate, s = log of profit margin, F = nominal Federal funds rate, and $\dot{D}$ = growth rate of total debt outstanding in the nonfinancial sector in nominal terms.

series of the focal variables quite well within the sample period. Most importantly, the simulation results for profit per share in Fig. 6.1(e) closely track the actual series and appear to identify periods when profits per share temporarily exceeded its long-run path. Relevant to the large stock market decline in 2008, the results for 2006 and 2007 indicate that profits exceeded their long-run trend, which was a warning sign that they may not be sustainable in 2008.

6.1.5 Estimating S&P's Industrial Index of the Stock Market

Based on Table 6.1's stock index model in equation (6.1.6), discounting actual profit per share generates the time series of estimated fundamental values for SPXI index. Alternatively, as demonstrated above, we can utilize the simulated (instead of actual) profit series estimated by the profit system model for these firms. Not only can

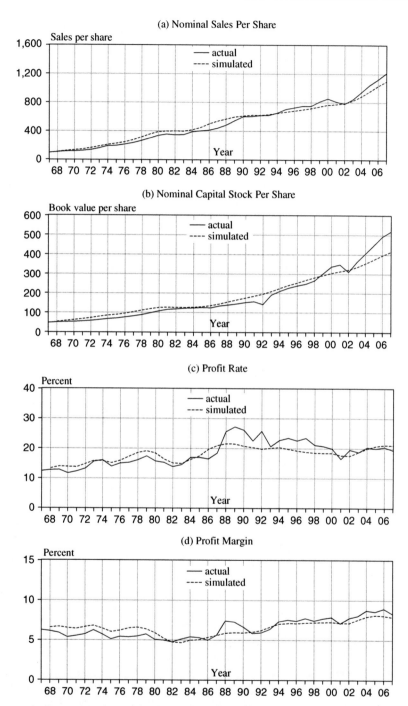

Fig. 6.1 (continued)

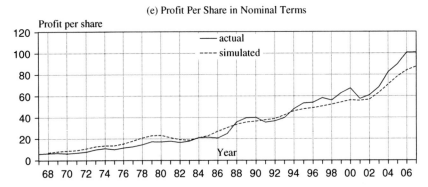

Fig. 6.1 Actual and simulated values of the variables in the profit system model for SPXI firms, 1967–2007: (**a**) nominal sales per share; (**b**) nominal capital stock per share; (**c**) profit rate; (**d**) profit margin; and (**e**) profit per share in nominal terms

in-sample profit series be estimated but out-of-sample profit series can also be estimated. In turn, the latter forecasted profit series can be discounted with expected future discount rates to gain insights into the future possible direction of the stock market index (based on future estimates of the fundamental values of sales, profit, capital stock, profit rate, and profit margin). For discounting the actual or simulated profit per share, we need a marketwide discount rate $(\hat{R})$ to proxy for the required rate of return by equity investors. For this purpose we use equation (6.1.7), which sums the after-tax corporate profit rate in the corporate sector (R_c), GDP inflation rate $(\dot{P})$, and business risk premium (I). The after-tax profit rate (R_{ct}) in the corporate sector from Chapter 4 is used because it is the broadest measure of profitability computed by dividing the aggregate profit for all corporations by their aggregate capital stock (both in nominal terms). This profit rate is measured on a time-varying basis in each period t. The average GDP inflation rate $(\dot{P})$ over the sample period[9] is added to the corporate rate due to the fact that the after-tax profit rate (R_{ct}) is in real terms (i.e., the effects of inflation are removed when nominal profit is divided by nominal capital stock). Nominal discount rates are needed to discount nominal profits.[10]

The time-varying risk premium (I_t) is the spread between Moody's seasoned AAA and BAA corporate bond yields. During the Great Depression, the spread reached an all-time high of 564 basis points (i.e., 5.64 percent) in May 1932 as shown by Fig. 6.2. More recently, in May 2008 the spread was 136 basis points and rose to 338 basis points in December 2008, the highest in the post-Depression era.

Figure 6.3 shows time series of annual closing prices for the SPXI over the sample period from 1967 to 2007. Results shown there give the estimated values of the

---

[9]We assume here that the long-run average inflation rate over the period 1959–2008 is a reasonable proxy for capital market investors' expected inflation rate.

[10]See Modigliani and Cohn (1979).

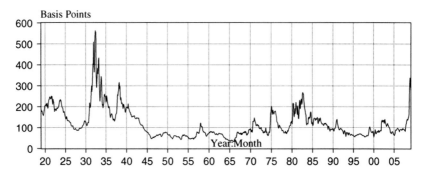

Fig. 6.2 Spread between Moody's seasoned AAA and BAA corporate bond yields: 1919–2008

SPXI based on discounted actual profits per share (Fig. 6.3(a)) and discounted simulated profits per share (Fig. 6.3(b)) from 1967 to 2007. As Fig. 6.3(a) illustrates, the
time series of discounted actual profit per share lies above the time series of SPXI
until 1996. That is, the SPXI was undervalued in the sense that market participants
used discount rates larger than our discount rates. This undervaluation most likely
is due to market participants' use of higher expected inflation rates for discounting
corporate profits in the inflationary environments prior to the 1990s (e.g., the average GDP inflation rate for the period 1959–1996 was 4.3 percent compared with 3.7
percent for the sample period from 1959 to 2008). The actual and estimated SPXI
time series were close to each other in 1996 when the SPXI was 869.9 and estimated
SPXI was 882.1. The actual SPXI then climbed to a peak of 1,841.9 in 1999, but
the estimated SPXI series reached its peak 2 years later in 2001 at 1,334.9. From
its peak in 1999, the actual SPXI fell to 1,005.9 in 2002 (i.e., a decline of 45 percent), while the estimated SPXI fell to 1,061.6 in the same year (i.e., a decline of 20
percent). Because equation (6.1.6) discounts one-period-ahead profit for estimation
purposes, our estimated SPXI series ends in 2006. Figure 6.3(c) shows that the two
estimated SPXI series with actual profits and simulated profits are similar to one
another.

As noted from Fig. 6.1(e), the time series of the simulated profit per share suggests that the post-2002 rapid growth rate of profit cannot be sustained. This is also
reflected in the time series of the discounted simulated profit per share in Fig. 6.3(b),
which lies below the actual SPXI from 2002 to 2007.

Table 6.3 presents out-of-sample projections of per share profit, per share sales
(output), per share book value (capital stock), profit rate, and profit margin for industrial companies in the SPXI. Panel A gives projections when forecasting begins from
2008 based on lagged actual data in 2007. Panel B gives the same projections for
2008–2012 from simulating the profit system model beginning in 1967. This case is
considered to investigate the long-run trajectory of the estimated discounted profit
series (see the dotted line in Fig. 6.1(e)). Panel C of Table 6.3 presents projections
of the discount rate and its components in the out-of-sample period 2008–2012. The
corporate profit rates are forecasts produced from the corporate model in Chapter 4.

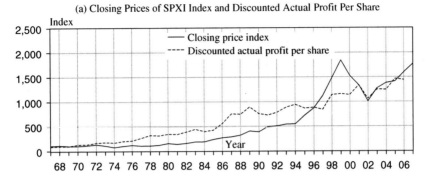
(a) Closing Prices of SPXI Index and Discounted Actual Profit Per Share

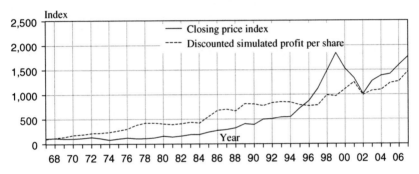
(b) Closing Prices of SPXI Index and Discounted Simulated Profit Per Share in Dollars

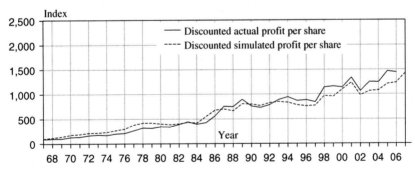
(c) Discounted Actual Profit Per Share and Discounted Simulated Profit Per Share in Dollars

Fig. 6.3 Profit system model for SPXI firms: closing prices, discounted actual profits per share, and discounted simulated profits per share: 1967–2007: (**a**) closing prices of SPXI and discounted actual profit per share; (**b**) closing prices of SPXI and discounted simulated profit per share in dollars; (**c**) discounted actual profit per share and discounted simulated profit per share in dollars

The *GDP* inflation rate is the average inflation rate over the sample period 1967–2007. And, the risk premium in 2008 is the spread between Moody's seasoned AAA and BAA corporate bond yields. We assume the same risk premium for 2009 and then decreasing risk premiums to their historical average of 1.1 percent in 2011 and

Table 6.3 Out-of-sample forecasts of the estimated profit system model for Standard and Poor's industrial index firms

	2008	2009	2010	2011	2012
A. Forecasts based on actual 2007 data					
Profit per share, $	102.6	103.8	110.2	113.4	113.4
Sales per share, $	1,269.0	1,288.6	1,305.3	1,310.9	1,305.2
Book value per share, $	532.1	545.9	567.5	589.7	609.1
Profit rate, %	19.4	19.1	19.6	19.4	18.8
Profit margin, %	8.1	8.1	8.4	8.7	8.7
Discounted profit per share	1,244.5	1,342.3	1,526.2	1,678.4	1,671.7
Actual stock price	1,150.6	1,019.0[a]			
B. Forecasts based on historical simulations beginning in 1967					
Profit per share, $	89.5	92.1	99.3	103.5	104.8
Sales per share, $	1,151.9	1,178.2	1,203.5	1,217.8	1,222.2
Book value per share, $	430.2	449.1	475.0	501.4	525.8
Profit rate, %	20.9	20.6	21.0	20.7	20.0
Profit margin, %	7.8	7.8	8.3	8.5	8.6
Discounted profit per share	1,104.0	1,209.5	1,393.5	1,551.0	1,560.6
Actual stock price	1,150.6	1,019.0[a]			
C. Discount rate components					
Discount rate, %	11.9	11.8	11.0	10.4	10.2
Corporate profit rate, %	5.3	5.2	5.4	5.5	5.6
GDP inflation rate, %	3.7	3.7	3.7	3.7	3.7
Risk premium, %	2.9	2.9	1.9	1.1	0.9

[a]Based on April 2009 values.

to 0.9 percent in 2012. Of course, other assumptions about future discount rates can be readily explored. Importantly, both forecast SPXI series in panels A and B point to increasing stock market valuation from 2009 to 2012. Panels A and B predict that industrial stocks will increase somewhere in the range of 53 percent to 64 percent from 2009 to 2012.

6.2 Stock Market Capitalization

Market capitalization is a measurement of the aggregate value of a corporation or its stocks equal to the product of the market value of its shares and the number of shares outstanding. Stock market capitalization is the aggregate market value of all stocks for a group of corporations included in a stock market. In the US stock market capitalization is the sum of American Stock Exchange, NASDAQ, and New York Stock Exchange market capitalizations.

Dividing the time series of total corporate profit (from Chapter 4) by the time series of discount rates results in a time series of fundamental stock market capitalization. Figure 6.4(a) presents the time series of US corporate market capitalizations from CRSP over the sample period from 1959 to 2008 based on the discounted actual after-tax corporate profits from 1960 to 2007, where the discount rate is the

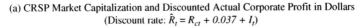

(a) CRSP Market Capitalization and Discounted Actual Corporate Profit in Dollars
(Discount rate: $\hat{R}_t = R_{ct} + 0.037 + I_t$)

(b) CRSP Market Capitalization and Discounted Out-of-Sample Corporate Profit
Forecasts in Dollars
(Discount rate: $\hat{R}_t = R_{ct} + 0.037 + I_t$)

(c) CRSP Market Capitalization and Discounted Simulated Corporate Profit
Forecasts in Dollars (Discount rate: $\hat{R}_t = R_{ct} + 0.037 + I_t$)

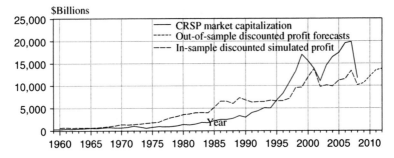

Fig. 6.4 (continued)

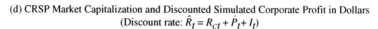

(d) CRSP Market Capitalization and Discounted Simulated Corporate Profit in Dollars
(Discount rate: $\hat{R}_t = R_{ct} + \dot{P}_t + I_t$)

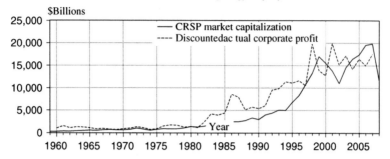

(e) CRSP Market Capitalization and Discounted Simulated Corporate Profit in Dollars
(Discount rate: $\hat{R} = E(R_c) + E(\dot{P}) + E(I) = 0.047 + 0.037 + 0.011 = 0.095$)

Fig. 6.4 CRSP index results comparing actual values, discounted actual profits, and discounted simulated profits, 1959–2008: **(a)** CRSP market capitalization and discounted actual corporate profit in dollars (discount rate: $\hat{R}_t = R_{ct} + 0.037 + I_t$); **(b)** CRSP market capitalization and discounted out-of-sample corporate profit forecasts in dollars (discount rate: $\hat{R}_t = R_{ct} + 0.037 + I_t$); **(c)** CRSP market capitalization and discounted simulated corporate profit forecasts in dollars (discount rate: $\hat{R}_t = R_{ct} + 0.037 + I_t$); **(d)** CRSP market capitalization and discounted simulated corporate profit in dollars (discount rate: $\hat{R}_t = R_{ct} + \dot{P}_t + I_t$); and **(e)** CRSP market capitalization and discounted simulated corporate profit in dollars (discount rate: $\hat{R} = E(R_c) + E(\dot{P}) + E(I) = 0.047 + 0.037 + 0.011 = 0.095$)

same discount rate used in the previous section. Our estimated CRSP series ends in 2007, as equation (6.1.6) discounts one-period-ahead profits.

Comparison of the actual CRSP market capitalization series and estimated CRSP series in Fig. 6.4(b) suggests that the US stock market was undervalued before 1996, as the actual series lies below the estimated series from 1959 to 1995. As mentioned in the previous section, this market undervaluation may have been due to market participants expecting higher inflation rates in the future than the average inflation rate for the sample period 1959 to 2008. The two time series were close to each other in 1996, with actual CRSP at $8,298.2 billion and estimated CRSP at $8,154.5 billion. Subsequently, the actual CRSP series climbed to $17,009.5 billion by year-end 1999 and diverged considerably from the estimated CRSP series at only $7,926.7 billion. Hence, the estimated CRSP series could discern that market capitalization was severely overvalued during the dotcom bubble in the mid-to-late 1990s. The actual CRSP series then fell by 35 percent to $11,033.6 billion by year-end 2002 to a level closer to the estimated CRSP at $10,121.0 billion. Both actual and estimated CRSP series turn upward from 2002 to 2006 (i.e., the actual and estimated series rose in 2007 to $19,850.9 billion and $14,420.7, respectively), but the estimated series is consistently below the actual series in line with overvaluation in this period.

Using the out-of-sample forecasts of aggregate corporate profit from the profit system corporate model in Chapter 4, Fig. 6.4(b) shows discounted after-tax corporate profit forecasts from 2009 to 2012 as well as the actual CRSP series from 1959 to 2008. The value of the estimated CRSP for 2008 is $11,129.1 billion, which is close to the actual CRSP value at year-end 2008 equal to $11,697.5 billion. The 2009 forecast of CRSP market capitalization is $10,064.9 billion. This decline is mainly due to high-risk premiums (i.e., the spread between Moody's seasoned BAA and AAA corporate bond yields) in 2009 that increase the discount rate. Thereafter, the stock market is projected to increase in value by about 25 percent from 2009 to 2012.

To investigate the long-run trajectories of the discounted corporate profit series, we use simulated (as opposed to actual) aggregate corporate profit generated from the stochastic simulation of the corporate model in Chapter 4. Figure 6.4(c) shows actual CRSP series from 1959 to 2008 and the discounted simulated profit series from 1962 to 2012. The simulation process begins in 1962 due to using 1959–1961 values of the fundamental variables in the US corporate sector as initial values. Comparison of the two series shows a pattern of overvaluation in the stock market in both 1999 and 2007. For the period 1995–2008, the simulated CRSP series tends to lie below the actual CRSP series. From 2009 to 2012 the forecasted CRSP series predicts about a 40 percent increase in the value of the stock market.

We also considered the following two cases: (1) inflation rates are also time-varying variables and (2) the discount rate is a constant equal to the sum of the expected values of after-tax corporate profit rates, inflation rates, and the risk premiums over the sample period from 1959 to 2008 equal to 9.5 percent. Figure 6.4(d) shows the actual CRSP series and the discounted actual after-tax corporate profits series when the discount rate is the sum of time-varying corporate profit rates, inflation rates, and risk premiums. Figure 6.4(e) repeats the analyses in Fig. 6.4(d) using a constant discount rate. It is interesting that the use of time-varying inflation rates in Fig. 6.4(d) produces an estimated CRSP series that reaches levels achieved in the actual CRSP series in the late 1990s dotcom bubble and recent market surge from 2002 to 2007. However, the use of a constant discount rate (based on average profit rates, inflation rates, and risk premiums in the past) in Fig. 6.4(e) successfully identifies the late 1990s dotcom bubble as an overvalued market. Also, the market surge from 2002 to 2007 is identified to end in 2005, with an overvalued market from 2005 to 2007 due to the falling estimated CRSP series.

In sum, we can use our profit system model of the corporate sector in Chapter 4 to estimate and forecast aggregate corporate profit and then discount aggregate profit using an appropriate discount factor for investigating changes in stock market values based on fundamental business variables. Actual profits can be discounted for in-sample data series also. Our DCF valuation approach is fundamental in that it uses basic accounting values for business sales, capital stock, profit rate, profit margin, and total profit. Also, our discount factor is based on the fundamentals of after-tax real corporate profit rates, inflation rates, risk premiums, and real profit growth rates.

6.3 Conclusion

In this chapter we applied our profit system model to stock market valuation. The profit system model was used to produce in-sample estimates and out-of-sample forecasts of corporate profits. These profits were then input into a discounted cash flow (DCF) stock valuation model to estimate the fundamental values of stocks. DCF models were developed for SPXI and CRSP market capitalizations. The models were applied to in-sample estimates based on discounted actual profits and discounted simulated profits, in addition to out-of-sample forecasts of these stock market capitalizations. Given repeated stock market over- and undervaluations in the past, our fundamental models of stock market valuation can potentially provide valuable information on the expected direction of the aggregate stock market based on fundamental values of underlying business sales, capital stocks, profit rates, profit margins, and total profits. For example, our DCF valuation model was able to detect the tech stock market bubble in the late 1990s and early 2000s and predict its return to the long-run path of discounted profits. More recently, our DCF model suggests that the stock market will trend higher from 2009 to 2012. These analyses show that the key variable explaining rising stock market values over long periods of time is profits. In this regard, we observed that, even though the US stock market in 2009 collapsed to 1997 valuations, profit levels in the US corporate sector were considerably higher in early 2009 than they were in 1997. Since shareholders own claims on firm profits, stock valuations are projected to adjust over time to the discounted value of profits. Our results confirm the long tradition of fundamental analysis as a foundation for stock market valuation.

Applications of our profit system model to the national economy in Chapter 2, the corporate sector in Chapter 4, and stock market aggregates in this chapter demonstrate that there is no dichotomy between modeling the real economy and the financial sector. Our profit system model can be applied to all sectors of the economy due to the fact that profit, profit rate, and profit margin variables serve as links between the real and the financial parts of the economy. Hence, the "power of profit" is a binding force that impacts not only business firms, industries, and the national economy but investors in the financial marketplace also.

Table 6.1A: Firms in the Standard and Poor's Industrial Index: Dollar Values Per Share Data for Fundamental Variables

Year	Sales	Profit	Book value of equity
1967	94.71	5.92	47.78
1968	104.15	6.38	50.21
1969	111.95	6.62	51.70
1970	114.41	6.14	52.65
1971	122.61	6.79	55.28
1972	134.56	7.73	58.34
1973	157.14	9.80	62.84
1974	189.62	10.89	67.81
1975	193.14	9.87	70.84
1976	210.46	11.44	76.26
1977	232.98	12.53	82.21
1978	263.20	14.41	89.34
1979	299.08	17.17	98.71
1980	336.47	17.04	108.33
1981	355.98	17.73	116.06
1982	345.44	16.42	118.60
1983	347.93	17.78	122.32
1984	389.79	21.04	123.99
1985	402.23	21.36	125.89
1986	413.15	20.60	124.87
1987	441.14	24.72	134.19
1988	481.66	35.72	139.50
1989	544.15	39.58	145.34
1990	600.72	39.89	152.71
1991	605.23	35.40	157.05
1992	617.88	36.68	142.46
1993	622.12	39.59	191.82
1994	653.75	47.92	210.98
1995	706.13	53.33	227.12
1996	727.40	53.94	238.76
1997	750.71	58.19	247.83
1998	750.48	55.93	264.63
1999	812.00	62.67	302.08
2000	853.86	67.29	337.51
2001	811.04	57.42	348.38
2002	781.65	60.78	310.61
2003	847.38	68.25	363.74
2004	944.36	82.49	405.59
2005	1043.61	89.59	448.62
2006	1123.34	100.73	492.65
2007	1211.90	100.86	519.04

Source: *Analyst's Handbook*, Standard and Poor's.

Chapter 7
A Profit System Model of the Firm for Business Analysis and Stock Valuation

As discussed in Chapter 2, dynamic relationships exist between sales (output), profit, profit rate, profit margin, and capital stocks of firms – that is, the values (magnitudes) of these fundamental variables in any period depend on the current and past values of the other variables. Consequently, for purposes of business analysis, an integrated business model of firms must contain all the dynamic relationships among these variables. Our profit system models in Chapter 2 provide analytical frameworks for short-run and long-run analyses of these fundamental variables over time. Here we apply the profit system model to individual firms for business analysis, forecasting, and stock market valuation. Regarding stock market valuation, we integrate the profit system model and the popular discounted cash flow (DCF) stock valuation model to perform in-sample analyses and out-of-sample forecasts of individual firms' stock values.

This chapter is comprised of three parts. The first part presents the model, discusses data issues in the application of the model to firms, and demonstrates its application to two well-known US corporations. The second part applies the model to the valuation of these two corporations' stocks. Lastly, the third part contains discussion of other important applications of our profit system model to firms, including strategic business planning, budgetary control, and capital budgeting decisions.

7.1 Application of the Profit System Model to Firms

7.1.1 Empirical Model

Here we apply the profit system model derived in Chapter 2 to individual firms. Using available data on sales, profit, and book equity values for two well-known US corporations, we estimate different empirical representations of the profit system model shown there. We found that the model in Table 2.1 (i.e., basic profit system model of the goods and services market with output and capital stock in current dollars) is the most suitable for empirical application in terms of statistical significance of the estimated coefficients as well as out-of-sample forecast accuracy. Panel A of Table 7.1 presents the model as a system of five equations. The fundamental

A. Anari, J.W. Kolari, *The Power of Profit*, DOI 10.1007/978-1-4419-0649-6_7,
© Springer Science+Business Media, LLC 2010

Table 7.1 Profit system model for individual firms and DCF stock valuation model

---

A. Models of focal variables

Capital stock model

$$k_t = \alpha_0 + \alpha_1 y_{t-1} + \alpha_2 r_{t-1} + \alpha_3 s_{t-1} + \alpha_5 \dot{D}_{t-L} + \alpha_6 F_{t-L} \tag{7.1.1}$$

Output model

$$y_t = \beta_0 + \beta_2 r_{t-1} + \beta_3 s_{t-1} + \beta_4 k_{t-1} + \beta_5 \dot{D}_{t-L} + \beta_6 F_{t-L} \tag{7.1.2}$$

Profit rate model

$$r_t = \theta_0 + \theta_1 y_{t-1} + \theta_3 s_{t-1} + \theta_4 k_{t-1} + \theta_5 \dot{D}_{t-L} + \theta_6 F_{t-L} \tag{7.1.3}$$

Profit margin model

$$s_t = r_t + k_t - y_t \tag{7.1.4}$$

Total profit model

$$Z_t = Y_t \times S_t \tag{7.1.5}$$

B. DCF stock valuation model

$$\hat{Z}_{t+1} = \frac{Z_{t+1}}{O} \tag{7.1.6}$$

$$V_t = \frac{\hat{Z}_{t+1}}{\hat{R} - \dot{Z}} \tag{7.1.7}$$

$$\hat{R} = R_c + \dot{P} + I \tag{7.1.8}$$

Bold numbered equations are empirically estimated (see Tables 7.2 and 7.3), and other equations are derived from their forecasts. All equations are solved simultaneously or recursively in forecasting and simulation analyses (see Table 7.4 as well as Figs. 7.2 and 7.3).

The variables are defined as follows:

Panel A

$Y(y)$ = sales in current dollars (log)
$K(k)$ = capital stock in current dollars (log)
$R(r)$ = profit rate (log)
$S(s)$ = profit margin (log)
Z = after-tax profit in current dollars
F = Federal funds rate in percent (maximum of monthly rates in a year),
D = growth rate of total debt outstanding of nonfinancial sector in nominal terms
$L = 0, 1, 2$ generic number of lags to be determined empirically,
where K_t = antilog k_t, Y_t = antilog y_t, R_t = antilog r_t, and S_t = antilog s_t.

Panel B

O = number of shares outstanding
$\hat{Z}$ = after-tax profit per share in nominal terms
V = stock price in nominal terms
$\hat{R}$ = average required rate of return on equity in the sample period
$\dot{Z}$ = growth rate of after-tax profit per share in real terms (deflated by GDP deflator).
R_c = after-tax corporate profit rate from corporate sector profit system model in Chapter 4 (average in the sample period)
$\dot{P}$ = GDP inflation rate from the macroeconomic profit system model in Chapter 3 (average in the sample period)
I = default spread between average interest rates on corporate bonds with the same rating as the firm and average interest rates on bonds with little or no default risk

---

variables of sales, capital stock, and profit are in nominal terms. As explained in Chapter 2, equations (7.1.1), (7.1.2), and (7.1.3) are specified for estimating logarithms of capital stocks (k), output (y), and profit rate (r) from the values of lags of these variables and profit margin (s). We also added the growth rate of nonfinancial debt outstanding ($\dot{D}$) and the Federal funds rate (F) to equations (7.1.1), (7.1.2), and (7.1.3), as these two financial sector variables are expected to influence our fundamental business variables. Equation (7.1.4) computes the logarithm of profit margin (s) from logarithms of capital stock (k), output or sales (y), and profit rate (r). The antilogs of k, y, r, and s give the levels of the corresponding variables K, Y, R, and S in levels. Equation (7.1.5) computes total profit as the product of sales or output (Y) and profit margin (S). This model can be applied to different kinds of business firms, including single proprietorships, partnerships, and corporations.

Equation (7.1.6) is added when the model of firm is applied to corporations with common stock outstanding in order to estimate earnings (or profits) per share ($\hat{Z}$), which is total profit (Z) divided by the total number of shares outstanding (O). The expected (one-period-ahead) profit per share is discounted in the fundamental model of stock valuation shown in equation (7.1.7) of panel B in Table 7.1. Equation (7.1.7) is based on the Gordon stock valuation model, where $\hat{R}$ is the required return on equity and $\dot{\hat{Z}}$ is the growth rate of after-tax profit per share in real terms (deflated by GDP deflator). Equation (7.1.8) defines the required return on equity $\hat{R}$ as the sum of R_c, $\dot{P}$, and I, where R_c is the after-tax real corporate profit rate (based on the corporate sector profit system model in Chapter 4), $\dot{P}$ is the *GDP* inflation rate (based on the macroeconomic profit system model in Chapter 3), and I is a proxy for the market risk premium represented by the yield spread between the average yield of corporate bonds with the same rating as the firm and the average yield on bonds with little or no default risk in a particular year. As discussed in Chapter 6, the latter yield spread captures risk aversion by investors in financial markets. Previous research studies have shown that risk premiums on stocks are related to bond default yield spreads.

7.1.2 Data Issues

When applied to an individual firm, our empirical profit system model requires time series of sales, profit, and capital stock at market values. These are the minimum data required. If employment time series data for firms are available, then the extended profit system model presented in Chapter 2 can be used, which includes employment, labor productivity, and other equations shown there.

Two data problems that arise in the case of individual firms is the lack of capital stock data in market value terms and the existence of negative profits in some periods.

Accounting data on the physical capital stock of firms are normally in historical book value terms, while the capital stocks in our profit system model are in market value terms. Historical book values contain less information on the productivity of capital stocks and exclude the impact of inflation on the nominal values of capital stocks. The gap between market values and book values of capital stocks may be particularly important bearing in mind that the capital stock in the business model consists of real estate properties, equipment, software, and inventory. For example, when the values of real estate properties are expressed in book values, they can be substantially lower than their market values due to inflation and other market factors.

Difficulties in measuring capital stocks affect profit rate time series, which is defined as profit divided by capital stock. Thus, there are measurement errors in two fundamental variables (K and R) out-of-four fundamental variables (Y, K, R, and S) in the model.

Given these data availability issues, we use capital stock measured in book value terms in forthcoming individual firm analyses. As the empirical results will show, the estimated equations for profit rate do not have high R^2 values reflecting weaker goodness-of-fit than similar corporate sector equations. Of course, firms know the approximate market values of their capital stocks and can compile time series of capital stocks in market values for use in our model. The authors hope that this publication will encourage firms, institutions, and government agencies to report individual firms' capital stock data in market value terms.

Another problem in application of the model to individual firms is the existence of losses in some periods. Naturally, expected profits are always positive as firms do not embark on production or capital formation activities unless they foresee positive expected profits. In application of the profit system model to individual firms – including the estimation of the model as well as model simulation – we treated losses as missing values in profit time series. The economic interpretation of this treatment is that losses are missed profit targets. We view making profit as a long-run goal, while incurring losses is an exception that can occur in the short run. Hence, the model is initially estimated as if there are missing values of negative profit rates and profit margins, and the subsequent simulation of the estimated model generates positive expected values of profit rates and profit margins (as well as total profits). This approach may be criticized for dropping information contained in losses. An alternative is to compute a moving average profit time series based on the notion that firm owners and investors normally form their profit expectations based on moving averages of profits in several periods. However, there are some problems with this approach. To generate a series of positive profits in all periods, it may be necessary to average over a long period, thus losing a number of initial observations. Also, it may be necessary to construct moving average time series of sales (output) and capital stock in order to be consistent with the time series of moving average profits. Due to this data smoothing, the data observations in the generated time series of moving averages may contain little information relevant to each period contained in the original time series.

7.2 Empirical Results for Two US Corporations

This section presents the profit system model results for two large US firms: International Business Machines (IBM) Corporation and Johnson & Johnson (JNJ). The annual profit time series of IBM contains losses in the early 1990s, which makes this firm a suitable case study for the application of our model when there are profit losses. The JNJ data set does not contain any negative profits. Both companies issue investment grade bonds and, therefore, have high credit quality. However, JNJ commands an AAA rating, while IBM is an A-rated firm consistent with the fact that it historically has experienced some profit dips.

The sample period 1959–2008 is used for (1) estimating profit system models for these two firms; (2) in-sample and out-of-sample forecasts of sales (output), capital stock, total profit, profit rate, profit margin, and profit per share; and (3) the present stock value of discounted profit per share and stochastic simulations of stock valuation.

7.2.1 Data for Firms

The data used for IBM and JNJ are annual data series for sales, profits, and capital stock downloaded from Wharton Research Data Services (WRDS) of the University of Pennsylvania. The Compustat North America database contained in WRDS offers annual data from 1950 and quarterly data from 1975Q4 on these fundamental business variables. Since annual time series of fundamental business variables contain more long-run information than quarterly data, we opted to use annual data from 1959 to 2008.

As mentioned earlier, the capital stock data are normally in book value terms, but our profit system model requires capital stock data in market value terms. Compustat provides two annual time series of capital stocks – namely, total assets (TA) and property, plant, and equipment (PPENT). We used both of these series for estimating the profit system model for IBM and JNJ. Since the PPENT time series of capital stocks resulted in higher R^2 values than the TA series for the estimated log of profit rate equation, it was selected for estimating profit system models for both IBM and JNJ. For profit data series we used income after income taxes but before extraordinary items. Consistent with convention, we chose this profit measure to compute earnings per share (EPS) for share valuation purposes.

7.2.2 Empirical Results for International Business Machines Corporation

As shown in Fig. 7.1(a), IBM Corporation experienced negative profits (losses) from 1991 to 1993. As discussed above, we treated these losses in model estimation as missing values, which are shown in the time series of profit in Fig. 7.1(b). Table 7.2 presents the estimated profit system model for IBM employing OLS and SUR regression methods. In the capital stock equation (k) the estimated coefficients for the lags of logarithms of sales (y), profit rate (r), and profit margin (s) are all significant at the 1 percent level in OLS and SUR regressions. In this equation the estimated coefficient for the second lag of growth rate of nominal nonfinancial debt

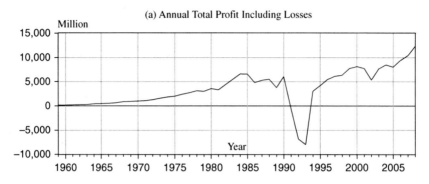

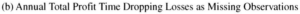

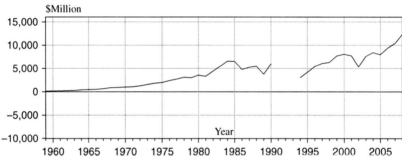

Fig. 7.1 Total profits for IBM Corporation: 1959–2008: (**a**) annual total profit including losses; (**b**) annual total profit time dropping losses as missing observations

outstanding ($\dot{D}$) is statistically significant at the 1 percent level in OLS and SUR regressions. The lag order for this variable is empirically determined. The R^2 value of 0.98 for the estimated capital stock equation suggests strong goodness-of-fit.

In the IBM logarithm of sales (y) equation, the estimated coefficients for lags of logarithms of profit rate (r), profit margin (s), and capital stock (k) are statistically significant at the 1 percent level in OLS and SUR regressions. The estimated coefficient for the contemporaneous growth rate of nonfinancial debt outstanding ($\dot{D}$) is statistically significant at the 10 percent level in the OLS regression. The R^2 value for the estimated sales equation is 0.99.

In the profit rate equation the estimated coefficients for lags of output (y), capital stock (k), and profit margin (s) are statistically significant at the 1 percent level in OLS and SUR regressions. The estimated coefficient for the Federal funds rate was not statistically significant and therefore was dropped from the equation. The R^2 value for the estimated profit rate equation is 0.80 in OLS and SUR regressions.

Using the estimated model based on the SUR method, Fig. 7.2(a)–(e) shows the results of 1,000 trials generated by running a Monte Carlo simulation of the estimated IBM model using the Broyden algorithm. This algorithm solves the model

Table 7.2 Estimatedprofit system model for IBM Corporation

A. OLS regression estimates

$k_t = 0.597 + 0.900\ y_{t-1} - 0.911\ r_{t-1} + 0.824\ s_{t-1} + 2.327\ \dot{D}_{t-2}$ $\qquad R^2 = 0.98 \quad DW = 1.70$

$\quad (3.14)^{**}\ (30.54)^{**}\ (14.51)^{**}\quad (6.85)^{**}\quad (2.56)^{**}$

$y_t = 0.242 + 0.927\ r_{t-1} - 1.017\ s_{t-1} + 0.958\ k_{t-1} + 1.154\ \dot{D}_t$ $\qquad R^2 = 0.99 \quad DW = 2.13$

$\quad (1.70)^{+}\ (30.88)^{**}\ (15.96)^{**}\quad (62.45)^{**}\ (1.89)^{+}$

$r_t = -0.582 + 0.929\ y_{t-1} + 0.603\ s_{t-1} - 0.951\ k_{t-1}$ $\qquad R^2 = 0.80 \quad DW = 1.65$

$\quad (1.82)^{+}\ (11.72)^{**}\ (4.77)^{**}\quad (9.85)^{**}$

B. SUR regression estimates

$k_t = 0.547 + 0.928\ y_{t-1} - 0.952\ r_{t-1} + 0.921\ s_{t-1} + 1.599\ \dot{D}_{t-2}$ $\qquad R^2 = 0.98 \quad DW = 1.70$

$\quad (3.22)^{**}\ (41.28)^{**}\quad (17.49)^{**}\ (9.88)^{**}\quad (2.59)^{**}$

$y_t = 0.293 + 0.929\ r_{t-1} - 0.982\ s_{t-1} + 0.965\ k_{t-1} + 0.748\ \dot{D}_t$ $\qquad R^2 = 0.99 \quad DW = 2.16$

$\quad (2.31)^{*}\ (32.84)^{**}\quad (18.29)^{**}\ (73.11)^{**}\quad (1.60)$

$r_t = -0.439 + 0.951\ y_{t-1} + 0.619\ s_{t-1} - 0.988\ k_{t-1}$ $\qquad R^2 = 0.80 \quad DW = 1.67$

$\quad (1.48)\ (12.70)^{**}\quad (5.20)^{**}\quad (10.91)^{**}$

Notes: Figures in parentheses are *t*-values associated with estimated coefficients, where the superscripts **, *, and + denote significance at the 1, 5, and 10 percent levels, respectively. The variables are defined as follows: k = log of capital stocks, y = log of output, r = log of profit rate, s = log of profit margin and $\dot{D}$ = growth rate of debt outstanding in the nonfinancial sector in nominal terms.

each time assuming that all error terms in the estimated model are normally distributed. The simulation incorporates coefficient uncertainty, uses the actual values of the variables from 1959 to 1961 as initial values, and generates the trajectories of all variables in the model from 1962 to 2008.

The simulation process generates positive expected profits from 1991 to 1993 when IBM incurred losses (see Fig. 7.1(a) and (b) with actual profit series and the same profit series with negative profits dropped as missing values, respectively). Figure 7.2(c)–(e) compares the actual values for profit rate, profit margin, and total profit, respectively, for IBM to their simulated values from 1960 to 2008. Figure 7.2(f) shows the number of shares outstanding. Dividing the actual and simulated total profits by the number of shares outstanding gives the time series of actual and simulated profit per share in Fig. 7.2(g).

Finally, Fig. 7.2(h) and (i) gives the time series of actual prices of IBM stocks and the discounted actual profit per share and the discounted simulated profit per share

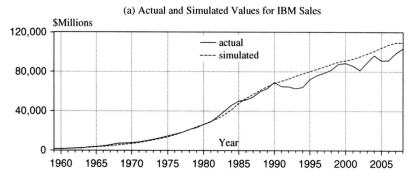

(a) Actual and Simulated Values for IBM Sales

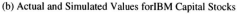

(b) Actual and Simulated Values forIBM Capital Stocks

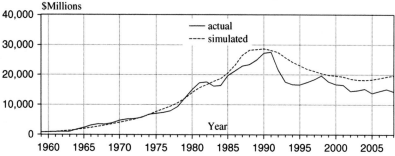

(c) Actual and Simulated Values for IBM Profit Rates

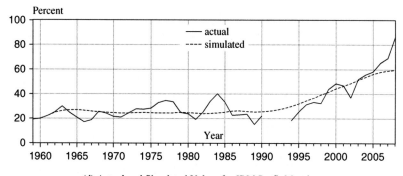

(d) Actual and Simulated Values for IBM Profit Margins

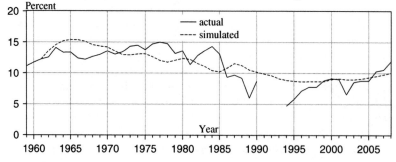

Fig. 7.2 (continued)

(e) Actual and Simulated Values for IBM Total Profits

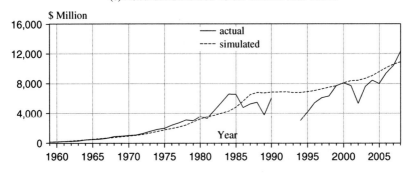

(f) Total Number of Shares Outstanding for IBM

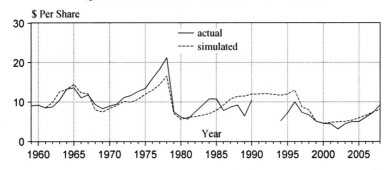

(g) Actual and Simulated Values of IBM Profit Per Share

(h) Actual IBM Stock Prices and Discounted Actual Profit Per Share

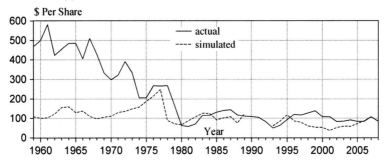

Fig. 7.2 (continued)

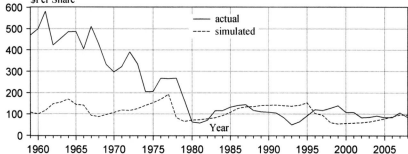

Fig. 7.2 Actual and simulated values of the variables in the profit system model for IBM Corporation (1959–2008): (**a**) actual and simulated values for IBM sales; (**b**) actual and simulated values for IBM capital stocks; (**c**) actual and simulated values for IBM profit rates; (**d**) actual and simulated values for IBM profit margins; (**e**) actual and simulated values for IBM total profits; (**f**) total number of shares outstanding for IBM; (**g**) actual and simulated values of IBM profit per share; (**h**) Actual IBM stock prices and discounted actual profit per share; and (**i**) actual IBM stock prices and discounted simulated profit per share

using a discount rate of 9.3 percent. The discount rate is computed as the average corporate profit rate plus average GDP inflation rate in the sample period plus the average risk premium on A-rated bonds equal to 0.785 percent.[1] Comparison of the actual price of IBM stocks with the discounted actual profit per share in Fig. 7.2(h) shows that the two series converge after 1975, where actual prices fell from over $581.2 in 1961 to about $205 in 1975, when the discounted actual profit per share was $187.7. Comparison of the actual price of IBM stocks with the discounted simulated profit per share in Fig. 7.2(i) shows that the two series converged from 1980 to 1982 and that the stock was undervalued in the early 1990s (when profit losses occurred) as the stock rebounded from 1993 to 1999.

Using the latest data for 2007 and 2008 as the initial values for forecasting 2009 stock price, a short-run forecast is generated from the model. Long-run forecasts are generated from simulating the model with data from 1962 to 2008. Table 7.4 shows these forecasts. At the time of this writing in 2009, the 52-week range for IBM's stock price was $69.50–$124.00. Our forecasts for 2009 and 2010 are in the middle of this range. A caveat here is that our forecasts are biased to some extent due to using historical values of capital stocks (PPENT) rather than market values.

---

[1] This value is based on Elton et al. (2001), who estimated the average interest rate spread between 10-year A-rated corporate bonds and comparable maturity Treasury bond rates over the period 1987–1996.

Table 7.3 Estimated profit system model for JNJ

A. *OLS regression estimates*

$k_t = 0.472 + 0.971 \, y_{t-1} - 0.973 \, r_{t-1} + 1.062 \, s_{t-1} + 0.628 \, \dot{D}_{t-1}$ $R^2 = 0.99$ $DW = 1.76$

   (1.30) (62.79)**   (8.71)**   (7.07)**   (1.60)

$y_t = 0.793 + 0.882 \, r_{t-1} - 0.751 \, s_{t-1} + 0.963 \, k_{t-1} + 0.470 \, \dot{D}_{t-1}$ $R^2 = 0.99$ $DW = 1.76$

   (2.34)* (7.78)**   (4.93)**   (66.52)**   (1.28)

$r_t = -2.360 + 1.317 \, y_{t-1} + 0.478 \, s_{t-1} - 1.198 \, k_{t-1} - 1.437 \, F_{t-1}$ $R^2 = 0.84$ $DW = 2.21$

   (3.08)** (5.13)**   (3.58)**   (5.01)**   (2.42)*

B. SUR regression estimates

$k_t = 0.543 + 0.968 \, \bar{y}_{t-1} - 0.994 \, r_{t-1} + 1.098 \, s_{t-1} + 0.802 \dot{D}_{t-1}$ $R^2 = 0.99$ $DW = 1.79$

   (1.59) (66.29)**   (9.43)**   (7.74)**   (2.20)*

$y_t = 0.894 + 0.848 \, r_{t-1} - 0.697 \, s_{t-1} + 0.959 \, k_{t-1} + 0.715 \, \dot{D}_{t-1}$ $R^2 = 0.99$ $DW = 1.79$

   (2.80)** (7.95)**   (4.86)**   (70.33)**   (2.13)*

$r_t = -2.343 + 1.310 \, y_{t-1} + 0.480 \, s_{t-1} - 1.191 \, k_{t-1} - 1.436 \, F_{t-1}$ $R^2 = 0.84$ $DW = 2.22$

   (3.23)** (5.40)**   (3.81)**   (5.27)**   (2.64)**

Notes: Figures in parentheses are *t*-values associated with estimated coefficients, where the super-scripts ** and * denote significance at the 1 and 5 percent levels, respectively. The variables are defined as follows: k = log of capital stocks, y = log of output, r = log of profit rate, s = log of profit margin, F = nominal Federal funds rate, and $\dot{D}$ = growth rate of debt outstanding in the nonfinancial sector in nominal terms.

7.2.3 *Empirical Results for Johnson & Johnson*

Johnson and Johnson (JNJ) did not suffer any losses over our sample period from 1959 to 2008. Table 7.3 presents the estimated profit system models of fundamental variables for JNJ using OLS and SUR regression methods. The estimated coefficients for lags of logarithms of sales (y), profit rate (r), and profit margin (s) in JNJ's capital stock (k) equation are statistically significant at the 1 percent level in OLS and SUR regressions. The estimated coefficient for the lag of the growth rate of nominal nonfinancial debt outstanding in the capital stock equation is statistically significant at the 5 percent level in the SUR regression. Again, the lag order for this variable is empirically determined. The R^2 value for the estimated capital stock equation is 0.99, which indicates strong goodness-of-fit.

In the JNJ logarithm of sales (y) equation, the estimated coefficients for lags of logarithms of profit rate (r), profit margin (s), and capital stock (k) are statistically significant at the 1 percent level in OLS and SUR regressions. The estimated coefficient for the lag of growth rate of nonfinancial debt outstanding ($\dot{D}$) is statistically significant at the 5 percent level in the SUR regression. The R^2 value for the estimated sales equation is 0.99.

In the logarithm of profit rate (r) equation for JNJ, the estimated coefficients for lags of logarithms of output (y), capital stock (k), and profit margin (s) are statistically significant at the 1 percent level in OLS and SUR regressions. The estimated coefficients for the lag of the Federal funds rate (F) are negative and statistically significant at the 5 percent level in OLS and 1 percent in SUR regressions. The R^2 value for the estimated profit rate equation is 0.84 in both OLS and SUR regressions.

Since the estimated coefficients for the growth rate of nonfinancial debt outstanding and the Federal funds rate in the fundamental equations using SUR methods are statistically significant, we chose this model for simulations. Figure 7.3(a)–(e) shows the results of 1,000 trials generated by running a Monte Carlo simulation of the estimated JNJ profit system model using the Broyden algorithm (see the IBM discussion). Unlike the more turbulent sales and capital stocks for IBM, the corresponding actual and simulated values of sales and capital stocks for JNJ reveal steady trajectories of growth (see Figs. 7.3(a) and (b)). Actual and simulated values for JNJ's profit rate, profit margin, and total profit in Fig. 7.3(c)–(e) are also less volatile compared with the corresponding series for IBM. Figure 7.3(f) shows the number of shares outstanding for JNJ. Dividing the actual and simulated total profits by the number of shares outstanding gives the time series of actual and simulated profit per share in Fig. 7.3(g).

With respect to stock valuation, discounting actual and simulated time series of profits per share using a discount rate of 8.5 percent gives time series of discounted actual and discounted simulated profit per share. Comparison of the actual stock price for JNJ with its discounted actual profit per share in Fig. 7.3(h) shows that the two series converge after 1980. Comparison of the actual stock price for JNJ with the discounted simulated profit per share in Fig. 7.3(i) shows similar results. In the late 1990s JNJ's stock price diverged considerably from its fundamental value based on our profit system model. No doubt the market bubble at that time contributed to this overvaluation. By 2008 the actual and simulated stock prices for JNJ converge again, which appears to suggest fair valuation consistent with fundamentals.

Table 7.4 reports short-run and long-run forecasts for JNJ's stock prices in 2009 and 2010. We used the same procedures as discussed above for IBM's stock price forecasts. At the time of this writing in 2009, the 52-week range for JNJ's stock price was \$46.25–\$72.76. Our short-run forecasts are higher than this range in 2009 and 2010. The long-run forecast in 2009 is at the upper end of this range, and the 2010 forecast is higher than this range. Again, these fundamental estimates based on profits may be biased to some extent due to using historical values of capital stocks (PPENT) rather than market values.

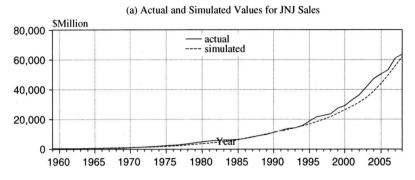

(a) Actual and Simulated Values for JNJ Sales

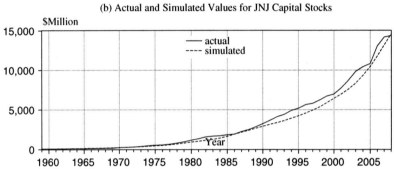

(b) Actual and Simulated Values for JNJ Capital Stocks

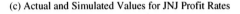

(c) Actual and Simulated Values for JNJ Profit Rates

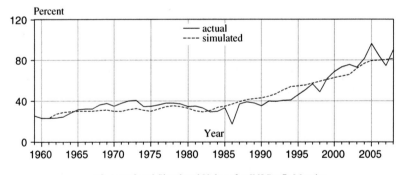

(d) Actual and Simulated Values for JNJ Profit Margins

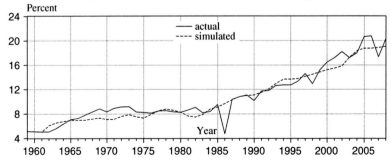

Fig. 7.3 (continued)

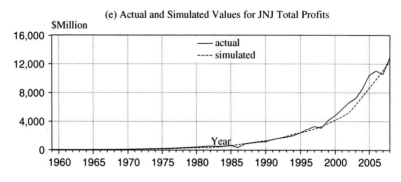

(e) Actual and Simulated Values for JNJ Total Profits

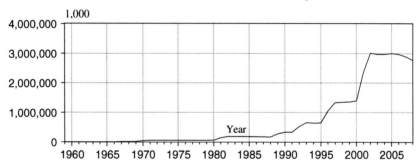

(f) Total Number of Shares Outstanding for JNJ

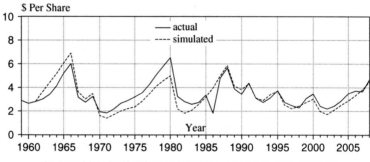

(g) Actual and Simulated Values for JNJ Profit Per Share

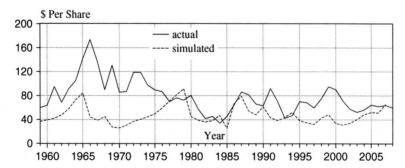

(h) Actual JNJ Stock Prices and the Discounted Actual Profit Per Share

Fig. 7.3 (continued)

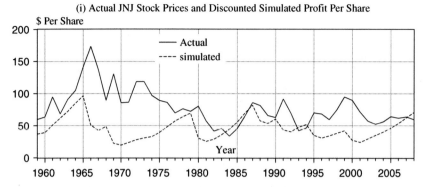

Fig. 7.3 Actual and simulated values of the variables in the profit system model for JNJ (1959–2008): (**a**) actual and simulated values for JNJ sales; (**b**) actual and simulated values for JNJ capital stocks; (**c**) actual and simulated values for JNJ profit rates; (**d**) actual and simulated values for JNJ profit margins; (**e**) actual and simulated values for JNJ total profits; (**f**) total number of shares outstanding for JNJ; (**g**) actual and simulated values for JNJ profit per share; (**h**) actual JNJ stock prices and discounted actual profit per share; and (**i**) actual JNJ stock prices and simulated discounted profit per share

Table 7.4 Long-run and short-run forecasts of stock prices

	2009	2010
A.IBM		
Long run	$87.77	$82.95
Short run	$91.80	$87.77
B.JNJ		
Long run	$72.20	$80.53
Short run	$84.20	$93.43

Since our estimated stock valuation model and related simulations are based on a set of fundamental variable assumptions, analysts can evaluate the sensitivity of simulation results to changes in the underlying assumptions. For instance, we assume a growth rate of profit per share in real terms of 1.4 percent per year for JNJ based on its past history. Analysts can estimate the stock valuation models under different assumptions regarding nominal future profits, after-tax real profit rates, expected inflation rates, risk premiums, growth rates of real profit per share, and so on.

7.3 Further Discussion

So far we have shown that our profit system model can be used to analyze and forecast key business variables for individual firms. While we applied the results to stock valuation, other important ways to utilize our model are strategic business planning, budgetary control, and capital budgeting (investment) decisions.

7.3.1 Strategic Business Planning

All enterprises, whether for-profit or not-for-profit, small or large, and so on, engage in informal or formal strategic planning regarding how to use their resources efficiently to attain their objectives. At the heart of strategic planning in business firms are forecasts of sales (revenues), profits, and other key variables. The profit system model developed in this book can be used as an analytical framework for strategic business planning with regard to fundamental business variables, such as sales (Y), total profits profit rates (R), profit margins (S), capital stocks (K), and human resources (H). The strength of the model stems from its inclusion of all relationships among these fundamental business and economic variables. These relationships are estimated by means of econometric techniques and computer-based simulation methods. This approach brings together accounting, economics, finance, and management information systems to develop an integrated model of the firm. The model begins with the accounting and economic concepts of profit rate, profit margin, capital stock, output or sales, and the production function. While the model contains all fundamental relationships among these variables, it can be adapted to include additional variables that may be relevant when applied to a country's business sector, an industry, or an individual firm. When applied to an individual firm, aggregate macroeconomic variables and macroeconomic policy instruments can be included in the model if there are reasons to believe that they may affect the firm's strategic planning. For instance, by adding the Federal funds rate and aggregate nonfinancial debt outstanding to the profit system model equations for sales (output), capital stocks, profit rates, and profit margins, we can investigate their impact on a firm's fundamental variables.

An important issue in strategic planning is the feasibility of sales plans, profit plans, investment plans, hiring plans, and so on. Using our profit system model, the viability of strategic plans can be tested by deterministic and stochastic simulation of the model. Inconsistent strategic plans can be detected when the variables in the model fall apart in simulations. Convergence of the levels or growth rates of business variables to their targets envisaged in strategic plans in simulation would be indicative of their feasibility.

7.3.2 Budgetary Control

Our profit system model is a potentially powerful tool for budgetary analysis and control. Budgetary control is closely related to strategic business planning in that continuous comparisons of planned and actual outcomes for sales, profit, profit rate, and so on are made. Our model represents a formal framework for generating targets for fundamental business variables. Throughout the budgetary process, targets are revised and operational changes are made in an effort to attain targets. In Chapter 2 we defined equilibrium to occur when the ex ante profit rate, which is the target or budgeted profit rate, equals the ex post realized profit rate.

Budgeting is dependent on forecasting. Budget preparation requires: (1) forecasts of sales or revenues, (2) forecasts of costs of goods sold or services to be rendered, (3) forecasts of profits computed as the difference between revenues and costs, and (4) forecasts of capital stocks (i.e., plants, equipment, buildings, etc.) and manpower for attaining business targets for sales, profit, profit rate, and so on. Our profit system model provides an integrated framework for the dynamic forecasting of these and other fundamental business variables and thereby seeks to exploit their simultaneous and recursive relationships. By relating the model to macroeconomic aggregates and macroeconomic policy instruments, the model is capable of analyzing their impacts on the likely paths of fundamental business variables in budgeting processes.

As in strategic planning, the viability of plans or budgets for sales or revenues, profits, and investments in physical and human capital is an important issue in the budgetary process. Our profit system model can be used to test the feasibility of budgets via deterministic and stochastic simulation by detecting potential inconsistencies. Feasible budget targets should converge to the levels or growth rates of forecasted target variables.

7.3.3 Capital Budgeting Decisions

Capital budgeting decisions concerning investment projects, including the evaluation of new products and services or abandonment of existing unprofitable economic activities, are normally based on evaluation criteria, such as payback period, discounted cash flow (DCF), or required rate of return on investment. For this purpose a worksheet is normally prepared containing projections of cash flows (i.e., revenues, costs, and profits) over the lifespan of investment projects. The projected cash flows are subsequently used for computing project evaluation criteria. Our profit system model offers a dynamic approach to investment evaluation that estimates potential future sales, profits, and capital stocks associated with an investment project. The model's simulation allows studying alternative investment strategies and their impacts on all business fundamental variables without the need to prepare numerous worksheets. Because three-out-of-five fundamental variables – that is, total profit, profit rate, and profit margin – are profit variables, it is essentially an investment evaluation model.

7.4 Conclusion

This chapter applied our profit system model to individual firms. The model is used to simulate long-run trends in fundamental business variables, such as sales, profits, profit rates, profit margins, and capital stocks. A discounted cash flow (DCF) model of stock valuation is proposed that discounts future estimated profits by the required rate of return on equity minus the growth rate of real profits. The profit system model and stock valuation model were applied to IBM Corporation and Johnson and Johnson, two members of the Dow Jones Industrial Average (DJIA). IBM was selected to demonstrate the application of our model to a corporation with negative profits in some periods, whereas Johnson and Johnson gives an example of a firm with no losses over time. The estimated models for both corporations were used for in-sample simulations of the fundamental variables and out-of-sample forecasting.

The actual and simulated values of total profits were divided by the number of shares outstanding to derive profit per share, which was then discounted using different discount factors to estimate time series of share values. Actual stock prices were then compared with time series of discounted simulated profits per share. The comparative stock valuation results lend insights into under- and overvaluation of IBM and JNJ relative to the present values of their fundamental profits over time. A major advantage of our profit system model is the ability to estimate in-sample and forecast out-of-sample profits over time as well as other fundamental variables to gain insights into the fundamental stock valuation of a firm. No other stock valuation model to our knowledge has this capability due to the lack of a business model of profits and other fundamental business variables. Modeling these variables is critical to implementing a fundamental analysis based on standard DCF methods.

Finally, we discussed potential applications of our profit system model to strategic business planning, budgetary control, and capital budgeting decisions. Simulation analyses based on our model can be used to evaluate the reasonableness of different strategic plans and budgetary targets, as well as help forecast future cash flows used in capital budgeting decisions. These contributions of our model highlight the "power of profit" in everyday business activities.

Chapter 8
Concluding Remarks

The famous economist Knut Wicksell defined economics as a practical science. Viewing the business world around us, we can see that modern market economies are comprised of a for-profit or business sector and a nonprofit sector. Practitioners in the business sector make investment and production decisions based on the fundamentals of expected and realized profit rate, profit margin, and total profit. In this book we presented a practitioner model of the firm in the sense that the model is derived from the definitions of profit rate and profit margin, which are well-known concepts among business people. With these concepts in hand, we defined output as the product of the profit rate and the market value of capital stock divided by profit margin. Similarly, capital stock was defined as the product of output and profit margin divided by profit rate. In effect, we formalized a model of the firm that informally is used by practitioners consisting of the five fundamental variables of total profit, profit rate, profit margin, capital stock, and output. Empirical representations of our theoretical model evolved as a system of dynamic equations given that each of the five fundamental variables is determined by the other variables. For this reason we referred to these equations as a profit system model of the firm.

Although we derived new formulations for output and capital stock, we have not proposed new economic theories of production and capital formation. Nonetheless, our approach for exploiting these relationships for economic and business analyses as well as forecasting is new. To this end we explored in Chapter 2 the impact of these and other variables in the economy (e.g., the availability and cost of debt) on the fundamental business variables, in addition to the issue of measuring output and capital stock in current or constant dollars. In Chapter 3 we applied the profit system model to the whole US economy demonstrating the application of the model for macroeconomic forecasting and policy analyses. The application of the model to the aggregate US business sector in Chapter 3, the US corporate sector in Chapter 4, 12 US industries in Chapter 5, and selected individual corporations in Chapter 7 demonstrated that the profit system model can be employed for business and economic analyses and forecasting at various levels of aggregation from individual firms to the national economy. Finally, in Chapters 6 and 7 we extended the profit system model to fundamental stock market valuation and forecasting. This innovation was made possible by linking the profit variables in the profit system model

A. Anari, J.W. Kolari, *The Power of Profit*, DOI 10.1007/978-1-4419-0649-6_8,
© Springer Science+Business Media, LLC 2010

of the macroeconomy to the valuation of financial claims such as stocks, thereby integrating financial and nonfinancial sectors of the national economy. Unlike the CAPM and other similar asset pricing models that focus on equilibrium in the financial markets, our proposed asset pricing model incorporates information from both the real economy and the financial markets. In sum, we have attempted to cover a wide variety of applications of our profit system model in business, economic, and stock market analyses. Our hope is that businesses, economists, investors, and others will find the profit system model a useful tool and discover other innovative applications.

In the course of the development of the models from theory in Chapter 2 to empirical applications throughout the remainder of the book, theories and methods developed in various academic disciplines – including accounting, economics, finance, management information systems, and statistics and econometrics – were employed. Hence, the profit system model embodies a multidisciplinary approach for teaching and research in business and economics schools as well as for practice in business organizations.

The profit motive has power in economies that produce the largest share of goods and services in the business sector. Profit has constructive, destructive, and reconstructive powers. The constructive power of profit stems from the ability of expected and realized profit rates to coordinate economic activities, especially capital formation and production activities, resulting in long periods of economic expansion. The destructive power of profit stems from honest miscalculation of expected profit rate as well as greed and corruption leading to recessions and slowing down of economies due to divergence between ex ante hurdle profit rates and ex post realized profit rates. And, the reconstructive power of profit is manifested in repeated economic recoveries in the aftermath of recessions and depressions.

At the time of this writing, many countries around the world were experiencing a deep recession, in contrast to other nations that have remained largely immune from crisis. The differences in current economic conditions among countries are due to differences between realized profit rates and expected profit rates used to select economic projects. While some countries are currently enjoying converging realized and expected profit rates, other nations are experiencing realized profit rates much lower than profit rates expected to be realized in several important sectors, notably housing, financial services, and manufacturing.

We have sought to explain models and their results in a simple and straightforward fashion in order to reach the largest possible audience. Consequently, some details of analyses were passed over. As an example, we did not report the estimated standard deviations for all of the variables and their growth rates in the estimated models generated from their stochastic simulations. Standard deviations together with means of the variables in the model would enable the application of Bayesian decision making to conduct risk analyses of various trajectories of the fundamental variables in the model in addition to risk analyses of various monetary and macroeconomic policies (e.g., inflation and recession risks). While we focused on US data series for firms, industries, business sector components, and the national economy, the methods outlined in the book can be readily utilized in other countries too. In this respect a major advantage of our profit system model is its intelligent simplicity that expands its scope of application to many different users.

Another unreported piece of evidence is Granger-causality tests on the channels of inflation transmission proposed by the profit system model. Based on quarterly data for the nonfinancial corporate sector presented in Chapter 4, empirical tests confirmed that the output price deflator Grange-causes nominal total profit which in turn Grange-causes capital stock which Grange-causes output. These empirical results support the theoretical propositions on the channels of inflation transmission.

A number of potential new venues for further economic research have been opened up by the profit system model: (1) an economic equilibrium attained by equalization of hurdle profit rates and realized profit rates, (2) a profit-based theory of economic growth, (3) a profit-based channel of transmission of inflation, and (4) a profit-based theory of business cycles.

This book showed that exploiting the power of profit for economic analysis and forecasting on micro- and macrolevels results in the development of profit system models founded on economic fundamentals. It is the authors' sincere wish that practical applications of the profit system models presented herein will result in more smooth and sustainable paths of future economic growth on both micro- and macrolevels, not to mention more realistic valuations of asset prices in financial markets.

While we have emphasized the role and power of profit in the economy, the macroeconomic profit system model embodies an analytical framework for the study of relationships between the private and the public sectors. Private–public coordination is imperative for a successful economy on both the micro- and the macrolevels. In the macroeconomic model developed in Chapter 3, the public sector is included in the nonprofit sector, and two-way relationships between output and prices in the business sector and nonprofit sector are specified. By recognizing the economy to consist of both a for-profit (or private) sector and nonprofit (including public) sector, the macroeconomic profit system model has the ability to analyze and forecast private–public interactions for policy analyses and other purposes.

George Box, an expert in statistical models, observed that "Most models are wrong, but some are useful." In our opinion the profit system model is a practical and useful tool for business and economic analyses, forecasting, and stock valuation.

References

Abel, A. (1979). *Investment and the Value of Capital*. Garland: New York, NY.

Abel, A., N. G. Mankiw, L. Summers, and R. Zeckhauser (1989). Assessing Dynamic Efficiency: Theory and Evidence. *Review of Economic Studies* 5, 1–20.

Aftalion, A. (1913). *Les Crises Périodiques de Surproduction*. Rivière: Paris.

Aghion, P. and S. N. Durlauf (2005). *Handbook of Economic Growth*. North-Holland: Amsterdam, Netherlands.

Alchian, A. (1955). The Rate of Interest, Fisher's Rate of Return Over Cost, and Keynes' Internal Rate of Return. *American Economic Review* 45, 938–943.

Anari, A. and J. Kolari, (2002). House Prices and Inflation. *Real Estate Economics* 30, 67–84.

Asimakopulos, A. (1971). The Determination of Investment in Keynes's Model. *Canadian Journal of Economics* 4, 382–388.

Asimakopulos, A. (1991). *Keynes's General Theory and Accumulation*. Cambridge University Press: Cambridge, UK.

Barberis, N., A. Shleifer, and R. Vishny (1998). A Model of Investor Sentiment. *Journal of Financial Economics* 49, 307–343.

Barro, R. J. (1997). *Determinants of Economic Growth: A Cross-Country Empirical Study*. MIT Press: Cambridge, MA.

Baumol, W. J. (1974). The Transformation of Values: What Marx 'Really' Meant (An Interpretation). *Journal of Economic Literature* 12, 51–62.

Bernanke, B. S. (1986). Alternative Explanations of the Money-Income Correlation. *Carnegie-Rochester Conference Series on Public Policy* 25, 49–100.

Bernanke, B. S. and I. Mihov (1998). Measuring Monetary Policy. *Quarterly Journal of Economics* 113, 869–902.

Beveridge, W. H. (1909). *Unemployment: A Problem of Industry*. Longmans, Green and Co.: London, UK.

Blanchard, O. J. and M. W. Watson (1986). Are Business Cycles All Alike? In: R. Gordon (ed.) *The American Business Cycle: Continuity and Change*. NBER and University of Chicago Press: Chicago, 123–156.

Böhm-Bawerk, E. (1895). The Positive Theory of Capital and Its Critics. *Quarterly Journal of Economics* 9, 113–131.

Böhm-Bawerk, E. (1921, 1959). *Capital and Interest* (3 vols. in one). Libertarian Press: South Holland, IL. Translation by G. D. Huncke and H. F. Sennholz.

Boudoukh, J., M. Richardson, and R. F. Whitelaw (2008). The Myth of Long-Horizon Predictability. *Review of Financial Studies* 21, 1577–1605.

Brainard, W. and J. Tobin (1968). Pitfalls in Financial Model-Building. *American Economic Review* 58, 99–122.

Brealey, R. A., S. C. Myers, and F. Allen (2008). *Principles of Corporate Finance*, 9th edn., McGraw-Hill/Irwin: New York, NY.

Broyden, C. G. (1965). A Class of Methods for Solving Nonlinear Simultaneous Equations. *Mathematics of Computation* 19, 577–593.

Bureau of Economic Analysis (1999). Notes on Rates of Return for Domestic Nonfinancial Corporations, 1960–98, *Survey of Current Business*. U.S. Department of Commerce: Washington, DC.

Campbell, J. R. and S. Krane (2005). Consumption-Based Macroeconomic Forecasting. *Economic Perspectives* 29, 52–70.

Campbell, J. Y. and R. J. Shiller (1987). Cointegration and Tests of Present Value Model. *Journal of Political Economy* 95, 1062–1088.

Campbell, J. Y. and R. J. Shiller (1988a). Stock Price, Earnings, and Expected Dividends. *Journal of Finance* 43, 661–676.

Campbell, J. Y. and R. J. Shiller (1988b). The Dividend-Price Ratio and Expectations of Future Dividends and Discount Factors. *Review of Financial Studies* 1, 195–228.

Campbell, J. Y. and S. B. Thompson (2008). Predicting Excess Stock Returns Out of Sample: Can Anything Beat the Historical Average? *Review of Financial Studies* 21, 1510–1531.

Caporale, T. (1993). Knut Wicksell: Real Business Cycle Theorist. *Scottish Journal of Political Economy* 40, 471–476.

Carver, T. N. (1903). A Suggestion for a Theory of Industrial Depressions. *Quarterly Journal of Economics* 18, 497–500.

Cassel, G. (1918). *Theoretische Sozialökonomie*. Leipzig: C. F. Winter. English translation (1923). *The Theory of Social Economy*. T. F. Unwin: London, UK.

Chang, T. (2002). An Econometric Test of Wagner's Law for Six Countries, Based on Cointegration and Error-Correction Modelling Techniques. *Applied Economics* 34, 1157–1169.

Charles, J. (2002). *Introduction to Economic Growth*. W. W. Norton & Company: New York, NY.

Chenery, H. B. (1952). Overcapacity and the Acceleration Principle. *Econometrica* 20, 1–28.

Christiano, L. J., M. Eichenbaum, and C. L. Evans (1999). Monetary Policy Shocks: What Have We Learned and to What End? Chapter 2. In: J. Taylor and M. Woodford (eds.), *Handbook of Macroeconomics*. Elsevier Science Publication: Amsterdam, Netherlands.

Clark, J. M. (1917). Business Acceleration and the Law of Demand: A Technical Factor in Economic Cycles. *Journal of Political Economy* 25, 217–235.

Cobb, C. and P. H. Douglas (1928). A Theory of Production. *American Economic Review* 18, 139–195.

Cochrane, J. H. (1992). Explaining the Variance of Price-Dividend Ratios. *Review of Financial Studies* 5, 243–280.

Cochrane, J. H. (1994). Shocks. Carnegie-Rochester Conference Series on Public Policy, Vol. 41, 295–364.

Cochrane, J. H. (1998). What Do the VARs Mean? Measuring the Output Effects of Monetary Policy. *Journal of Monetary Economics* 41, 277–300.

Cochrane, J. H. (2008). The Dog That Did Not Bark: A Defense of Return Predictability. *Review of Financial Studies* 21, 1533–1575.

Cooley, T. and LeRoy, S. (1985). Atheoretical Macroeconometrics: A Critique. *Journal of Monetary Economics* 16, 283–308.

Culter, M. D., J. M. Poterba, and L. H. Summers (1990). Speculative Dynamics and the Role of Feedback Traders. *American Economic Review* 80, 63–68.

Daniel, K., D. Hirshleifer, and A. Subrahmanyam (1998). Investor Psychology and Security Market Under- and Overreaction. *Journal of Finance* 53, 1839–1885.

Dechow, M. P., A. P. Hutton, L. Meulbroek, and R. G. Sloan (2001). Shortsellers, Fundamental Analysis and Stock Returns. *Journal of Financial Economics* 61, 77–106.

Delong, J. B., A. Shleifer, L. H. Summers, and R. J. Waldmann 1990. Positive Feedback Investment Strategies and Destabilizing Rational Speculators. *Journal of Finance* 45, 379–395.

Denton, F. T. and J. Kuiper (1965). The Effect of Measurement Errors on Parameter Estimates and Forecasts: A Case Study Based on the Canadian Preliminary National Accounts. *Review of Economics and Statistics* 47, 198–206.

Duesenberry, J. S (1949). *Income, Saving, and the Theory of Consumer Behavior*. Harvard University Press: Cambridge, MA.

Duménil, G. and D. Lévy (1993). *The Economics of the Profit Rate*. Edward Elgar Publishing: Aldershot, UK.

Elton, E., M. Gruber, D. Agrawal, and C. Mann (2001). Explaining the Rate Spread on Corporate Bonds. *Journal of Finance* 56, 247–277.

Fair, R. C. and R. Shiller (1990). Comparing Information in Forecasts from Econometric Models. *American Economic Review* 80, 375–389.

Fama, E. F. and K. R. French (1988). Dividend Yields and Expected Stock Returns. *Journal of Financial Economics* 22, 3–25.

Fama, E. F. and K. R. French (1992). The Cross-Section of Expected Stock Returns. *Journal of Finance* 47, 427–465.

Fama, E. F. and K. R. French (1993). Common Risk Factors in the Returns on Stocks and Bonds. *Journal of Financial Economics* 33, 3–56.

Fama, E. F. and K. R. French (1995). Size and Book-to-Market Factors in Earnings and Stock Returns. *Journal of Finance* 50, 131–155.

Feldstein, M. S. (1977). Does the United States Save Too Little? *American Economic Review* 67, 116–121.

Feldstein, M. S. (1996). The Missing Piece in Policy Analysis: Social Security Reform. *American Economic Review* 86, 1–14.

Felipe, J. and C. A. Holz (2001). Why Do Aggregate Production Functions Work? Fisher's Simulations, Shaikh's Identity and Some New Results. *International Review of Applied Economics* 15, 271–285.

Feltham, A. G. and J. A. Ohlson (1995). Valuation and Clean Surplus Accounting for Operating and Financial Activities. *Contemporary Accounting Research* 11, 689–731.

Fisher, I. (1907). *The Rate of Interest*. Macmillan: New York, NY.

Fisher, I. (1911). *The Purchasing Power of Money*. Macmillan: New York, NY.

Fisher, I. (1930). *The Theory of Interest*. Macmillan: New York, NY.

Fisher, I. (1932). *Booms and Depressions: Some First Principles*. Adelphi Company: New York, NY.

Flavin, M. A. (1983). Excess Volatility in the Financial Markets: A Reassessment of the Empirical Evidence. *Journal of Political Economy* 96, 929–956.

Foley, D. K. (1999). *Growth and Distribution*. Harvard University Press: Cambridge, MA.

Francis, J., P. Olsson, and D. R. Oswald (2000). Comparing the Accuracy and Explainability of Dividend, Free Cash Flow, and Abnormal Earnings Equity Value Estimates. *Journal of Accounting Research* 38, 45–70.

Friedman, M. (1961). The Lag in Effect of Monetary Policy. *Journal of Political Economy* 69, 447–466.

Friedman, M. (1962). *Capitalism and Freedom*. University of Chicago Press: Chicago, IL.

Friedman, M. (1993). The 'Plucking Model' of Business Cycle Fluctuations Revisited. *Economic Inquiry* 31, 171–177.

Frisch, R. (1933). Propagation Problems and Impulse Problems in Dynamic Economics. In: *Essays in Honor of Gustav Cassel*. Allen & Unwin: London, UK, 171–205.

Gabisch, G. and H. W. Lorenz (1987). *Business Cycle Theory: A Survey of Methods and Concepts*, 1989 edition. Springer-Verlag: Berlin, Germany.

George, H. (1879, 1962). *Progress and Poverty*. Robert Schalkenbach Foundation: New York, NY.

Gilles, C. and S. F. LeRoy (1991). Econometric Aspects of the Variance-Bounds Tests: A Survey. *Review of Financial Studies* 4, 753–791.

Gillman, M. J. (1957). *The Falling Rate of Profit: Marx's Law and Its Significance to the Twentieth-Century Capitalism*. Dennis Dobson: London, UK.

Goodwin, R. M. (1951). The Non-Linear Accelerator and the Persistence of Business Cycles. *Econometrica* 19, 1–17.

Goodwin, R. M. (1967). *A Growth Cycle in C. Feinstein (ed.) Socialism, Capitalism, and Economic Growth*. Cambridge University Press: Cambridge, MA.

Gordon, M. J. (1962). *The Investment, Financing, and Valuation of the Corporation*. R.D. Irwin: Homewood, IL.

Gottschalk, J. (2001). *An Introduction into the SVAR Methodology: Identification, Interpretation, and Limitations of SVAR Models*. Kiel Institute of World Economics: Kiel, Germany.

Haberler, G. (1932). Money and the Business Cycle. In: Q. Wright (ed.), *Gold and Monetary Stabilization: Lectures on the Harris Foundation*. University of Chicago Press: Chicago, IL.

Haberler, G. (1937a). *Prosperity and Depression*. League of Nations: Geneva, Switzerland.

Haberler, G. (1937b). *Prosperity and Depression*. League of Nations: Geneva, Switzerland.

Hall, R. E. and D. W. Jorgenson (1967). Tax Policy and Investment Behavior. *American Economic Review* 57, 391–414

Hamilton, E. J. (1942). Profit Inflation and Industrial Revolution, 1751–1800. *Quarterly Journal of Economics* 56, 256–273.

Hamilton, J. D. and Ò. Jordà (2002). A Model of the Federal Funds Rate Target. *Journal of Political Economy* 110, 1135–1165.

Hansen, A. H. (1927). *Business-Cycle Theory: Its Development and Present Status*. Ginn: Boston, MA.

Hansen, A. H. (1937). Harrod on the Trade Cycle. *Quarterly Journal of Economics* 51, 509–531.

Hansen, A. H. (1938). *Full Recovery or Stagnation?* Norton: New York, NY.

Harrod, R. F. (1936). *The Trade Cycle: An Essay*, 1961 reprint. Augustus M. Kelley: New York, NY.

Harrod, R. F. (1948). *Towards a Dynamic Economics*. Macmillan: London, UK.

Hawtrey, R. G. (1913). *Good and Bad Trade*. Constable: London, UK.

Hawtrey, R. G. (1919). *Currency and Credit*. Longmans Group: London, UK.

Hawtrey, R. G. (1932). *The Art of Central Banking*. Longmans Group: London, UK.

Hayashi, F. (1982). Tobin's Marginal Q and Average Q: A Neoclassical Interpretation. *Econometrica* 50, 213–224.

Hayek, F. A. (1929). Geldtheorie und Konjunkturtheorie, Hölder-Pichler-Tempski, Vienna; English edition, *Monetary Theory and the Trade Cycle*. J. Cape, London, 1933; reprint, 1966, Augustus M. Kelley: New York, NY.

Hayek, F. A. (1931). *Prices and Production*, 2nd edn., Reprint 1935, Routledge & Kegan Paul: London, UK.

Hayek, F. A. (1939). *Profits, Interest and Investment and Other Essays on the Theory of Industrial Fluctuations*. Routledge: Longdon, UK.

Hayek, F. A (1941). *The Pure Theory of Capital*. University of Chicago Press: Chicago, IL.

Hayek, F. A. (1942). Professor Hayek and the Concertina Effect. *Economica*, New Series 9, 383–385.

Hicks, J. R. (1950). *A Contribution to the Theory of the Trade Cycle*. 1956 reprint, Clarendon: Oxford, UK.

Hood, W. C. and T. C. Koopmans (eds.) (1953). *Studies in Econometric Methods*. Cowles Commission Monograph 14. Wiley: New York, NY.

Howrey, P. (1996). Forecasting GNP with Noisy Data: A Case Study. *Journal of Economic and Social Measurement* 22, 181–200.

Hull, G. H. (1911). *Industrial Depressions: Their Causes Analyzed and Classified, with a Practical Remedy for Such a Result from Industrial Derangements*. Frederick A. Stokes Company: New York, NY.

Jennergren, L. P. (2008). A Tutorial on the Discounted Cash Flow Model for Valuation of Companies. SSE/EFI Working paper series in business administration No. 1998:1, Stockholm School of Economics, Stockholm, Sweden.

Johanssen, N. A. (1908). *A Neglected Point in Connection with Crisis*. The Bankers Publishing Company: New York, NY. Reprinted in 1971.

Jorgenson, D. W. (1963). Capital Theory and Investment Behavior. *American Economic Review* 53, 247–257.

Jorgenson, D. W. (1967). The Theory of Investment Behavior. In: R. Ferber (ed.), *Determinants of Investment Behavior*. NBER: New York, NY.

Jorgenson, D. W. (1971). Econometric Studies of Investment Behavior: A Survey. *Journal of Economic Literature* 9, 1111–1147.

Jorgenson, D. W. and K.-Y. Yun (2001). *Lifting the Burden: Tax Reform, the Cost of Capital, and U.S. Economic Growth*. The MIT Press: Cambridge, MA.

Juglar, C. (1862). *Des Crises Commerciales et der Leur Retour Periodique en France, en Anglettere et aux Etas-Unis*. Guillaurrin: Paris (2nd edn. 1889), translated in part as A Brief History of Panics and Their Periodical Occurrence in the United States. A.N. Kelley: New York, NY, 1966.

Kaldor, N. (1939). Capital Intensity and the Trade Cycle. *Economica* 6, 40–66.

Kaldor, N. (1940a). The Trade Cycle and Capital Intensity: A Reply. *Economica* 7, 16–22.

Kaldor, N. (1940b). A Model of the Trade Cycle. *Economic Journal* 50, 78–92.

Kaldor, N. (1942). Professor Hayek and the Concertina Effect. *Economica* 9, 359–385.

Kalecki, M. (1935). A Macroeconomic Theory of the Business Cycle. *Econometrica* 3, 327–344.

Kalecki, M. (1937). A Theory of the Business Cycle. *Review of Economic Studies* 4, 77–97.

Kalecki, M. (1939). *Essays in the Theory of Economic Fluctuation*. 1972 edition, Allen and Unwin: London, UK.

Keynes, J. M. (1930). *A Treatise on Money*. Macmillan: London, UK.

Keynes, J. M. (1936). *The General Theory of Employment, Interest, and Money*. Harcourt, Brace and Company: New York, NY.

Khoury, S. S. (1990). The Federal Reserve Reaction Function: A Specification Search. In: T. Mayer (ed.), *The Political Economy of American Monetary Policy*. Cambridge University Press: Cambridge, UK.

King, R. G., C. I. Plosser, and S. T. Rebelo (1988). Production, Growth, and Business Cycle I. The Basic Neoclassical Model. *Journal of Monetary Economics* 35, 195–232.

Kleidon, A. W. (1986a). Bias in Small Sample Tests of Stock Price Rationality. *Journal of Business* 59, 237–261.

Kleidon, A. W. (1986b). Variance Bound Tests and Stock Price Valuation Models. *Journal of Political Economy* 94, 953–1001.

Koenig, E. F. and S. Dolmas (1997). Real-Time GDP Growth Forecasts. Federal Reserve Bank of Dallas Working Paper 97–10.

Koopmans, T. C. (ed.) (1950), *Statistical Inference in Dynamic Economic Models*. Cowles Commission Monograph 10. Wiley: New York, NY.

Kydland, F. E. and E. C. Prescott (1982). Time to Build and Aggregate Fluctuations. *Econometrica* 50, 1345–1370.

Laidler D. (1999). *Fabricating the Keynesian Revolution. Studies of the Inter-war Literature on Money, the Cycle, and Unemployment*. Cambridge University Press: Cambridge, UK.

Lee, B.-S. (1996). Comovements of Earnings, Dividends, and Stock Prices. *Journal of Empirical Finance* 3, 327–346.

Lee, B.-S. (1998). Permanent, Temporary, and Nonfundamental Components of Stock Prices. *Journal of Financial and Quantitative Analysis* 33, 1–32.

Lee, C. M. C. (1999). Accounting-Based Valuation: Impact on Business Practices and Research. *Accounting Horizons* 13, 413–425.

Lee, C. M. C, J. Myers, and B. Swaminathan (1999). What Is the Intrinsic Value of the Dow? *Journal of Finance* 54, 1693–1741.

Leeper, E. M., C. A. Sims, and T. Zha (1996). What Does Monetary Policy Do? *Brookings Papers on Economic Activity* 2, 1–78.

Lerner, A. P. (1953). On the Marginal Product of Capital and the Marginal Theory of Investment. *Journal of Political Economy* 61, 3–4.

LeRoy, S. and R. Porter (1981). The Present Value Relation: Tests Based on Implied Variance Bounds. *Econometrica* 64, 555–574.

Lescure, J. 1906. *Des Crises Générales et Périodiques de Surproduction.* Domat-Montchrétien: Paris, France, 5th edition in 1938.

Long, J. B. and C. I. Plosser (1983). Real Business Cycles. *Journal of Political Economy* 91, 39–69.

Lucas, R. E. (1975). An Equilibrium Model of Business Cycle. *Journal of Political Economy* 83, 1113–1144.

Lucas, R. E. (1976). Econometric Policy Evaluation: A Critique. In: K. Brunner and A. Meltzer (eds.), *Phillips Curve and the Labor Market.* North Holland Press: Amsterdam, Netherlands.

Lucas, R. E. (1977). Understanding Business Cycles. In: K. Brunner and A. H. Meltzer (eds.), *Stabilization of the Domestic and International Economy,* Carnegie-Rochester Conference Series on Public Policy 5, 7–29. North-Holland Press: Amsterdam, Netherlands.

Lucas, R. E. (1981). *Studies in Business Cycle Theory.* MIT Press: Cambridge, MA.

Lucas, R. E. (2004). Lectures on Economic Growth, ed. Harvard University Press: Cambridge, MA.

Lucas, R. and E. Prescott (1971). Investment Under Uncertainty. *Econometrica* 39, 659–681.

Mankiw, G. N. (1985). Small Menu Costs and Large Business Cycles: A Macroeconomic Model of Monopoly. *The Quarterly Journal of Economics* 100, 529–539.

Mankiw, N. G. and R. Reis (2002). Sticky Information Versus Sticky Prices: A Proposal to Replace the New Keynesian Phillips Curve. *Quarterly Journal of Economics* 117, 1295–1328.

Marsh, T. A. and R. C. Merton (1986). Dividend Variability and Variance Bounds Tests for the Rationality of Stock Market Prices. *American Economic Review* 76, 483–498.

Marsh, T. A. and R. C. Merton (1987). Dividend Behavior for the Aggregate Stock Market. *Journal of Business* 60, 1–40.

Marshall, A. and M. P. Marshall (1879). *The Economics of Industry.* Macmillan: London, UK.

Marx, K. (1867, 1885, 1894). *Capital, I, II & III.* Progress Publishers: Moscow, Russia.

McGrattan, E. R. and E. D. Prescott (2000). Is the Stock Market Overvalued? *Quarterly Review* 24, Federal Reserve Bank of Minneapolis, 20–40.

Mehra, Y. P. (1997). A Federal Funds Rate Equation. *Economic Inquiry* 35, 621–330.

Menger, C. (1871). *Principles of Economics,* Translated in English by Dingwall and Hoselitz, New York University Press: New York, NY (1981).

Metzler, L. A (1941). The Nature and Stability of Inventory Cycles. *Review of Economic Studies* 23, 113–129.

Mill, J. S. (1948). *The Principles of Political Economy: With Some of Their Applications to Social Philosophy.* Routledge and Kegan Paul Ltd.: London, UK.

Miller, M. and F. Modigliani (1961). Dividend Policy, Growth and the Valuations of Shares. *Journal of Business* 34, 411–433.

Mises, L. (1912, 1953). *The Theory of Money and Credit.* Yale University Press: New Haven, CT.

Mises, L. (1959). Capital and Interest: Eugen von Böhm-Bawerk and the Discriminating Reader. *Freeman* 9, 52–54.

Mitchell, W. C. (1913). *Business Cycles.* University of California Press: Berkeley, CA.

Modigliani, F. and R. A. Cohn (1979). Inflation, Rational Valuation and the Market. *Financial Analysts Journal* 39, 24–44.

Mohun, S. (2003). The Australian Rate of Profit, 1965–2001. *Journal of Australian Political Economy* 52, 83–112.

Mohun, S. (2006). Distributive Shares in the US Economy, 1964–2001. *Cambridge Journal of Economics* 30, 347–370.

Odean, T. (1998). Volume, Volatility, Price, and Profit When All Traders Are Above Average. *Journal of Finance* 53, 1887–1934.

Ohlin, B. (1937a). Some Notes on the Stockholm Theory of Savings and Investment I. *The Economic Journal* 47, 53–69.

Ohlin, B. (1937b). Some Notes on the Stockholm Theory of Saving and Investment II. *The Economic Journal* 47, 221–240.

Ohlin, B. (1937c). Alternative Theories of the Rate of Interest: Three Rejoinders. *The Economic Journal* 47, 423–427.

Ohlson, A. J. (1991). The Theory of Value and Earnings, and an Introduction to the Ball-Brown Analysis. *Contemporary Accounting Research* 8, 1–19.

Ohlson, A. J. (1995). Earnings, Book Values, and Dividends in Equity Valuation. *Contemporary Accounting Research* 11, 661–687.

Pasinetti, L. L. (1960). Cyclical Growth and Fluctuations, Oxford Economic Papers. Also reprinted in Pasinetti, 1974, *Growth and Income Distribution: Essays in Economic Theory*. Cambridge University Press: Cambridge, UK.

Persons, W. M. (1914). Review: Books on Cycles: Mitchell, Aftalion, Bilgram. *Quarterly Journal of Economics* 28, 795–810.

Pigou, A. C. (1920). *The Economics of Welfare*. Macmillan: London, UK.

Pigou, A. C. (1927). *Industrial Fluctuation*. Macmillan: London, UK.

Plosser, C. I. (1989). Understanding Real Business Cycles. *Journal of Economic Perspectives* 3, 51–77.

Pontiff, J. and L. D. Schall (1998). Book-to-Market Ratios As Predictors of Market Returns. *Journal of Financial Economics* 49, 141–160.

Poterba, J. M. (1997). The Rate of Return on Corporate Capital and Factor Shares: New Estimates Using Revised National Income Accounts and Capital Stock Data, National Bureau of Economic Research, Working Paper No. 6273.

Prescott, E. C. (1986). Theory Ahead of Business Cycle Measurement, *Quarterly Review* 10, Federal Reserve Bank of Minneapolis, 9–22.

Ricardo, D. (1815). Essay on Profits. In: P. Sraffa (ed.), *The Works and Correspondence of David Ricardo*. Cambridge University Press (1962): Cambridge, UK.

Robertson, D. H. (1915). *A Study of Industrial Fluctuations*. Aldwych: London, UK.

Robertson, D. H. (1934). Industrial Fluctuation and the Natural Rate of Interest. *The Economic Journal* 44, 650–656.

Robertson, D. H. (1936). Some Notes on Mr. Keynes' General Theory of Employment. *Quarterly Journal of Economics* 51, 168–191.

Robertson, D. H. (1937). Alternative Theories of the Rate of Interest: Three Rejoinders. *The Economic Journal*, 428–436.

Robertson J. C. and E. W. Tallman, (1998). Data Vintages and Measuring Forecast Model Performance. *Economic Review*, Federal Reserve Bank of Atlanta, Fourth Quarter, 83(4), 4–20.

Rosser, J. B. (1991). *From Catastrophe to Chaos: A General Theory of Economic Discontinuities*. Kluwer: Boston, MA.

Ruback, R. S. (2002). Capital Cash Flows: A Simple Approach to Valuing Risky Cash Flows. *Financial Management* 31, 85–103.

Rudebusch, G. D. (1998). Do Measures of Policy in a VAR Make Sense? *International Economic Review* 39, 907–931.

Samuelson, P. A. (1939a). A Synthesis of the Principle of Acceleration and the Multiplier. *Journal of Political Economy* 47, 786–797.

Samuelson, P. A. (1939b). Interaction Between the Multiplier Analysis and the Principle of Acceleration. *Review of Economics and Statistics* 21, 75–78

Samuelson, P. A. (1974). Insight and Detour in the Theory of Exploitation: A Reply to Baumol. *Journal of Economic Literature* 12, 62–70.

Schumpeter, J. A. (1927). The Explanation of the Business Cycle. *Economica*, Dec., 286–311, in *Essays of J.A. Schumpeter*, edited by R. V. Clemence. Addison-Wesley Press, Inc. (1951): Cambridge, MA, 21–46.

Schumpeter, J. A. (1934). *The Theory of Economic Development: An Inquiry into Profits, Capital, Credit, Interest, and the Business Cycle*. Harvard University Press: Cambridge, MA.

Schumpeter, J. A. (1939). *Business Cycles: A Theoretical, Historical, and Statistical Analysis of the Capitalist Process*. McGraw-Hill: New York, NY.

Schumpeter, J. A. (1942). *Capitalism, Socialism and Democracy*. Harper (1975): New York, NY.

Shaikh, A. M. and E. A. Tonak (1994). *Measuring the Wealth of Nations*. Cambridge University Press: Cambridge, MA.

Shapiro, M. D. (1986). Investment, Output, and the Cost of Capital. *Brookings Papers on Economic Activity* 1, 111–152.

Sharpe, W. F. (1964). Capital Asset Prices: A Theory of Market Equilibrium Under Conditions of Risk. *The Journal of Finance* 19, 425–442.

Shiller, J. R. (1981). Do Stock Prices Move Too Much to Be Justified by Subsequent Changes in Dividends? *American Economic Review* 71, 421–436.

Sims, C. A. (1980). Macroeconomics and Reality. *Econometrica* 48, 1–48.

Sims, C. A. (1986). Are Forecasting Models Usable for Policy Analysis. *Quarterly Review*, Federal Reserve Bank of Minneapolis, 2–16.

Sims, C. A. (1992). Interpreting the Macroeconomic Time Series Facts: The Effects of Monetary Policy. *European Economic Review* 36, 975–1000.

Sims, C. A. (1998). Comment on Glen Rudebusch's 'Do Measures of Monetary Policy in a VAR Make Sense?' *International Economic Review* 39, 933–941.

Sims, C. A. (1999). The Role of Interest Rate Policy in the Generation and Propagation of Business Cycles: What Has Changed Since the '30s? In: J. C. Fuhrer and S. Schuh (eds.), *Beyond Shocks: What Causes Business Cycles?* Federal Reserve Bank of Boston Conference Series 42, 121–160.

Slutsky, E. (1927). The Summation of Random Causes as a Source of Cyclical Processes. Conjecture Institute, Moscow, reprinted in *Econometrica* 5, 105–146.

Smith, A. (1776). *An Inquiry into the Nature and Causes of the Wealth of Nations Published*. Edited by Edwin Cannan, fifth edition (1904), Methuen and Co., Ltd.: London, UK.

Smithies, A. (1957). Economic Fluctuations and Growth. *Econometrica* 25, 1–52.

Solow, R. M. (1956). A Contribution to the Theory of Economic Growth. *Quarterly Journal of Economics* 70, 65–94.

Solow, R. M. (1957). Technical Change and the Aggregate Production Function. *Review of Economics and Statistics* 39, 312–320.

Sombart W. (1902). Der Moderne Kapitalismus: Historisch-Systematische Darstellung des Gesamteuropäischen Wirtschaftslebens von Seinen Anfängen bis zur Gegenwart (quoted as MK), 2 vols., Leipzig; 3 vols., Duncker&Humblot, Munich and Leipzig (1916–27); reprinted Deutscher Taschenbuch. Verlag (1987): Munich, Germany.

Sombart, W. (1904). Versuch einer Systematik der Wirtschaftskrisen. *Archiv für Sozialwissenschaft und Sozialpolitik* n. 19, 1–21.

Sombart, W. (1930). *Capitalism, Encyclopedia of the Social Sciences*. Macmillan: New York, NY, Vol. 3, 195–208.

Spiethoff, A. (1902, 1903, 1909). Vorbemerkungen zu Einer Theorie der Überproducktion. *Schmoller's Jahrbuch* (1902), 721–59, (1903), 670–708, (1909), 445–67, 1417–37.

Spiethoff, A. (1902, 1925). Vorbemerkungen zu Einer Theorie der Überproduktion, in *Jahrbuch für Gesetzgebung, Verwaltung und Volkswirtschaft im Deutschen Reich*, n. 26, 721–59. (1925), Krisen, in *Handwörterbuch der Staatswissenschaften* 6, 8–91. English translation: Business Cycles. *International Economic Papers* n. 3 (1953), 75–171.

Sraffa, P. (1960). *Production of Commodities by Means of Commodities*. Cambridge University Press: Cambridge, MA.

Summers, L. H. (1981). Taxation and Corporate Investment: A q-Theory Approach. *Brookings Papers on Economic Activity* 1, 67–127.

Swan, T. W. (1956). Economic Growth and Capital Accumulation. *Economic Record* 32, 334–361.

Swanson, N. R. and W. Halbert (1997a). A Model-Selection Approach to Real-Time Macroeconomic Forecasting Using Linear Models and Artificial Neural Networks. *The Review of Economics and Statistics* 79, 265–275.

Swanson, N. R. and H. White (1997b). Forecasting Economic Time Series Using Flexible Versus Fixed Specification and Linear Versus Nonlinear Econometric Models. *International Journal of Forecasting* 13, 439–461.

Taylor, J. B. (1979). Estimation and Control of an Econometric Model with Rational Expectations. *Econometrica* 47, 1267–1286.

Taylor, J. B. (1993). Discretion Versus Policy Rules in Practice. *Carnegie-Rochester Conference Series on Public Policy* 39, 195–214.

Tobin, J. (1969). A General Equilibrium Approach to Monetary Theory. *Journal of Money, Credit and Banking* 1, 15–29.

Trivellato, U. and E. Rettore (1986). Preliminary Data Errors and Their Impact on the Forecast Error of Simultaneous-Equations Models. *Journal of Business & Economic Statistics* 4, 445–453.

Tugan-Baranovsky, M. (1894). Industrial Crises in Contemporary England, Their Causes and Immediate Consequences on National life. (In Russian). I. Schorochodov.

Veblen, T. (1904). *The Theory of Business Enterprise*. Charles Scribner's Sons: New York, NY.

Veblen, T. (1923). *Absentee Ownership and Business Enterprise in Recent Times: The Case of America*. Kelley: New York, NY.

Wagner, A. (1892). *Grundlegung der Politischen Ökonomie*, Part 1, Vol. 1. 3rd edn., Winter: Leipzig, Germany.

Wagner, R. E. and W. E. Weber (1977). Wagner's Law, Fiscal Institutions, and the Growth of Government. *National Tax Journal* 30, 59–68.

Welch, I. and A. Goyal (2008). A Comprehensive Look at the Empirical Performance of Equity Premium Prediction. *Review of Financial Studies* 21, 1456–1508.

West, D. K. (1988). Dividend Innovations and Stock Price Volatility. *Econometrica* 56, 37–61.

Wicksell, K. (1898). The Influence of the Rate of Interest on Commodity Prices. In: K. Wicksell (ed.) (1969). *Selected Papers on Economic Activity*, Augustus M. Kelley Publishers: New York, NY.

Wicksell, K. (1907a). The Influence of the Rate of Interest on Prices. *The Economic Journal* 17, 213–220.

Wicksell, K. (1907b). Krisernâs Gata, in *Statsôkonomisk Tidsskrift*, n. 21, 255–284. English translation: The Enigma of Business Cycles, *International Economic Papers* n. 3 (1953), 58–74.

Williams, J. B. (1938). *The Theory of Investment Value*. Harvard University Press: Cambridge 1938; 1997 reprint, Fraser Publishing.

Willis, J. L. and J. Wrobleski (2007). What Happened to the Gains from Strong Productivity Growth? *Economic Review* 92, Federal Reserve Bank of Kansas City, 5–23.

Wolff, E. N. (2003). What's Behind the Rise in Profitability in the US in the 1980s and 1990s? *Cambridge Journal of Economics* 27, 479–499.

Woodford, M. (2003). *Interest and Prices: Foundations of a Theory of Monetary Policy*. Princeton University Press: Princeton, NJ.

Zellner, A. (1962). An Efficient Method of Estimating Seemingly Unrelated Regression Equations and Tests for Aggregation Bias. *Journal of the American Statistical Association* 57, 348–368.

Zellner, A. (2001). Keep It Sophisticatedly Simple. In: A. Zellner, H. A. Keuzenkamp, and M. McAleer (eds.), *Simplicity, Inference and Modelling*. Cambridge University Press: Cambridge, UK.

About the Authors

Dr. Ali Anari obtained his PhD in Industrial Economics and Business Studies at the University of Birmingham, UK, in 1978. He has more than 30 years research experience in developing computer-based economic models for economic analysis and forecasting in the areas of business economics, macroeconomics, real estate economics, and regional economics. In his professional career Dr. Anari has been a research economist in the areas of national and regional economic modeling at the Real Estate Research Center for Business and Economic Analysis in the Mays Business School at Texas A&M University; Visiting Scholar in the Anderson School of Management of the University of California, Los Angeles; research economist at the Imperial College of Science and Technology, London; research fellow at the University of Birmingham, UK; and economic analyst at the Economics and Statistics Department of National Iranian Oil Company. He has presented papers on economic modeling at conferences around the world and published book chapters and articles in such scholarly publications as the *Journal of Money, Credit, and Banking*, *Journal of Applied Economics*, *Journal of Financial Research*, *Journal of Real Estate Economics*, *Journal of Economics and Business*, *Journal of Energy Policy*, and *Journal of Emerging Markets*. Current research interests include developing economic models for early warning of real estate bubbles, profitability and economic growth, and regional profitability analysis.

Prof. James W. Kolari obtained his PhD in Finance at Arizona State University in 1980 and thereafter has taught financial markets and institutions at Texas A&M University in the Finance Department. In 1994 he was awarded the JP Morgan Chase Professorship in Finance in the Mays Business School. He has more than 30 years research experience in the areas of computer-based modeling of financial markets (including stock, bond, and real estate markets), financial institutions (such as banks and insurance companies), and financial regulation. Over the years, he has been a Visiting Scholar at the Federal Reserve Bank of Chicago, Fulbright Scholar at the University of Helsinki and Bank of Finland, Faculty Fellow with the Mortgage Bankers Association of America, and Senior Research Fellow at the Swedish School of Business and Economics (Hanken) in Finland, in addition to being a consultant to the US Small Business Administration, US Information Agency, American Bankers Association, Independent Bankers Association of America, and numerous banks and other organizations. He has published over 100 articles in refereed journals, numerous other papers and monographs, and 12 co-authored books. His papers have appeared in such domestic and international journals as the *Journal of Finance*, *Journal of Business*, *Journal of Money, Credit and Banking*, *Journal of Economic Dynamics and Control*, *Journal of Banking and Finance*, *Real Estate Economics*, *Journal of International Money and Finance*, and *Scandanavian Journal of Economics*. Papers in Dutch, Finnish, Italian, Swedish, and Russian have appeared outside of the United States. He is a co-author of leading college textbooks in commercial banking and international business courses.

Author Index

Subject Index